The international wool trade

The international wool trade

JULIAN ROCHE

WOODHEAD PUBLISHING LIMITED
Cambridge England

Published by Woodhead Publishing Ltd,
Abington Hall, Abington,
Cambridge CB1 6AH, England

First published 1995

British Library Cataloguing in Publication Data
A catalogue record for this book is available from the British Library

ISBN 1 85573 191 6

Designed by Andrew Jones (text) and The Colour Studio (jacket).
Typeset by BookEns Ltd, Baldock, Herts.
Printed by St Edmundsbury Press, Suffolk, England.

Contents

Preface

> Sheep are bountiful animals unto man for, let us blunder as we will, they feed us, they clothe us, and can hardly, under any bad management, be kept with loss ...
>
> Lord Somerville

The international wool trade has distinctive features for a commodities analyst which distinguish it from the international trade of other fibres.

Firstly, it is heavily weighed with history, much more so than similar trades of its competitors. Wool has a rich and ancient history and the trade is deeply aware of it. The benefit is continuity; the disadvantage is a reluctance to change fundamentals in the private sector.

Secondly, what can and is changed very frequently is the institutional framework in the public or quasi-public sector, which is both more extensive proportionately than other traded textile fibres and also more dominant in questions of marketing (and until recently many more issues as well). The benefit of this to an author is immeasurable, however, and I am extremely grateful to the British Wool Marketing Board, the International Wool Secretariat, the New Zealand Wool Marketing Board and the South African Wool Marketing Board for their kind and invaluable assistance in creating this book. In saying that I should also like to thank Bruce Rainsford of Bradford and Ilkley College, Dr Peter Glover of Marks and Spencer, and Jonathan Todhunter of AusTop, for casting their eyes over chapters of this book in draft form. Thanks also to the editor of *Wool Record*, Mark Keighley, for allowing me access to previous editions of this important journal.

Thirdly, the international wool trade is characterised by more insecurity and introspection than its competitors. This is accounted for by the combination of the loss of market share that wool has experienced since World War II, the ever prevalent closeness - especially in countries other than Australia - of the profitable sheepmeat business, a proximity in activity unique to wool, and particularly the loss of confidence and huge losses caused by the steep price rise and then catastrophic fall with the collapse of the Reserve Price Schemes that occurred between 1989 and 1992.

All this can and will change. The history is gradually being put in its place, as it must be. The public organisations are divesting their responsibilities to the private sector which is beginning the slow process of rationalisation itself - only lastly, it seems, with respect to brokers and exporters. Whatever prices do from the mid-nineties will be the dictate of the market with no stockpiles accumulating with public authorities - and risk management instruments must come into their own eventually. The medium and long term for the international wool trade look worth watching very closely indeed as lost time is made up.

CHAPTER

1

The history of wool production

Ancient times

Awareness of the ancient origin of sheep and wool and the existence of valued traditions are key distinguishing features of the wool industry and even the current international wool trade. More than for other commodities, a sense and understanding of history is useful for the analysis of the international wool trade.

Sheep's ability to provide for many human needs such as meat, milk, skins and wool was the main reason for their domestication, although even in pre-history people clothed themselves in the skins of killed animals. Sheep were most likely to have been domesticated originally as a flock because their herding instinct is highly developed, and this, together with their docility, makes them easy to domesticate and manage, especially with the aid of trained dogs.

No evidence of wild sheep has been found in Europe, so it seems that sheep were already domesticated before being brought there. Sheep have been domesticated since 6500 BC, judging from carbon dating of the Mesopotamian village of Qualat Jarmo in the Tigris Valley of Iraq and the city of Anau in Turkmenistan, and some estimates place domestication at as early as 10 000 BC. This places the original domestication of sheep, in the Near East, in the Middle Stone Age. There is evidence from a Maltese temple dating from 4000 BC of a Mouflon sheep, recognised since 1805 as the ancestors of our domestic sheep. Mesopotamian civilisations had wool dealers, several different types of sheep (at least three) and Babylonia was even referred to as 'the land of wool'. In the famous law code of Hammurabi (c 1792–1750 BC), corn, oil and wool are mentioned as the three main products of the country. Food sheep were already categorised differently from wool sheep; wool was graded into three categories and there were taxes paid on it. At the time of Nebuchadnezzar II (604–561 BC), the Hanging Gardens of Babylon were lit up by 18 000 braziers each holding one pound of sheep's tallow, the product of about 2000 fat sheep daily and 60 000 head monthly.

Sheep were also kept in Ancient Egypt where as early as 1700 BC sheep are known to have been shorn and lambing occur twice annually. Later Pharaohs, influenced by Syrian and Mesopotamian experience, introduced flocks and new breeds of sheep into Egypt.

Sheep raising in Greece also dates back to prehistoric times: the basis of any kind of ownership was the possession of flocks, not of land itself. All the native traditions of Greece describe its first inhabitants as living a settled life as shepherds and hunters, and not a nomadic one. The Minoans were familiar with sheep, as were their invaders. The Mycenaean, Homeric Greeks also tended sheep, and they were kept for their milk, meat and wool, as Homer himself frequently relates. Archaeological evidence suggests that at this time there were some privately owned fields but the majority were left for grazing. Flocks were the main portion of the property of the rich, the chief means of payment for goods and services and the principal cause of disputes. They were also offered in sacrifices and figure in myth, pre-eminently that of Jason and the Golden Fleece. Aristotle gave special attention to sheep in his works, commenting for example on the special breeds of very large sheep owned by Pyrrhus.

Rome actually imported sheep from Colchis; the fine-wooled sheep of Asia Minor were transported around the Mediterranean by the Phoenicians who were active traders (including of Cornish wool) after 1000 BC; some believe that the Merino stock came to Spain from North Africa with the Moors. The name is derived from the 'Beni Merinos' tribe of Tuareg Africans. During this period Sicily was a very important wool producer, as was Spain subsequently under Carthaginian influence. Spain became famous throughout the Mediterranean world at this time for the excellence of its woollen cloths. At the same time the Ptolemies were improving Egypt's wool industry through better breeding methods and new breeds of sheep. They kept sheep for wool, used for their households, and they had their own shepherds. They were also kept for cheese which became a staple food. The Egyptian state considered itself theoretically the owner of all sheep, and collected a tax on flocks, but in practice many were privately owned or leased, though grazing on public pastures.

Varro wrote that the Romans were first and foremost shepherds: much of ancient Italy's prosperity depended on sheep breeding, on the ranches and at the villas, many of them laid waste by Hannibal during his invasion of Italy. Gradually, Asiatic, Greek and other breeds of sheep were imported to improve the quality of the wool and its colour – the finest wool of Roman times came from Tarentum but these were replaced through interbreeding with sheep that eventually, it is thought, became the ancestors of the modern Merino, and which were exported to Spain. The Romans were selective and scientific sheepbreeders: Virgil was aware of subtle colour differences that would influence future generations and also of the effect of luxurious pasture in giving coarseness to the fleece. The Bible is another frequent source of sheep references and it is clear that a high economic and religious value was placed on sheep and their pasture. Lambs have long been identified as symbols of innocence, Christian archbishops, prelates and patriarchs wear woollen pallia and carry shepherds' crooks as symbols of their office even now.

United Kingdom

In the UK, sheep breeding existed from the Stone Age, reinforced with each successive invasion. It was woven into cloth as early as the Bronze Age around 1900 BC. The clearance of British forests enabled sheep to become as numerous as cattle. The Romans, typically, set up a wool factory to supply their occupying forces with clothing. British sheep fleeces were already highly valued at the time of Emperor Constantine. By 925 the English wool industry had advanced so that a fleece was valued at two-fifths of the whole sheep. Sometime between AD 500–1000 the spinning wheel was invented. The Normans intensified sheepbreeding, and an export trade in wool and fells began. The Domesday Book of William I, compiled in 1086, showed that sheep were practically everywhere; their numbers exceeded those of all other farm animals. Their main function was to provide milk: wool, manure and meat were by-products.

In the Middle Ages, the monastic (especially Cistercian) tradition reinforced sheepbreeding: by the 14th century, records show nearly 200 abbeys in England and Scotland supplying wool for export. Richard I was ransomed entirely with wool. In 1297 Parliament asserted that wool represented half the country's wealth – mainly very fine, high quality wool. The product of the looms of Winchester became so well known that it was said that 'the wool of Britain is often spun so fine that it is in a manner comparable to the spider's thread'. This reputation was maintained throughout medieval times and there was a large demand from the Low Countries and other parts of the Continent; export duties levied became an important part of royal revenue.

From the days of William I Flemish weavers had settled in Carlisle, and later in Pembrokeshire in Wales. Flemish weavers continued to immigrate and could be found throughout the country; by the 12th century wool was becoming the country's main national asset; cloth manufacture was especially prevalent in the large towns of southern and eastern England; carters charged a set fee per mile which amounted to 1.5% of the value of wool. Henry II set up a cloth fair in the churchyard of St Bartholomew priory; the weavers set up guilds; the exclusive right to export woollen cloth was given to the City of London. Wool exports increased from 5500 tons in 1273 to 8300 tons by 1305, largely under the 'staple' (authorised entrepots) system established by Edward I although they declined later amidst political uncertainty. Edward III revived the industry, bringing weavers, dyers and fullers from Flanders, wearing British cloth himself and prohibiting – with the usual violent penalties for transgression – the export of English wool, despite the export taxes imposed mainly to finance the war with France and the effects of the Black Death from 1349 which actually increased the sheep population as there were insufficient people left to cultivate the arable crops. The law was found to be unworkable, however, and wool smuggling began. Edward IV moderated the policy, such that only English citizens were allowed to export wool and that it should only be exported to Calais.

Different parts of England began to specialise in different wools, for example worsted cloth in East Anglia; and wool traders became more specialised, buying from producers to be able to supply many different wools of various origins and grades for specific customers. In the 14th and 15th centuries Italian ships importing spices, perfumes and fruit usually returned laden with English wool and later, cloth. In the 16th century Huguenot refugees brought their weaving skills to England and the country began to produce better quality wool than Flanders.

But with the spread of enclosures for sheep farming which provided improved grassland feeding, the fine medieval wool of the Midlands and Lincolnshire was gradually replaced with a longer and courser staple. Spanish wool began to be held in greater esteem and by the early 16th century English wool was losing its reputation for fineness. The export regime stayed until Elizabeth I's reign, when free trade was instituted and manufacturing increased. The previous regime was reinstituted in 1660, and stayed in force until 1825. Economists and historians agree that the effects of this legislation were not beneficial to the development of domestic industry; on the contrary, wool production greatly exceeded consumption, wool prices of course fell, smuggling became well organised and the whole industry became disorganised. The English authorities took extreme measures to encourage the consumption of woollen manufactures; for example in Charles II's reign an Act was passed demanding that all corpses be buried in woollen shrouds - an Act which remained, at least on the Statute Books, for 120 years. In the colonies strenuous efforts were made to encourage the use of English cloth, and manufacture was discouraged and on occasion prohibited in Ireland. As late as the 17th century, sheep were kept in England for milk and indirectly cheese.

Wool remained 'the flower and strength and revenue and blood of England' (H Purvis, *Talking about Newbury)* and until the development of the cotton trade, towards 1800, the wool industry was the most important source of wealth in the kingdom. In about 1700 £2m of wool was produced annually, producing about £8m of manufactured goods, of which 25–35% was exported. At its peak in the mid-eighteenth century, the Weyhill Fair in Hampshire saw a turnover of 140 000 sheep every day. In 1774 the number of sheep in England was estimated at 10–12m, the value of wool produced at £3m (about 5 s/lb), manufactures at £12m and exports at £3–4m. The number of people employed by the industry was estimated to be 1m (see John Campbell, *Political Survey of Great Britain*, London, 1774).

King George III brought Spanish Merino sheep to England and these were interbred with English sheep. The British Wool Society, founded in 1791 at Edinburgh, researched the best ways to improve native Scottish breeds. By 1800 there were some 20 recognizable sheep breeds in Britain, distributed largely geographically; the total national wool crop was estimated at 96m lb (44 000 tonnes), and with import duty not being imposed until 1802, a further 8.6m lb (4000 tonnes) was imported, 6m lb (2700 tonnes) from Spain. Eventually some of King George's flock was auctioned off and in 1811 a Merino Society was established in the UK. But Merino breeding did not itself succeed in England as the sheep herded too close for sparse Scottish hills, the sheep despite interbreeding were still not very heavy, and the wool could anyway be produced more cheaply in Australia. In 1825 the import of wool from the UK's colonies became tariff-free, the duty for several years before having been as high as 6 d/lb. In 1844 the duty was finally lifted on foreign wool generally. However the number of breeds continued to multiply; as Fraser noted in 1950: 'There is practically no corner of Britain where some breed of British sheep under suitable management will not pay its way' (*Sheep husbandry*, 5th ed, 1950).

Continental Europe

Originally the Moors rejuvenated Spanish sheep breeding, from the 8th to the 13th centuries. The Spanish established a central sheep organisation, the Mesta, which dominated the whole of the Spanish economy, bound up as it was with the sheep and the wool industry. Columbus' voyage was paid for from sheep revenue, and the industry reached its peak during the 17th and 18th centuries when there were 20m sheep in Spain, over half being Merinos. No Merinos were exported and Spain had a monopoly on fine wool during this period. It was eventually the Napoleonic Wars which led to the break-up of the Spanish flocks and the wholesale distribution of the breed to other parts of the world.

Meanwhile in France and in other European countries sheep were imported, especially after the impetus provided by Napoleon, and French breeds were specifically developed. In Germany sheep breeding became important after the 12th century, particularly when the influence of the Flemish merchants spread throughout the large cloth and wool-producing centres of Eastern Europe. Wurttemberg was the oldest German Land where sheep were raised, and in 1719 Prussian authorities issued an edict against the importation of any foreign cloth or woollen goods. Merino sheep were imported into Germany, starting in the late 18th century, but the production of Saxon superfine wool ceased when the first worsted plant was founded in Saxony and less crimped wools were needed. The last German Merino flock producing fine wool – in Silesia – was destroyed during World War II although there are still some mutton sheep. Limited numbers of wool sheep survive in Austria, the Netherlands, Ireland, Belgium and Switzerland, amongst other European countries.

America

Spanish sheep were exported with Coranado and then Juan de Onate in Mexico and what became Texas, in the mid-16th century. English sheep were shipped to North America in the 17th century although Rambouillet sheep did not reach Argentina until 1844 despite the fact that the Spanish had bred some sheep there since the early 16th century. Wool production rose rapidly in Argentina in the 19th century until very wet weather between 1877 and 1884 caused heavy Merino losses, and a tremendous switch occurred to mutton breeds to meet the new frozen mutton industry. Uruguay's sheep are said to date from Captain Hernandrias de Saavedra in 1617 and the country has had a wide variety of different sheep, increasingly also not Merino.

Australia

The first Australian sheep were from Bengal in India as there were no native sheep. In 1788 there were only 29 sheep in Australia, 70 having been imported from the Cape by the first Governor of Australia, Arthur Phillip. In 1793 Captain John MacArthur, known as 'The Father of Australia', started a flock, joined by the Rev Marsden, the two founders of the Australian Merino wool industry. South Africa was the first country outside Europe to obtain Merino sheep, sent as a gift from the Spanish to the Dutch to Colonel Gordon in the Cape. After the export of these Merinos to Australia by his widow, and the addition of sheep sent by King George III, the Australian flocks developed rapidly through cross-breeding.

As early as the first decade of the 19th century, when Australian wool first began to be sold in London coffee houses, it was recognised that Australian wool was as good as Spanish and Parliament reduced its duties on imported Australian wool. In 1824 the Australian Agricultural Company was formed in London to produce fine wool in Australia. The Saxons competed, but the Australians succeeded: the industry flourished, despite periodic crashes. The first auction of Australian wool was held at Garraway's Coffee House in London in 1821. By 1830 Australia was Merino wool-conscious, and the saying was 'put everything on four feet' with the first auction held in Adelaide in 1840. Quality deterioration caused by the rapid spread of the industry without effective quality control was noted as early as 1844.

The gold rush period (1851-80) brought about a revolution in sheep management: it was discovered that shepherding was not necessary: the sheep thrived when left to their own devices and yielded heavier and better fleeces when allowed to roam freely in search of food. The mechanism starting from the Australian farms and ending in the European industry was created by Thomas Mort in 1844 when he wrenched control from the London wool brokers, work continued by Richard Goldsborough, who started the first colonial auctions of wool and later built the first Australian-designed wool store in Melbourne, although the majority of Australian wool continued to be sold at auction in London in the 19th century. Peppin Merino sheep better suited to the dry plains were bred. A significant trend in the last four decades of the 19th century was the shift from the production of clothing wool for the woollen industry to combing wool for the worsted. Between 1851 and 1891 the flocks of the six colonies of Australia (New South Wales, Victoria, Queensland, South Australia, Western Australia, Tasmania) grew from 21m to 107m and the weight of the clip sevenfold, from 78m lb (35 000 tonnes) in 1861 to 545m lb (247 000 tonnes) in 1891. Around this time unsuccessful attempts to introduce the Vermont sheep were made. The prolonged droughts from 1892–1902 nearly halved the sheep population and it took almost thirty years to rebuild to over 100m. Since the 19th century Merino breeding has been intensive. Cross-bred sheep with fine and medium wools did not begin to flourish until the 1880s and then they expanded mostly at the expense of Merino in all except the dryest, wettest and roughest areas of the sheep world.

New Zealand

The first permanent sheep flock was established in New Zealand in 1834, although some sixty years earlier Captain Cook had unsuccessfully tried to introduce sheep to New Zealand. These first sheep were Merinos, and for the rest of the 19th century their numbers increased rapidly, to peak at 14m. However, with the introduction of refrigerated meat shipments to England in 1882, this slow maturing fine wool specialist was rapidly replaced by the dual purpose breeds. They were able to give the farmer a quick return on their carcasses as well as significant supplementary income from their heavier fleeces. Also counting against the Merino was its inability to cope with the wetter, newly developed pasture of North Island.

South Africa

In South Africa the sheep was primarily kept for mutton production until the last decade of the 18th century. In 1891, after just over a century of sheepfarming, it was estimated that there were just over 13.5m woolled sheep in the Cape Colony, but quality was poor until Merinos were imported from Australia after the Boer War.

Global marketing

In the 19th century the international wool market was already segmented between apparel - which dominated production and trade, and continues to do so - and carpet wool. Although the amount of wool used worldwide rose from 222 000 tonnes in 1800 to 850 000 tonnes in 1900, 'wool failed to have the same impact as cotton simply because the manufacture and sale of woollens were less suited than cotton to the methods of mass production' (*An illustrated history of the sheep and wool industry*, SAWB, 1970). As a result, well-known trading firms willing to trade most commodities traded increasingly little of the commodity and by as early as 1860 wool had been pushed back into fifth place in English trade after cotton fabrics, pig-iron, machinery and coal.

Before World War I, wool marketing was outside government control internationally, and London was the main auction market worldwide, followed by Boston, Mass. The auction market especially emphasised the particular quality characteristics of every individual clip of wool which was useful when the quality varied so substantially between lots. During World War I wool prices fluctuated substantially and governments made large scale purchases. Raw wool was not controlled until 1916, when scarcity led the British government to acquire successively the Australian, New Zealand, and then South African clip. Prices fell dramatically after the war when surplus supplies were sold off, first by the government directly and then by the British Australian Wool Realisation Association.

Meanwhile, auction sales had developed elsewhere in the world. Sydney was already trading more than London and there were other spot markets in Australia as well as in New Zealand and South Africa. By the mid-1920s, nearly half the Australian wool clip was still bought by the UK, but the USA and Japan were emerging as major buyers at auction sales throughout Australia. Relatively more wool was produced in those countries, and was almost all marketed by public auctions at central marketing points; the first reserve price support scheme was introduced in Australia in the 1920s, to stop prices falling below eight pence a pound, and a Merino ram export ban was imposed in 1929. In 1936 the first Australian Wool Board was established.

Throughout America and Europe, however, farmers continued to sell their wool individually at private sale or at local auctions. An arrangement which was effectively bulk purchase was made between South Africa and the UK in 1934 and was in force until World War II. In that war, control of apparel wool was swiftly arranged, with the British government agreeing to buy both the New Zealand and the Australian clips for all the war and one year thereafter, at an initial average price of 13s 4d/lb for greasy wool, later increased to 15s 5d. In Australia this work was carried out by the Central Wool Committee appointed by the government which contained representatives of all wool interests in wool production and trade. Much of the wool concerned was stored in the USA, though remaining under British ownership, and was not sold until 1947.

Marketing in the USA

In the USA, for example, which had always been a significant wool producer and a very major importer, there has been a long history of wool control measures passed: a tariff on wool imports was enacted in 1816. In 1922 a specific duty per pound of clean fibre content was introduced. Under the Tariff Act of 1930 all wools no finer than 40s (see Chapter 2, Table 2.4) became duty free if they were used for the manufacture of floor coverings, press cloths, knit or felt boots, heavy-fulled socks and other such products. The USA also enacted price support and purchase programmes for US wool from the 1930s onwards. In 1938/39 non-recourse loans were extended and thereafter the US military took up the domestic production: the US government responded to war conditions first by guaranteeing the price of the domestic clip and then in 1943 taking it over. The Defense Supplies Corporation, which was the US government organisation responsible, also bought some Australian wool from the UK government, as well as wool from South America, New Zealand and South Africa.

After World War II

Post-war wool production began at levels that were slightly down from the average of the last years before the war, see Table 1.1. Surplus US government supplies were sold off at the conclusion of World War II, South American wool continuing to be a free market with a high percentage going to the USA. In fact, during World War II consumption had fallen behind production by about a third, with the result that at the end of the war, there was a large accumulation of apparel wools controlled by the Joint Disposals Organisation, a private company with representatives from the UK, Australia, New Zealand and South Africa. About two years' supply was held, and there was great pessimism as to production and prices in 1945–46; then current estimates suggested that it would take thirteen years to dissipate the stock if existing and future production levels were not to be heavily disrupted. Partly as a result of this perceived problem, the International Wool Study Group was formed by a resolution adopted at the international wool talks which were held in London in November

Table 1.1 World wool production, m kg clean, Jul–Jun

	Fibre Organon (Fibre Economics Bureau, Inc)	Wool Statistics (Commonwealth Secretariat)		Fibre Organon (Fibre Economics Bureau, Inc)	Wool Statistics (Commonwealth Secretariat)
1890	720	720	1930	995	995
1900	725	725	31	1004	1004
5	720	720	32	990	990
1910	797	797	33	976	976
11	788	788	34	954	954
12	801	801	35	972	972
13	779	779	36	1004	1004
14	774	774	37	1026	1026
15	765	765	38	1058	1058
16	734	734	39	1107	1107
17	752	752	1940	1125	1125
18	756	756	41	1142	1143
19	783	783	42	1121	1121
1920	801	801	43	1116	1116
21	824	824	44	1062	1062
22	819	819	45	1026	1026
23	810	810			
24	864	864			
25	905	905			
26	963	963			
27	976	976			
28	1013	1013			
29	1013	1013			

Table 1.1 cont'd

	Fibre Organon (Fibre Economics Bureau, Inc)	Wool Statistics (Commonwealth Secretariat)		Fibre Organon (Fibre Economics Bureau, Inc)	Wool Statistics (Commonwealth Secretariat)
1946	940	940	1970	1602	1602
47	945	945	71	1566	1566
48	973	973	72	1457	1547
49	1007	1007	73	1432	1432
1950	1049	1049	74	1531	1511
51	1060	1060	75	1538	1503
52	1148	1148	76	1487	1508
53	1161	1161	77	1488	1486
54	1181	1181	78	1538	1531
55	1255	1255	79	1576	1575
56	1328	1328	1980	1607	1599
57	1300	1300	81	1626	1616
58	1372	1372	82	1624	1667
59	1447	1447	83	1639	1683
1960	1451	1451	84	1655	1745
61	1470	1470	85	1722	1745
62	1466	1466	86	1790	1787
63	1494	1494	87	1835	1830
64	1468	1468	88	1883	1887
65	1481	1481	89	1933	1964
66	1541	1525			
67	1562	1574			
68	1625	1620			
69	1614	1607			

1946. Between 1945 and 1947 the USA had a wool purchase programme which allowed farmers to sell on a permissive basis either directly or indirectly to the Commodity Credit Corporation (CCC) at ceiling prices, which could not then sell at less than the parity price. As a result, sizeable wool stocks also accumulated with the US government.

But the pessimists were completely confounded. Consumption increased steadily, and at a higher rate than anticipated. Stocks had been used up by the 1951/52 season, by which time the Korean War had provided fresh problems for the wool market and supply. The Wool Committee of the International Materials Conference met in April 1951, but plans to consider whether international action was required came to nothing and the committee dissolved in September 1952 when the increase in world wool production and the 1951–52 slump in wool textile production improved the demand/supply balance.

For 44s and finer (see Chapter 2, Table 2.4) the US tariff

agreement following the 1948 GATT agreement were variable; 44s and less carried lower rates. President Truman vetoed one price support measure in 1947 but in August 1947 price support measures were resumed at the 1946 level and stayed in force until 1950. The CCC was also authorised to sell wool at less than the parity price. Under the Agricultural Act of 1949, in force until 1952, wool prices were buttressed by loans at a level between 60–90% of parity to encourage annual production of 360m lb (163 000 tonnes) of shorn wool. In practice because of the upturn of prices caused by the Korean War it was not necessary to implement the announced price support measures.

Although production was steady in Australia and up in New Zealand, Argentina, Uruguay, Spain and even Russia, China and Turkey to some extent, large falls in production were observed in the first post-war stage in South Africa, the USA (above all – US wool production between 1946–50 was 285m lb (129 000 tonnes) (greasy) compared to 425m lb (193 000 tonnes) in 1936–40), and more understandably the UK. The fall in US production more than compensated for increases elsewhere, and the result was world production of 3840m lbs (1.74m tonnes) compared to 3930m lb (1.78m tonnes) for the same period. Continued US decline, though more gradual, was more than offset in the second post-war phase by substantial further increases in New Zealand and other countries and a revival in UK and South African production.

In the mid-1950s there were approximately 800m sheep world-wide, producing an annual crop of about 4.3m lb (2000 tonnes) of greasy wool.

During 1966/67 there were 29m sheep in Britain and they produced 131m lb (59 000 tonnes) of wool (greasy). At the same time in Spain there were still 22m sheep producing 82m lb (37 000 tonnes) wool (greasy). In 1967–68 the Soviet Union was the second largest wool producer in the world after Australia, producing 871m lb (395 000 tonnes) greasy from 138.1m woollen sheep.

It was the collapse of prices after the Korean War that led to Australia's second attempt at a reserve prices scheme. In 1951, however, a grower referendum in Australia threw out the proposal, and again in 1965. In 1966 there were more than 120m Merinos in Australia. For almost a century, by the mid-1960s, Australia had maintained its position as the world's leading wool producer. In 1945/46 Australia produced 424.6m kg (936m lb) (greasy), of which 369.4m kg (814.4m lb) was shorn wool (including crutchings), 29.9m kg (65.9m lb) was dead and fellmongered wool and 25.3m kg (55.8m lb) was wool exported on skins. This compared to 677m kg (1493m lb) in

1977/78, for example, with 605.5m kg (1335m lb) now shorn, and 71.5m kg (158m lb) together of the other two categories. Sheep numbers in Australia were 106.4m in 1950; by 1960 they had reached 149m and in 1970 they reached a record 174.3m, thereafter declining to 132.7m in 1980 and 173.1m in 1990, a fall which continued. In 1989 Australia produced 35% of the world's wool on a clean basis from 14% of the world's sheep. The export ban remained in force until as late as 1970 and there are still restrictions on embryo and semen exports as well as a quota of 900 Merino rams.

The first minimum price scheme in New Zealand was established in 1952 by the New Zealand Wool Commission. The 1966/67 severe worldwide downturn saw 33% of the New Zealand clip held by the Commission. The rules were eased; in 1973 greater flexibility was introduced and a further intervention regime, strata price control, was introduced in 1976. In 1985, when the New Zealand dollar was floated, intervention and strata price control became the same. The New Zealand Wool Board (NZWB) began to buy on a flexible basis, changing intervention prices from sale to sale if necessary. The intervention prices remained confidential. Prices could change to reflect changes in the exchange rate. In 1988 the minimum price regime ceased to be statutory, and from 1990/91 the Board's market support operated on fixed intervention levels. From February 1991 onwards the whole system was suspended and subsequently terminated.

In 1970 wool prices collapsed and the Australian Wool Commission was established to operate a Reserve Price Scheme, which operated from 1970–91 and was designed to provide both wool growers and wool users with protection against the impact of fluctuating prices. A flexible system with no fixed and publicised minimum price was replaced by the formation of the Australian Wool Corporation in 1973 followed by the reserve price system being introduced on 2 September 1974. At all approved public wool sales, AWC staff valued each individual sale lot at the floor price level. Any lot which failed to reach this level was bought by the AWC at the floor price. This expensive scheme was funded by the growers from a levy and the AWC banked profits; at the height of the market in 1988/89 the AWC accumulated interest income at almost A$1m every day. During the controlled prices regime in Australia the wool combing industry overseas experienced continual difficulties. The AWC sometimes withdrew large amounts of wool from processing and commerce which in turn drove many processing firms out of business. This was especially true for topmakers who depended on a regular supply of wool from the farm through to the spinner.

Topmakers tended to be independent commission combing plants which were all in wool processing centres, processing on commission for merchants, a system found effective over many decades.

Events in Australia in 1991 had a direct bearing on the 1991 world wool market collapse and the NZWB's decision to follow the AWC. By 1991 Australia was producing some 20% more wool than the world wanted. The Australian reserve price (also known as the floor price) was a more rigid and federally rather than board funded system than the New Zealand minimum price scheme. The reserve price was an inflexible level; the AWC was obliged to buy all wool which did not reach the reserve price, and from 1989/90 this effectively meant that the reserve price was the world price - A700 ¢/kg in 1990/91 compared to A870 cents the season before. The AWC bought more wool than the NZWB; stocks peaked at almost 80% and 35% of annual clip respectively, and the AWC system was stopped. The New Zealand system was suspended the day after the Australian one, on 12 and 11 February 1991 respectively. NZ$260m of producers' funds had been frozen by the banks to provide security for NZWB loans. No government assistance or compensation was made available to New Zealand wool growers, in contrast to the situation in Australia (see Chapter 7).

World wool imports declined from a peak of 1.41bn tonnes in 1987 - before the record price increases of 1988 - falling to 983m tonnes in 1990. This fall in turn helped to create the large wool stocks that bedevilled the international wool trade in the early 1990s. Wool prices then fell. Demand in developed countries, especially in Europe, fell, supply remained inelastic, and the price falls that followed were inevitable. Criticising the prevailing wool production culture, the Arthur Little report of May 1992 pointed out that many producers, for example British hill farmers and New Zealand producers, were rooted in a culture that accepted low incomes in return for guaranteed production and profit levels. They entertained the familiar notion of a 'right' price for their commodity, which equalled production costs currently prevailing under established production modes, together with a modest profit. The industry internationally even during the 1980s found it difficult to accept the idea that the only right price was formed by the intersection of supply and demand on an international free market without the numerous government support schemes then in operation. In the early 1990s the next stage of the development of the international industry occurred when the support schemes were stripped away from the wool market in Australia, the UK and South Africa, freeing the industry at last to make sensible plans and to compete on the basis of productivity. The mid-1990s saw the consolidation of the new free market international wool trade and its associated industry, initially in a climate of depressed international trade, high stockpiles and exceptionally low prices, but from late 1993 onwards in more encouraging times.

CHAPTER

2

The production of wool

Sheep

There are over 1.1bn sheep worldwide which is about one sheep for every four people. Even now in Britain there are approximately four sheep to every five people. Numbers have been falling in the early 1990s in response to price falls and the need to demolish the stockpile. Numbers are expected to recover in the later years of the decade. Table 2.1 shows world woolled sheep population.

Sheep are tough, adaptable animals which can thrive in many different climates. There are 40 breeds in the UK alone, each individually suited to the different climate, soil, vegetation and ground found in the country. There are eleven main breeds in New Zealand, each with a different end product (see Table 2.2). By contrast, in Australia, Merinos comprise over 70% of the sheep flock. There are four basic strains of Australian Merino, Peppin, South Australian, Saxon and Spanish. It is prized for its ability to thrive in Australia's harsh environment and yet still produce high quality fleeces but it is intolerant of damp climates and subject to foot rot as well as having a low lambing rate. The second most populous Australian sheep is the Border/Merino Crossbred, the ewe progeny from Border Leicester rams mated to Merino ewes. In regions with longer and wetter winters the Merino has been crossed with other breeds, and these in turn have been fixed into recognised breeds. Foremost of these are the Corriedale and Polwarth, though the

Table 2.1 World woolled sheep population, millions

Year ending Sept of second year shown from 1986/87 onwards	**Census Month from 1986/87 onwards**	**Average 1980–81/ 1984–85**	**1986–87**	**1987–88**	**1988–89**	**1989–90**	**1990–91**	**1991–92**	**1992–93**
Albania	Dec	1.7	1.4	1.4	1.5	1.5	1.6	1.6	1.6
Argentina	June	32.4	28.8	29.2	29.3	28.6	27.6	25.7	
Australia (a)	Mar	132.9	153.2	156.6	165.2	175.2	166.6	150.7	141.4
Brazil	Dec	18.3	19.7	19.9	20.1	20.0	20.1	20.3	
Bulgaria	Jan	10.7	9.6	8.9	8.6	8.1	7.9	6.7	
Canada	June	0.8	0.7	0.7	0.7	0.8	0.8	0.8	
Chile	June	6.1	5.5	5.6	5.7	5.2	4.7	4.6	
China	Dec	104.8	99.0	102.7	110.6	113.5	112.8	110.9	110.9
Czechoslovakia	Jan	1.0	1.1	1.0	1.1	1.0	0.9	0.9	
Falkland Is	May	0.7	0.7	0.7	0.7	0.7	0.7	0.7	
France	Dec	12.6	10.8	12.1	11.5	11.2	11.1	10.6	
E Germany	Dec	2.2	2.6	2.7	2.6	2.6	} 3.2	} 2.5	
W Germany	Dec	1.2	1.4	1.4	1.5	1.5	}	}	
Greece	Dec	8.8	11.0	10.8	10.4	10.4	10.2	9.8	
Hungary	Dec	3.1	2.3	2.3	2.2	2.1	1.9	2.3	
India	May	40.0	39.0	39.0	39.0	40.0	40.0	40.0	40.0
Iran	Oct	34.2	45.0	45.0	45.0	45.0	45.0	45.0	
Iraq	Mar	11.8	9.0	9.0	9.5	9.6	7.8	9.0	
Irish Republic	June	3.5	5.6	6.7	7.7	8.7	8.9	8.9	
Italy	Dec	10.1	11.5	11.5	11.6	11.6	10.8	10.8	
Lesotho	Aug	1.2	1.4	1.4	1.4	1.5	1.5	1.5	
Mongolia	Dec	14.5	13.2	13.2	13.5	14.3	15.1	15.1	
Morocco	Mar	15.2	13.8	13.8	13.8	13.8	13.5	14.0	14.1
Namibia	Aug	5.3	6.2	6.3	6.4	6.5	6.7	6.7	
New Zealand	June	70.0	64.2	64.6	60.6	57.9	55.2	52.5	(50.3)
Pakistan	May	22.6	26.6	27.5	28.3	29.2	30.2	30.8	
Peru	Dec	14.7	13.1	13.2	12.9	13.0	12.3	12.2	
Poland	June	4.1	4.7	4.4	4.4	4.2	3.2	2.4	
Portugal	Dec	4.4	3.0	3.0	3.2	3.3	3.4	3.4	3.3
Romania	Jan	16.9	(17.0)	16.8	16.2	15.4	14.1	13.5	
South Africa (b)	Aug	27.3	23.8	24.2	25.9	25.6	24.4	23.2	22.3
Former Soviet Union (c)	Jan	143.0	142.2	140.8	141.0	138.9	134.6	119.8	117.4
Spain	Dec	16.3	17.9	20.3	23.1	22.7	24.0	24.3	
Turkey	Dec	48.3	48.7	48.8	49.0	48.8	47.5	47.3	
UK	June	33.1	38.7	40.9	43.0	43.8	43.6	44.0	
USA	Jan	12.4	10.6	10.9	10.9	11.4	11.2	10.8	10.2
Uruguay	June	20.6	24.4	24.1	24.9	25.2	25.9	25.6	25.0
Yugoslavia	Jan	7.4	7.8	7.8	7.6	7.6	7.4	7.5	
Other Africa (c)		113.8	119.0	121.3	123.9	121.8	126.9	125.7	
Other America (c)		22.9	23.4	23.7	24.3	24.6	24.7	24.9	
Other Asia (c)		48.0	45.9	45.3	48.2	49.9	50.8	50.2	
Other Western Europe (c)		5.8	5.5	5.8	5.7	6.1	6.3	6.4	
World total of which:		**1104.7**	**1129.0**	**1145.3**	**1172.7**	**1172.7**	**1165.1**	**1123.6**	
Soviet Union, China, Eastern Europe		299.8	290.5	291.6	299.0	299.1	292.1	273.1	

(a) Covers all farms.
(b) Official series plus fixed estimate for woolled sheep in Bantu areas.
(c) See note below for country coverage.

Other Africa includes Algeria, Botswana, Egypt, Ethiopia, Kenya, Libya, Mali, Mozambique, Sudan, Swaziland, Tanzania, Zambia, Zimbabwe.
Other America includes Bolivia, Colombia, Ecuador, Greenland, Mexico, Paraguay, Venezuela.
Other Asia includes Afghanistan, Bangladesh, Bhutan, Cyprus, Gaza, Indonesia, Israel, Jordan, Kuwait, Lebanon, Macao, Malaysia, Myanmar, Nepal, Saudi Arabia, Syria, Thailand, Yemen.
Other Western Europe includes Austria, Belgium, Denmark, Finland, Iceland, Luxembourg, Malta, Netherlands, Norway, Sweden, Switzerland.

Source: International Wood Textile Organisation

Perendale, Tukidale and Drysdale - genetic mutations or 'sports' derived from the New Zealand Romney - are also important, especially in New Zealand where they were first bred.

Sheep produced for their wool in the late 20th century have been specially bred for centuries. In the eighteenth century, Robert Bakewell in Leicestershire was the most notable among many breeders. They aimed first to improve the natural coat of the sheep. The coat contained not only wool fibre, but also hair and kemp which are brittle fibres that will not accept dye. Both these factors were bred

Table 2.2 Fibre characteristics and principal end uses of the main New Zealand breeds

Breed	Fibre diameter, µm	Staple length[1], mm	Bulk lustre	Fleece weight, kg	Average yield, %	End uses[2]
NZ Romney	33–40	125–175	Low/med	4.5–6.0	75–80	1 2 3 4 5
Perendale	31–35	100–150	Med/low	3.5–5.0	75–80	1 2 3 4 5
Coopworth	35–39	125–175	Low/high	4.5–6.0	75–80	1 3
Borderdale	30–35	100–150	Low/med	4.5–6.0	74–78	3 4 5 7
Border Leicester	37–40	150–200	Low/high	4.5–6.0	76–81	1 3 4
Drysdale	>40	200–300	Med/low	5.0–7.0	77–83	1
Corriedale	28–33	75–125	Med/med	4.5–6.0	65–72	2 4 5 8 9
NZ Halfbred	25–31	75–110	Med/low	4.0–5.0	65–72	4 5 6 8
Merino	17–24	65–100	Med/low	3.5–5.0	69–72	6 8
Cheviot	28–34	75–100	High/low	2.0–3.0	75–79	8 9
Downs	23–32	50–75	High/low	2.0–3.0	50–70	5 8 9 10

Notes:
1 Typical full year's growth
2 Principal end uses

1 Carpets
2 Blankets
3 Heavy woollens/overcoatings
4 Furnishing fabrics
5 Handknitting yarn
6 Fine apparel
7 Heavy apparel
8 Knitwear
9 Tweeds
10 Wool filling

Source: NZWB

out. Likewise in the Middle Ages sheep grew both coarse and fine wool in the same fleece, and this too has been bred out. The genetic improvement of sheep and selective breeding programmes have characterised sheep rearing for more than two decades. For example sheep can now be tested individually for facial eczema tolerance using sporedesmin and worm resistance through dung samples - in every case breeding the most effective together. Of course sheep can be subject to a wide variety of natural diseases as well as predators, but in comparison to other fibre products this is by no means as serious a problem. For example, foot rot, the most economically significant contagious disease of Australian sheep, costs the industry only $80m in production losses and control annually. Internal parasites are another problem for which genetic breeding programmes have been recognised as an answer. Cutbacks in the Commonwealth Scientific and Industrial Research Organisation (CSIRO) funding must threaten further advances in all these areas.

The relationship between wool production and sheepmeat production is clearly a close one. The British Wool Marketing Board (BWMB) states in reference to the situation in the UK: 'Meat production from lambs is more important to the lowland man but the hill producer can derive as much as a third of his income from wool. Breeders strive for the ideal - the animal that will meet the requirements both of the butcher and the wool manufacturer; one that will rear more lambs and have the milk to feed them.' Certainly, in the same way that Merino meat is not satisfactory except for petfood use, so the wool from pure lambing and mutton breeds is not worth shearing under most circumstances. When wool prices reached their nadir in late 1993 wool was contributing at best 5%, and a breed of 'easy-care' sheep has been developed that sheds its wool naturally.

Wool the product

Wool that is knitted into warm sweaters and woven into fine cloth comes from the fleece of sheep. Wool is the second most important natural fibre after cotton. The thick covering or coat of the domestic sheep consists of a mass of specialised fibres. Typically it is unlike hair in that there are minute overlapping scales or plates extending lengthwise on the surface of the fibre which give it an entangling or felting characteristic. Wool is an outgrowth of the epidermis and is generally believed to represent the evolutionary development of the undercoat of the animal from which domestic sheep were derived. Whether as a vestigial remnant of the past or as a new development associated with certain environmental conditions, some sheep do grow hair and kemp, especially in sub-tropical areas. In cross-section, a wool fibre consists of a two-part outer layer (cuticle) and an absorbent core (cortex). Many of the wool fibres are called non-medullated continuous fibres, i.e. they are solid and comprise just cutile and cortex. There are other types consisting of three layers: the cuticle, the cortex and the medulla (pith), and there are also mixed types which are part medullated and part non-medullated. There may also be kemps, which are periodically shed fibres thought to be relics of the former shiny outer coat. These are coarse and straight, are often white and shiny, and mostly sharply pointed, consisting of an outer cuticle and an inner medulla of loosely packed cells.

The cuticle regulates wool's dual ability to repel liquid, yet absorb moisture vapour. Seen under a microscope, it consists of a thin, porous membrane covering overlapping scales. These scales have a fine wax coating which causes liquid to bead and roll off the surface of wool fabric, while moisture vapour (e.g. perspiration) can be absorbed through the porous fibre. The cortex, which accounts for approximately 90% of the fibre, is composed of very small, cigar-shaped cells, each enclosed in a tough membrane and containing dense fibrous material. Many of the amino acids in the cortical cells are able to bond physically and chemically with water vapour. Consequently under humid conditions wool can absorb up to one-third of its weight in moisture without feeling damp – this makes wool ideal for underclothing which has to absorb perspiration from the body without clinging to the skin. As the atmosphere dries out the fibre releases the moisture, which is quickly dispersed through evaporation.

Wool fibres, whether short or long, grow in tufts of as many as a dozen fibres. Density of fibre varies widely with the breed and from one part of the body of the individual sheep to another. Merino lambs have been credited with 20m fibres and the superfine fleece of a fully grown Merino may have as many as 126m fibres, arranged in separate bundles (staples) of some thousands of fibres each. Other breeds have moderately or sharply lower densities, ranging from 10–50m fibres; staple size and shape also vary by breed e.g. Merino staples are blunted while strong wool sheep have tapering staples, and there may also be considerable variation within a fleece. The wool follicles of the sheep's skin are pits reaching into the dermis, formed by in-turning epidermal layers. The follicles are of two sorts, one provided with only the wax gland and the other, primary, with perspiration (suint) gland and arrestor pili muscle as well. Fibre growth is a continuous process, occurring through multiplication of the soft cells of the papilla at the base of the follicle, which is bathed in a nutrition medium. The flow of this fluid is greatly affected by the sheep's health, in turn affected by drought, poor forage and disease. If the process is defective, the result will be weak areas in the wool fibre, known as 'tender' wool. Differentiation of the cells into the wool protein (keratin) of the cuticle and cortex occurs about one-third of the distance above the follicle's base, beyond which point the wool fibre is no longer alive. Wax and protection salts are added near the exit.

Greasy wool, the form in which practically all wool is marketed initially, is mainly obtained by clipping or cutting the coat or fleece of fibres from the live animal. Smaller amounts, called pulled wool, or sometimes skin or dead wool, are obtained from the skins or pelts of dead sheep. The raw grease wool contains perspiration or suint salts, which along with varying amounts of natural grease are sometimes called yolk, plus wool fibres of possibly a number of different types, and foreign matter such as dirt, all of which can be between one-third and two-thirds - but usually about half - of the total weight of the unprocessed fleece.

The natural colour of wool ranges from the usual white through grey, fawn and brown to actual black. However the complex structures formed by the amino acids also bond with most dyestuffs, so that dye is absorbed into the core of the fibre, imparting true and lasting colour to the finished product.

Wool fibres are usually slightly elliptical, with an average diameter of between 1/400 and 1/2000 inch (0.063 and 0.013 mm). The range is dependent on the breed of sheep but there is considerable variation within the same fleece. The length of fibre, which depends not only on the breed but also on the time that the fibre has grown, is normally between less than 1 inch (25.4 mm) to several inches, although when shearing has not been carried out for several years, a growth of more than 40 inches (1.02 m) has been recorded in cross-breds. Growth and fineness depends on the length of daylight, especially for cross-bred sheep, while the latter applies to Merinos. Table 2.3 shows average yearly growths for some major sheep breeds. The first year's wool growth, sheared from what are termed hog or teg sheep, is usually longer than indicated by the table, because the lambs are born from February to April and the shearing does not occur until the next May or June. Hog wool is identified through its pointed fibre tips.

The cortex is further divided along its length into the ortho (soft) and para (hard) cortex. These two cells lie on opposite sides of the fibre, but grow at different rates so that the wool fibre develops its

Table 2.3 Average yearly growths of the more important breeds of sheep

	Inches	Centimetres
Black-faced	10–18	25.4–45.72
Southdown	3–4	7.62–10.16
Lincoln	12–18	30.48–45.72
Romney	6–8	15.24–20.32
Shropshire	4–6	10.16–15.24
Clothing Merino	1.5–3	3.81–7.62
Combing Merino	2.5–5	6.35–12.7

characteristic waviness or crimp structure, with the ortho-cortex on the outside. This curl in the fibres makes wool elastic. The fibres uncurl when stretched, but return to their original state when released. This explains why woollen garments resist creasing and crushing so well. Crimp frequency is often used as a subjective indicator of fibre diameter; as a rule finer wools have a more frequent and tighter crimp structure. The crimp or wave of wool fibre varies generally with the average finesse from about 6 per inch (25.4 mm) in cross-bred sheep to about 24 per inch in the finest Merino fibres. It is related to the period of rotation or curl of the major axis of the eclipse, since the fibre issues from the follicle. The overlapping scales of the cuticle point towards the outer tip of the fibre.

Some other important physical characteristics of wool are its lightness (a specific gravity of 1.3) and its resilience or springiness which is related to its elasticity. The elongated shape and length-wise arrangement of the cortical cells make the wool fibre very strong and flexible. It can resist a high level of abrasion, and can be bent and twisted many times without damage. The fibre crimp is reflected in the total structure of the fibre, right down to the coiled springs formed by the molecular chains which resembled miniature shock absorbers. It can be extended by as much as 30% for short periods without suffering permanent deformation, which is an important factor in its selection for high-grade clothing. Wool does not conduct electricity well, and will hold a charge of static electricity under some conditions. It is a warm fabric because the curled fibres enclose a great deal of insulating air; air is trapped in the crinkles when the fibre is twisted together to make yarn. The fibres themselves have a rough, scaly surface which also helps to hold the air. This air layer insulates the body of the garment wearer from both cold and heat. The effect is increased by weaving and knitting woollens loosely from soft-spun yarns. Some wools are lustrous. Severe drying fatigues the fibre by damaging the protein.

Chemically, wool keratin is an animal protein not unlike hair, feathers and horn. Chemical analysis of wool shows its average composition to be as follows: carbon 50%, hydrogen 7%, oxygen 22–25%, nitrogen 16–17% and sulphur 3–4%.

The relatively high sulphur content of wool is an unusual property amongst textiles. Wool is rich in cystine, an amino acid high in sulphur. The amino acids are arranged in large bundles, or chains, or large molecules, called polypeptide chains. In one keratin subtype, these chains apparently take a folded form, whereas the other subtype is built from the same chains pulled into straightened forms. These chains can be linked in two different ways: the cystine or disulphide one can be altered by some chemical reagents, with consequent alteration or destruction of the physical quality of the fibre. The other or salt linkages can be readily broken, a fact which is utilised to advantage in some stages of processing. If wool is burned, it largely resolves itself into ammonia gas with its characteristic odour.

The average production per sheep is about 5 lb (2.27 kg). However, 10 lb (4.54 kg) per animal is not unusual amongst the better wool-producing flocks, and it is possible to reach a yield of 15–20 lb (6.8–9 kg) per animal. The harvest is annual or biannual, usually in the middle or late spring or even early summer, with the sheep thereby getting the most benefit from its coat during the winter.

Woollen materials are attacked by moths. The moths lay eggs in the wool and the larvae which are then hatched feed on the wool fibres. Moth attack can be prevented by placing 'moth-balls' among the woollens. Wool can also be moth-proofed during manufacture.

The term wool is also applied to fibres made from other animals, including cashmere and angora goats, camels and other similar animals. These animals grow thick coats in the same way as sheep grow wool. The hair fibres are not as crimped as sheep wool, but they do have a slightly scaly surface.

The main fibre properties affecting the processing efficiency, product performance and cost of wool are diameter (Fig. 2.1), length (Fig. 2.2) and strength, colour (Fig. 2.3 and 2.4), medullation, bulk (crimp) and lustre. In addition, other constituents of the fleece such as wax, suint, dirt and vegetable matter must also be considered when assessing greasy wool. In general, yield values increase with fibre diameter. The average yield for New Zealand Merino is 65–70%, while for half-breeds it increases to 70–74% and cross-breeds achieve 75–80%. The yield from oddments can be 10% less than the fleece. Wool wax will average about 25% of a Merino fleece and 10% of a cross-breed. Suint can form up to 10% of weight and vegetable matter as well as soil can also represent a contamination problem.

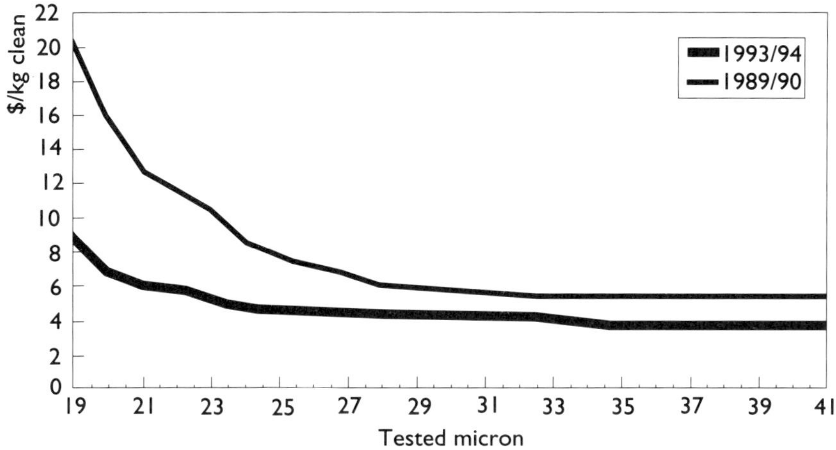

2.1 Price by diameter of wool sold at auction (source: Wools of New Zealand Statistical Handbook, 1993/94).

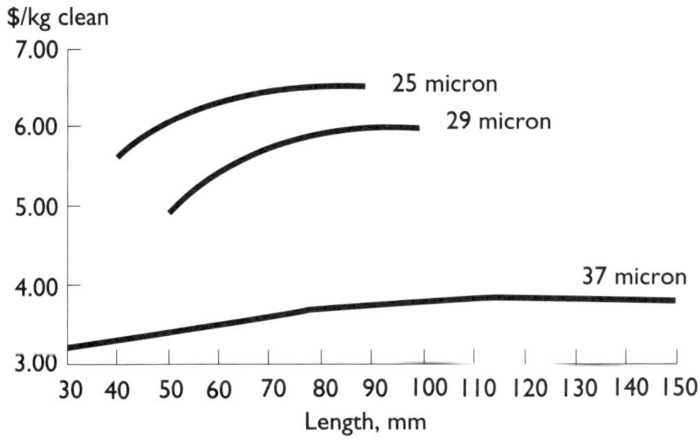

2.2 Price relativities based on variation in fibre length for the 1991/92 season (source: NZWB Statistical Handbook 1991/92 season).

Wool is also very storable - sometimes to the regret of growers. The Australian Wool Testing Authority in mid-1994 confirmed that none of the characteristics of the wool they tested - the most important ones - had changed in the two years they had been monitoring the wool.

The measurement of quality and type

Raw wool is suited to a great variety of different purposes depending on its type and grade. However, there is no one classification system

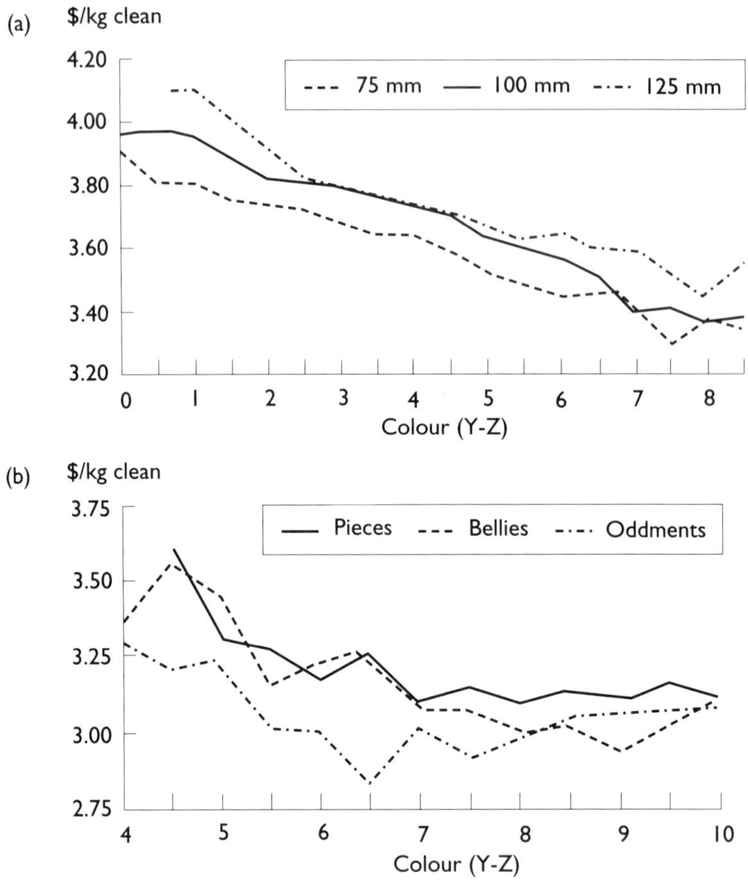

2.3 Price relativities based on variation in fibre colour for the 1991/92 season: a) Fleece; b) Skirtings (source: NZWB Statistical Handbook 1991/92 season).

for wool. This is explained by the differences in historical development and its many different uses, as well as the fact that many different characteristics can be found even in wool from the same origin. There are also many different varieties of sheep: the UK Government Purchase System recognised 1500 different types of Australian wool, 950 from New Zealand and 350 from South Africa, with relatively few types in any one clip common to the clip of another country. Fineness of diameter of the fibre, fibre length, uniformity, colour, lustre, elasticity, strength and suppleness all vary depending on area and breed, as well as between individual sheep and across an individual fleece. Classifying wool is still less precise than the measurements that are used for cotton, for example, for which increasingly accurate measurements have been created in the 1980s.

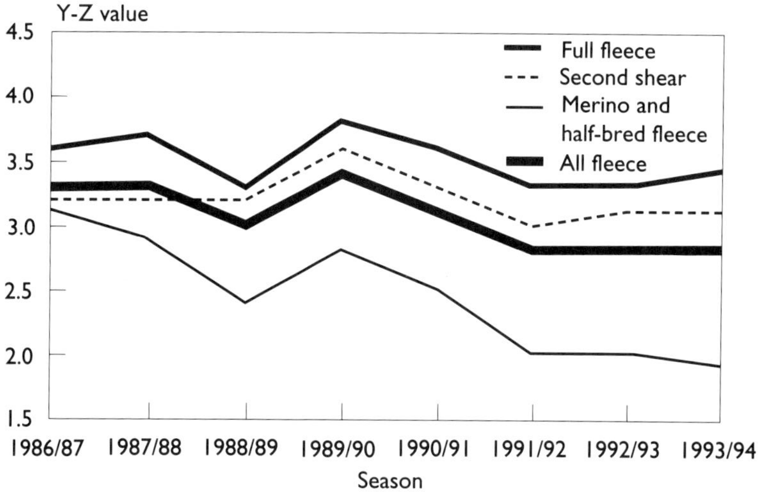

2.4 Average colour measurement for New Zealand fleece wool (source: Wools of New Zealand Statistical Handbook 1993/94).

'Micron' is the term used in the wool industry to indicate micrometre which is the linear measure for one millionth of a metre. Fine Merino wool is 16–20 microns, medium is 20–23 and strong is 23–27.

In the USA and Japan there are other systems based on the closeness of the relationship to Merino wool, the 'blood' system, or the 'numerical', 'count' or 'quality number' system which is used for Japanese futures contracts. The numerical or count system refers to the worsted count which it is estimated will be spun from the fibre, so for example a 50s count fibre should spin that many hanks of yarn each of 560 yards (512 m) length from one pound of combed wool. Table 2.4 gives the micron/quality number relationship.

Table 2.4 Micron/quality number relationship

Micron	Quality number	Micron	Quality number
19	70s	30	52/54s (50/48s lambs)
20	64/70s	31	52s (46/50s lambs)
21	64s	32	50/52s
22	60/64s	33	50s (44/48s lambs)
23	60s (Merino)	34	48/50s
24	60s (quarterbred)	35	46/50s or 48s
25	58/60s	36	46/48s
26	58s	37	44/48s or 46s
27	56/58s	38	46/40s
28	56s (52/56s lambs)	39	40/46s
29	54/56s (50/52s lambs)	40	36/44s

Source: New Zealand Wool Board

Other qualities are considered in classification than the fineness of the fibre (and hence spinning quality). Soundness, the absence of 'cotting' (matting of the wool caused by the combined effects of seasonal reduction in wool growth and the stress of lambing), pronounced weak areas in the fibre, caused by malnutrition or illness of the sheep during the growth of the fleece, and contamination caused by penstain are all very important in combing wools. Good tensile strength, enabling the fibre to undergo the seven pound pull of the comb without breaking is desired. This factor influences to a large degree the yield of valuable tops in relation to noils; 'tender' wool gives up to 25% of the less valuable noils. Combing wools must also be of good length. The condition of wool relates to the adhering wax, salts and moisture and these must be estimated to judge the probable yield when scoured. Colour, sheen and lustre are important with English breeds and cross-breeds, ranging from the rich glossy metallic sheen of the Lincoln and Leicester to the second dimilustre of the Romney Marsh.

Classifying or grading of wool has probably been most developed in Australia. On the large Australian sheep stations, classing is a key operation, taking the place of sorting from the other areas. Fleeces from the sheep are skirted and trimmed, then professionally classed according to their fineness in relation to worsted counts, or formerly as superclothing, ordinary clothing, etc, if they are shorter wools more suited to the woollen industry.

Wool classes in Australia emphasise the needs of different end users. Merino combing wool is classified into eight groups, from Super, AA, A, combing, first and second fleece, Merino clothing wool of four grades (super, first, clothing and fleece), then ordinary wool of six grades and cross-breed wool of eight grades, including that of the long-woolled and short-woolled British grades. Amongst Australian wools the Geelong wool of the Western district of Victoria and the New England tablelands of New South Wales are especially valuable. This highly skilled grading and related operations has been of great benefit in marketing Australian wool of known quality.

The first commercial application of objective measurement in New Zealand was carried out by the New Zealand Department of Agriculture in the 1950s. In the past two decades, WRONZ has developed the capacity to describe in objective terms those properties of wool that are important for trading and manufacturing. At first this research concentrated on techniques for the objective measurement of wool's important properties in terms of trading, this is the yield of greasy wools and condition (moisture content) of scoured wools. Now there is more concentration on the measurement of other commercially important properties such as fibre diameter, followed by colour and more recently length, strength and bulk. Initially tests were made after the wool was sold but now the development of accurate and representative sampling methods, together with tests for yield and fineness, have made it possible to apply objective measurement prior to sale, which occurred in parallel with the development of sale by sample in the 1970s.

Advocates - especially *Wool into the 21st Century*, the New Zealand Wool Board and virtually every other organisation that does not actually itself live or die by trading wool - suggest that all participants in the industry have benefited from objective measurement. Farmers can improve breeding and farm management; wool buyers and exporters benefit because they can value sale lots more easily through the availability of test data on yield, fibre diameter, vegetable matter and colour. In addition, the representativeness of the displayed grab sample (see below) allows an accurate assessment to be made of the commercial characteristics that are not currently tested. Not only does objective measurement allow more accurate assembly of mill deliveries, but claims are reduced where mutually accepted test data are used. Pre-sale testing also means that combination certificates can be quickly obtained covering mill consignments comprising individual sale lots, eliminating the delays involved in further post-sale testing. Overall the processor benefits from production efficiencies that can be achieved through the use of the data; they can more importantly specify relevant aspects of their requirements in precise, objective terms. Yet wool continues to be sold by sample despite what analysts call the 'cost savings and enhanced information flows' (*Wool into the 21st Century*, p 28) to be gained from sale on description from computers.

In South Africa the Wool Testing Bureau (Pty) Ltd is responsible for wool testing. In Australia the Australian Wool Surveillance Authority (AWSA) was established in 1988 as a Division of the National Association of Testing Authorities. SGS Wool Testing Services and the Australian Wool Testing Authority Ltd (AWTA) are the two accredited commercial test houses - in New Zealand similarly it is the New Zealand Wool Testing Authority Ltd and SGS Wool Testing Services, which carry out the pre- and post-sale measurement and certification of wool sold at auction in New Zealand as well as testing samples sent in by growers for breed information and cores taken from scoured deliveries. These must be registered with the Testing Laboratory Council of New Zealand (TELARC) and New Zealand wool test certificates can be issued only with New Zealand authorised test methods. Yield, including vegetable matter content, fibre diameter, colour and medullation (when specifically requested) are measured using internationally accepted standard test methods, and the results are available to the purchaser on test certificates.

The IWTO (International Wool Textile Organisation) yield test (IWTO-19) involves the removal of all impurities (wax, suint, vegetable matter and dirt), including moisture, to arrive at a percentage figure termed wool base (i.e. content of pure, dry wool). Wool base is then used to calculate a range of theoretical processing yields suitable for different sections of the industry although IWTO standards actually on certificates used in trading pre-suppose some different small percentages of remaining dirt, wax and moisture.

Three separate tests are carried out to determine the percentage of residual impurities left after scouring: for vegetable matter content, for ash content and for fatty matter content. There used to be two standard tests for measuring diameter: the airflow method (IWTO-28) and the projection microscope method (IWTO-8) which can also measure medullation (IWTO-12) as a percentage of the total fibres. Since November 1993 this has been joined by the CSIRO-developed SIROLAN -LASERSCAN method of which thirty were already in use by late 1993, seven with the AWTA alone and which has now been adopted as an IWTO standard test in early 1994.

Colour measurement is still a test method under evaluation, although for reliable and consistent dyeings from batch to batch, accurate information on the base colour properties of raw wool is essential and eye observations inadequate. Fine wool growers in New Zealand are being encouraged through subsidy to test their wool for pre-sale certification of length and strength, using the Australian developed ATLAS method. There are two standard test methods in New Zealand for length: the scoured wool length after carding test (NZS8719) and the greasy wool staple and strength test (IWTO-E-12). In 1992 Wool Services International commented that the length after carding test needs to be fully recognised before objective measurement can be fully effective in wool trading.

Although a draft test method for bulk is currently being assessed, it is not yet generally available to New Zealand wool exporters to measure their scoured deliveries despite the acknowledged importance that fibre crimp, which is a major factor influencing wool bulk value, is of commercial and technical importance. Wool is also tested for 'invoice mass' as agreed by the IWTO-33 method to take into account the moisture content of shipped wool (which can vary from 12 to 23% without noticeable consequences).

Test methods must be rigorously evaluated before national or international acceptance: test reports do not have the recognised status of a certified test result in terms of the 'Arbitration Agreement, Standard Contracts and Other International Decisions and Agreements' contained in the IWTO's Blue Book which is the internationally agreed collection of trading rules for wool.

Individual lots of wool purchased at auction by wool exporters in Australia and New Zealand may be brought together for scouring and combined and averaged test certificates can be requested for the resulting composite wool package, which can be modified 'by subtraction' if certain bales have subsequently to be removed.

Testing is available for condition, core sampling for moisture content, yield (including vegetable matter content), length after carding, fibre diameter and colour - these last two conforming to the same procedure as for greasy wool, and yield testing is also similar. The Comprehensive Scoured Wool Package, combining yield, residual grease, fibre diameter and colour tests, introduced from 1987 by the New Zealand Wool Testing Authority, is regarded by the NZWB as 'an important step towards the full objective description of New Zealand wool' and is the most common certificate accompanying exports of New Zealand scoured wool. New core bulk, length after carding and fibre diameter tests were introduced by the New Zealand Wool Board in 1994. The new length after carding test allows processors to specify to their suppliers the average fibre length required in their deliveries.

In 1992, CSIRO estimated that the costs of yield and fibre diameter testing costs were 2.3 ¢/kg, while staple length testing added another 3 ¢/kg. What is certain is that manufacturers are extremely concerned about yarn quality. As Brian Lodder of the UK textile manufacturer the Parkland Group stated in *Wool News* in March 1994: 'We have recently been having trouble with yarns which don't perform on our new looms. Our productivity requirements mean that we will not run yarns that cannot perform to 90% efficiency. Quality faults such as hairiness, black fibre or short fibres have to be eliminated because we don't want to grade inspect as this is an expensive process. We simply don't want poor quality fibres.' The problem for the wool industry is very real.

Existing test methods are constantly being revised and updated, and research is being done on new methods of measurement. For example, the current IWTO method for yield determination requires a substantial amount of time and effort to separate the wool from its contaminants - wax, suint, dirt and vegetable matter - and a more rapid method would be highly desirable. Work has been done using near infra-red spectroscopy to determine the amounts of various contaminants present in raw wool. Near infra-red reflectance analysis (NIRA) of moisture content and solvent extractable matter is already being used in quality control during scouring. However it is unlikely to present a possibly alternative for certification in the near future. Imaging techniques for the rapid measurement of fibre diameter distribution have been developed in Australia as a more economic alternative to the projection microscope method. Having established that NIRA can be used to measure medullation, WRONZ is currently developing the use of near infra-red techniques as a better way of measuring fibre bulk. The International Wool Secretariat (IWS) has used vitamin C and citric acid to develop an environmentally friendly way of selectively bleaching dark fibres which contaminate wool fabric. All these developments and more are needed for wool to meet the existing quality requirements of manufacturers, let alone those of the future.

The wool production process

Shearing

To harvest the wool crop, the farmer must confine the sheep so that each animal may be caught and clipped. This capture and confinement may not be easy over large rugged geographic areas. Historically, on some ranches, sheep would be washed with warm water to remove as much of the perspiration salts and dust as practicable, and allowed to dry before shearing. In New Zealand, shearing is done in the farm wool shed, either by shearing contractors or by the farmer and his family. In the UK, almost every sheep shearer uses efficient techniques demonstrated first in the UK by the late Godfrey Bowen during 1957-64 and there are still close links between the two countries' shearing practices and development. The cost of shearing was estimated at 45p/fleece in the UK in 1993.

Whether with traditional hand clippers, now hardly used anywhere, or with power clippers or blade shears (which leave about 5–10 mm (0.2–0.4 inch) of wool to protect sheep in cooler conditions), the sheep is held by the person doing the shearing, who concurrently clips the wool close to the body to leave the fleece essentially in one piece. Pelt damage costs New Zealand more than $650m annually. How the sheep is held, and the order and speed with which the parts of the sheep are sheared vary between workers, but it still remains hot, tiring work at an awkward angle. Although according to the NZWB 260 sheep/day is typical, a trained, skilled sheep shearer can remove

400 fleeces in a working day. One of the improvements in shearing, developed by Sunbeam Australia and the New Zealand Wool Board, has been the cover comb. This has skids and a wide gap between the teeth, leaving two to three times the normal amount of wool on sheep and protecting them against temperature changes.

Once removed from the sheep, on some Australian ranches the fleece is then skirted and rolled, after which it is classed, bale pressed and branded. Skirting is the operation of removing and packing separately the inferior parts of the fleece, such as the underside's short belly wool. Shorter, discoloured crutch wools, second cuts, rough, burry and coarse ends from the legs and head, dags and dirty, short and stained wool, and sweaty locks, especially from around the breech, are also removed. The fleece is then thrown on to a slatted table where it is skirted to remove faults (cotted portions, vegetable matter, shed stain, etc) and permanently discoloured or shorter wools. Loose pieces and second cuts still adhering to the fleece fall to the floor and are packed with the shearing board sweepings. The remaining wool is then divided and rolled so the rib and shoulder portions of the fleece can be seen. In other areas, the fleece is not skirted and each fleece is just tied with paper twine in a bale or bundle to be classed or sorted later.

Originally sheep were shorn once annually, producing full length fleece wool. Over the last quarter of a century, a more frequent shearing pattern has emerged, especially, for example, in northern New Zealand where relatively high rainfall and warm temperatures can cause yellowing of long wool. Wool from sheep shorn twice a year is called second shear, while that at eight-monthly intervals is called short shorn. Lower wool prices resulted in a diminution of these practices. For most farmers, annual shearing is in late spring or early summer. If shorn in early spring, if warm enough, wool is less affected by tenderness and is of a better colour. Twice-yearly shearing occurs in the autumn and spring giving farmers a better cashflow: autumn shorn wools tend to be of better colour and strength. However second shear wool is shorter with fewer uses; short shorn wool is a compromise.

Slipe wools (from dead sheep) are removed by machine; trimmed by, for example, a Slipemaster machine (the trimmings are sold separately), the wool is then chemically removed from the skins and subsequently sorted and dried ready for scouring.

Classing and sorting

Wool is classed by qualified wool-classers. The first stage of wool processing is usually sorting for baling which is necessary to ensure the maximum spinning result from each fleece. Even the bales of wool that have been classed carefully are examined fleece by fleece. Each fleece is spread out and examined by sight and touch, then pulled apart. All the different qualities, known as matchings, are placed in separate baskets, which is an efficient way to administer quality even if the different qualities are to be blended later. In the 19th century, sorting or stapling was an industry in itself, and it is still somewhat separate, although the work is now done on the farm rather than at wool brokers' stores.

Clothing wool is separated and classed differently from combing wool, and in sorting wool from different breeds of sheep, the classification used by the sorter is also different. For cross-bred wool, grading aims to achieve even, uniform lines by separating fleeces which are discoloured or very long, short or tender. Fineness is not a consideration because strong wools are usually sufficiently even across one flock and differences in diameter do not affect price. Lambswool and second shear wool are also generally sorted on differences in colour and length. Wools finer than 33 microns (Merino, half-breed and Corriedale) are usually sorted by registered classers. They are classed into fine, medium or strong lines, from which are separated fleeces of very different length, strength, colour or with significant faults.

Short-staple wool is given qualities by the woollen manufacturers. In descending order these are: picklock, prime, choice, super, head, seconds, abb and breech, and the class of fleece determines the proportions in which each is found. Worsted manufacturers classify from fine, blue, neat, brown, breech, downright seconds, to abb – these are for English wools. The last three are short wools not usually used by worsted manufacturers. Only rarely is more than 5–8% fine, or less quality than breech on the other, used in worsted manufacture. Usually, the best quality wool is found from the shoulders and side of the fleece, falling towards the tail end of the sheep; the 'britch' often being long, strong and irregular. Belly wool is short, worn and dirty, as is also the front of the throat; on the head and shins the wool is short, stiff and straight, more like hair than wool, and is liable to contain grey hairs. Australian and New Zealand wools come classed, and are usually sorted into only three or four qualities; a 60s fleece may be sorted into 56s, ordinary 60s, super 60s and skirtings.

Because of improvements in the wool selling industry, in

particular objective measurement and more carefully controlled wool classing, there is now a reduced need for sorting.

Scouring

Grease wool after sorting is still very dirty and greasy, containing bits of straw, soil natural wax, suint and varying quantities of foreign matter, dust, burs, etc, which must be removed before further processing is done. In fact, dirt and grease make up half the weight of the raw wool. The importance of scouring is considerable; if not done with proper care, the fibre qualities will suffer a great deal. If it is not cleaned evenly it will not dye evenly and manufacturing will become unsatisfactory. The grease is removed by scouring, which means treating the wool with soap, detergents, or with chemicals, and also mechanically through rakes pushing the wool through the scouring bowls.

On average, wool is in the scouring liquid about eight minutes, the temperature will range from 110–120° C and it will pass through approximately 15–25m (16.4–27.3 yards) of bath. The whole process is rather slow, and some chemical damage to the wool fibre through the alkaline solution may occur. There are also some difficulties in disposing of the wash water and the accompanying grease without breaking anti-pollution laws in most countries. Since World War II the technology in this area has moved on apace: CSIRO, WRONZ and machinery manufacturers have together ensured that Australian and New Zealand scouring technology has moved on swiftly in the past two decades. SIROSCOUR, introduced in 1988, was a step forward for aqueous scouring systems, splitting up the functions of removal. The new generation of scouring equipment, based on the ANDAR/WRONZ mini-bowl, was designed and built in New Zealand and has been installed in several overseas countries. The system typically consists now of six in-line bowls, with detergents at 60-65° C and then cold/hot rinse bowls. The WRONZ system allowing for continuous plant operation has been designed to improve energy efficiency, save water, recover grease and remove effluent. Automatic systems control and monitor the scouring process. Linked to the introduction of the WRONZ comprehensive scouring system has been the introduction of weigh belt feeders, computer blending and improved opening and dusting machinery. These developments have improved the efficiency of scouring. A more recent technical development has been the introduction of NIRA in several scours for the rapid measurement of residual grease and moisture regain to monitor the effectiveness of scouring and drying.

With nip rollers Australian and New Zealand wool is sufficiently dry to be passed on directly, usually by passing through a drying chamber on a conveyor belt through which hot air is blown, taking care not to overheat the fibre. Wool emerges at the other end in a dry and open state, some 30% lighter than its original weight.

For woollen spinning, however, the wool may need to be blended and so it may therefore need to be dry and in a suitable condition for oiling. If it is matted it is unravelled through the Willey machine, made out of rotating cylinders and hooked teeth. For English and cross-bred wools, more agitation in the scouring bath may be needed, in which case the eccentric fork action machine is used, in which the degree of movement is controlled by the setting of the forks moving the wool along.

The services provided by scourers are similar but do vary to some degree. The scouring is done to exporters' requirements - this may include machining, opening, picking out yellow wool, dusting and bleaching as well as mixing auction lots before scouring to form homogeneous types to meet exporters' specifications. Some scourers have high density presses and others have conventional pressing systems and the wool is double or triple dumped after pressing. Wool grease is extracted from the scouring liquor during the process and this is sold to overseas markets from Australia and New Zealand. Once the wool is scoured it is high density packed ready for export.

Some scours are located in main centres in Australia and New Zealand whilst others are located in smaller towns and have to centralise wool to and from their scouring plants. Due to the installation of modern scouring equipment and a decline in sheep numbers in the 1990s there is an over-capacity of scouring plant in Australia and New Zealand, and several plants have been shut down. This is despite encouragement from the Boards for exporters to export scoured not greasy wool and the commercial success of companies such as ANDAR in New Zealand, which reported that whilst the emphasis in 1992/93 had been on fine wool processing upgrading, this had changed to strong wool in the following season. Currently in the USA there are four wool scourers.

Topmaking

Once bought and often after shipment topmakers make the wool into tops which is raw wool in industrial form ready for the spinner. The wool must be washed and then combed into a long white continuous sliver which can then be spun and woven. The sliver is called wool top (so called, quite possibly, from the top of the hand spindle) or combed wool (see Chapter 8).

In 1992 70% of Australia's wool was transformed by nine companies who in turn control the transforming (wool combing) capacity of the world. AusTop is the only 'commission topmaker' in Australia; they scour and comb wool on others' behalf. They argue that because they do this close to the source they produce a much higher quality than the northern hemisphere topmakers. In the USA in 1993 there were two commission topmakers.

AusTop's Chairman Jonathan Todhunter believes that the way forward for Australian wool exports is to create wool combing plants in the heart of the Australian rural wool production base. The aim is to cut the costs of the transformation from wool into yarn and cloth. In 1992 he estimated that from the farm to the Italian spinning plant Biella there were 17 physical handlings of wool, one million transactions to sell the wool clip, 50 000 semi-trailer turnarounds and 'the transport over the seas of thousands of tons of grease, mud, burr and dirt' as well as unnecessary storage costs and interest costs which he estimated added as much as 20% unnecessarily to the cost of wool and which the Australian Bureau of Agriculture and Research Economics (ABARE) calculated in 1992 at 1.52 kilo (clean) - 26% of the indicator quote. Both BWK, on the coast, and AusTop are active in this area, the latter currently establishing two such complexes in Parkes and Hamilton in the heart of the wool producing area and is trying to move towards what Todhunter has described as 'Agro industrial complexes in Australia that guarantee a much more efficient interface from the agricultural product to the industrial product' (*Eco di Biella*, 18/6/92) and which would produce export earnings for Australia more like $9bn than the current less than $5bn.

Wool sterilisation

Wool can cause disease in humans. The most important problem is anthrax, which can be caught prior to weaving and finishing. Coarse wools from countries and districts where anthrax is a major problem are the main sources, and greasy wool is not as likely to be contaminated as pulled wool. Washing and scouring may actually cause the micro-organism to spread to previously uncontaminated wool; in general the risk falls after scouring, which reduces spores and removes extraneous material. High drying temperatures are advised against; but dyeing of raw wool eliminates the risk.

In the UK, raw wool is sterilised by being washed for ten minutes in 0.5% sodium carbonate solution at 37.8 °C, followed by another washing in 3.5% soap solution for 10 minutes at the same temperature. Thirdly it is subjected to 10 minutes of 2% formaldehyde at the same temperature, and then a second formaldehyde wash of 1.8% for 10 minutes. Fifthly the wool is washed in a 0.25% formaldehyde solution at again the same temperature. Then the wool is pressed out and dried in hot air at 100 °C, the temperature dropping rapidly so that the wool is not scorched. Then it is blown into bailing presses.

CHAPTER

3

Wool consumption

The uses of wool

The use of wool for clothing stretches back into antiquity if not into pre-history. Its outstanding properties of insulation against heat and cold and sudden temperature changes as well as moisture resilience, water repellency, fire resistance, resilience and longevity, versatility, static resistance, noise insulation, dirt and wrinkle resistance, hygroscopic quality, felting property, easy to sew qualities, easy dyeing and low heat conductivity long ago gave it a usefulness not just for clothing but for blankets, upholstery, floor coverings and for animals to wear. Worsted yarn is mainly used for suiting fabrics and tailored materials with a smooth finish such as serges, gabardines and twills. This smooth finish is also used to advantage in upholstery fabrics and carpets. Because combing wools are used and extra processes are required for worsted yarns, they usually command a higher price than woollen yarns.

Woollen yarns are used to produce products such as upholstery, bulky knitwear, blankets, flannels, tweeds and carpets. In mens' suits, wool had in 1990 a 63% share, a 39% share for womens' coats, 38% for mens' jackets and 28% of mens' knitwear. Blends such as the SIROFILL technology are another important apparel use of wool. In 1994, for example, Nikke, Japan's largest wool manufacturer, and Nissinbo, the country's best quality cotton spinner, jointly produced a high quality wool/cotton blend for casual wear. In general, the relationship between micron and end use is as shown in Table 3.1.

Wool has numerous uses for clothing; amongst its important uses are military: no other fibre has yet been discovered with properties

Table 3.1 The micron range/end-use relationship

Micron range	End-uses
19–25	• Single/double knit piecegoods • Fully fashioned knitwear • Underwear • Half and ankle socks
25–27	• Single/double knit piecegoods • Fully fashioned knitwear • Half and ankle socks
23	• Handknitting: 'Baby wool'
27	'3-ply'
27	'4-ply'
28–32	Double knit
28–32	Triple knit
28–32	Bulky knit

Source: NZWB

that are suitable for the clothing of armies, and also for felt washers for military equipment and lining for water bottles. A soldier's clothing and equipment takes between four and ten times a civilian's wool needs. This explains the very considerable importance of wool in both World Wars and it accounted for a great deal of Soviet wool.

In 1992 the NZWB stated that 45% of New Zealand wool was used in machine-made carpets, and 15% for hand-knotted carpets, a percentage which rose steadily during the 1980s but whose rise was arrested by the recession in 1991–94. Clothing usage accounted for 31%, split between woven apparel 11%, knitwear 11% and hand knitting yarn 9%. Bedding took 5%, mainly for blankets and quilt fillings, upholstery 3% – for example for aircraft and cars – and other uses 1%. New manufacturing processes such as Pebblemill for carpets and the use of Treotek worsted yarn to produce durable lightweight wool upholstery fabrics and flame resistant clothing are all part of the continued effort by the New Zealand industry to make better use of wool. End use consumption of wool is shown in Fig. 3.1.

The BWMB says that, British wool is also particularly suited to the carpet industry because of its 'bounce' and resilience. Great attention is therefore focused within the UK wool industry on the housing market – which was consistently disappointing during the early 1990s but which began to show some signs of revival by 1994/95. The BWMB also states that British wool is suitable for 'hosiery and

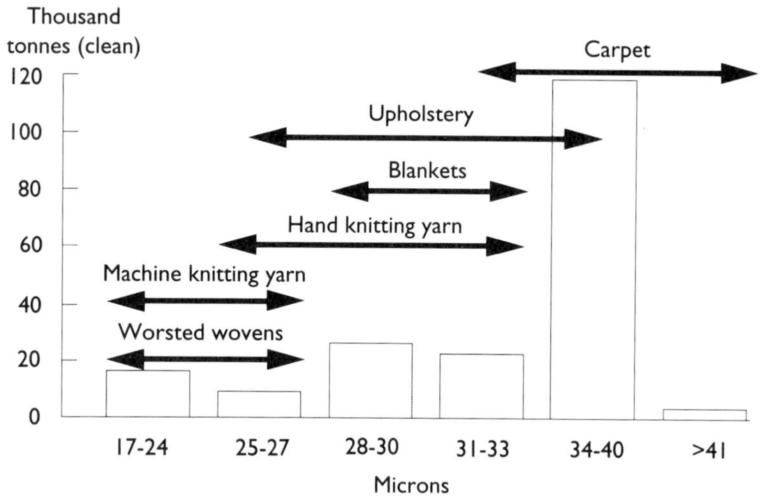

3.1 Principal end uses of New Zealand wool (source: New Zealand Wool Board).

knitwear, suitings, dress and furnishing fabrics, and speciality pile fabrics for soft toys, upholstery, seat covers and linings'. The Japanese and British futon market is increasingly important.

In the Western European contract market, wool is primarily used in the hospitality sector which includes hotels, restaurants and theatres. The IWS is optimistic, however, that wool's use can be expanded in other areas such as offices and shops and car upholstery.

In the USA, wool provided fibre for 2.4% of apparel (taking 66.4% of US wool consumption), 0.4% of home furnishings (taking 5.1% of wool consumption), 0.7% of floor coverings (taking 7.6% of wool consumption), 0.4% of industrial and other consumer type products (taking 6% of wool consumption) and 3.8% exports of domestic products (taking 10.6% of wool consumption). Since the mid-1980s wool has declined as a fibre for apparel - although that may now reverse - home furnishing use has fallen, as has use for floor coverings, but industrial use has remained constant and exports of domestic products have increased.

Wool soft knops (tiny balls of rolled wool) are used for furniture filling - Woolfill, for example, using the new water-based process introduced in October 1993 which replaces the previous less environmentally-friendly solvent-based treatment - and for bedding. In 1993, a new furniture filling product was introduced by Woolfill which should increase this use. Other products include Woolspill, a product used to mop up oil spills: wool can absorb up to 20 times its

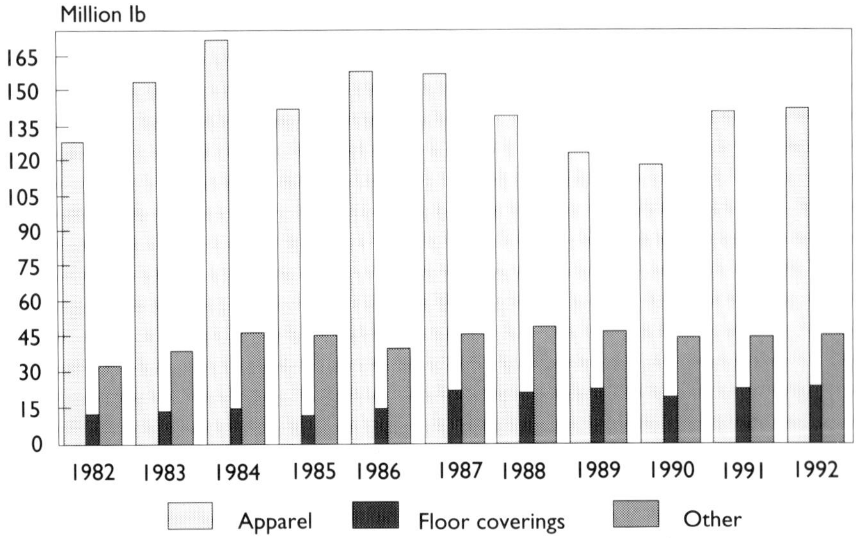

3.2 End-use consumption of wool including semi-manufactured imports (source: New Zealand Wool Board).

weight in oil, 'Woolover' covers for lambs and wool building insulation. End-use consumption of wool is shown in Fig. 3.2.

Currently global wool demand - net world consumption - is steadily increasing - up 3% in 1994 - despite warnings from the IWS in early 1995 that a 'cold snap' was required to prevent unsold garment stocks having a significant downward pressure on future pipeline orders. The recovery in demand was widely spaced geographically, too (see Table 3.2): although in Asia, countries such as China, Korea, Taiwan and India showed significant recoveries, as did the North American and UK/Nordic markets. This was not matched either in the Japanese, Continental European, Eastern European or Turkish markets.

Wool consumption in 1994/95 was closely reflecting the level of economic recovery in individual countries. The IWS argue that consumers in Continental Europe are still postponing their major textile item purchases - and wool, on the whole, features more heavily in such major textile purchases than does cotton or synthetics as a percentage of its total sales - and even in the UK, where apparel sales as a whole increased in 1994, mens' formalwear and interior textile sales remain 'difficult'. Japanese demand for wool apparel remained flat over 1994 and into 1995, largely because of mild weather and - allegedly - saturation in the mens' suit sector which is large. If this is the case it must be worrying for the industry.

The carpet sector has also not improved significantly, except for an increase of imports of cheaper hand-knitted carpets from China.

Table 3.2 Net domestic absorption of virgin wool at retail stage – by region (ranked), m kg clean

Region/country	1989	1990	1991	1992	1993	1993 % share
Western Europe	**495.2**	**492.0**	**543.5**	**571.6**	**470.7**	**28**
Germany	124.2	124.8	128.7	136.7	133.1	28
Italy	94.3	107.3	123.3	130.7	89.3	19
UK	81.2	69.9	79.0	83.2	79.9	17
France	60.7	50.9	62.2	66.9	40.5	9
Spain	26.7	31.9	39.3	36.3	24.5	5
Netherlands	20.6	21.1	20.2	20.0	16.4	3
Austria	10.9	10.8	12.8	13.1	13.0	3
Switzerland	15.6	14.8	14.3	14.6	12.1	3
Belgium	14.4	10.3	9.8	16.1	11.7	2
Portugal	10.5	10.3	12.7	14.3	11.5	2
Greece	9.2	12.4	12.6	8.1	8.9	2
Ireland	7.3	8.8	7.8	6.6	7.8	2
Sweden	5.9	5.7	6.6	7.1	7.1	2
Denmark	5.0	4.5	5.5	6.6	6.6	1
Norway	4.1	4.2	4.9	7.0	4.2	1
Finland	3.9	3.3	2.6	3.1	3.0	1
Others	0.7	1.0	1.2	1.2	1.1	–
Eastern Europe*	**411.1**	**317.8**	**290.8**	**218.6**	**206.7**	**12**
Former USSR	329.3	251.2	243.4	184.5	172.8	84
Romania	14.0	14.3	12.1	11.0	8.4	4
Bulgaria	12.6	12.5	9.9	6.6	6.7	3
Poland	20.7	11.2	8.7	4.5	6.3	3
Former Yugoslavia	15.8	14.6	10.2	7.5	6.0	3
Former Czechoslovakia	14.0	11.9	4.7	2.7	4.3	2
Others	4.7	2.1	1.8	1.8	2.2	1
Far Asia	**477.1**	**354.9**	**500.9**	**513.0**	**512.2**	**30**
China	219.0	136.2	229.9	246.4	266.7	52
Japan	204.6	176.3	198.7	200.3	170.0	33
Korea	21.2	27.2	31.4	32.7	36.4	7
Taiwan	18.8	5.2	26.9	17.2	27.2	5
Hong Kong	13.5	10.0	14.0	16.4	11.9	2
Other Asia	**41.5**	**40.1**	**41.4**	**42.0**	**42.0**	**2**
India	17.9	18.0	18.2	18.2	18.2	43
Pakistan	13.5	12.8	15.0	14.5	14.5	35
Afghanistan	5.7	4.1	3.4	4.5	4.5	11
Mongolia	2.6	3.4	3.0	3.0	3.0	7
Bangladesh	0.8	0.8	0.8	0.8	0.8	2
Nepal	0.5	0.5	0.5	0.5	0.5	1
Malaysia	0.3	0.3	0.3	0.3	0.3	1
Thailand	0.2	0.2	0.2	0.2	0.2	–
North America	**147.5**	**116.4**	**124.0**	**134.1**	**147.2**	**9**
USA	127.8	102.0	109.5	118.8	129.1	88
Canada	19.7	14.4	14.5	15.3	18.1	12

Region/country	1989	1990	1991	1992	1993	1993 % share
Central and S America	**53.5**	**52.2**	**57.2**	**59.6**	**54.8**	**3**
Argentina	23.4	21.5	25.0	28.0	23.0	42
Brazil	5.7	7.5	6.5	6.5	6.5	12
Chile	7.6	6.5	7.0	6.5	6.5	12
Bolivia	6.2	6.4	6.6	6.4	6.4	12
Mexico	4.7	4.8	6.2	5.7	6.0	11
Colombia	2.6	3.0	3.0	3.5	3.5	6
Ecuador	1.0	1.1	1.1	1.1	1.1	2
Peru	1.9	0.9	1.0	1.0	1.0	2
Venezuela	0.3	0.4	0.8	0.9	0.8	1
Middle East	**96.9**	**109.7**	**113.1**	**116.0**	**128.6**	**8**
Turkey	56.0	68.3	66.6	68.7	83.0	65
Syria	15.0	17.3	15.2	15.7	15.0	12
Saudi Arabia	6.7	6.0	13.2	12.0	12.0	9
Iran	10.5	10.5	10.5	12.0	11.0	9
Iraq	5.0	4.0	4.0	4.0	4.0	3
Jordan	1.8	1.8	1.8	1.8	1.8	1
Israel	1.9	1.8	1.8	1.8	1.8	1
Africa	**64.7**	**63.3**	**65.5**	**62.9**	**62.0**	**4**
Algeria	21.9	21.0	22.2	21.0	20.0	32
Morocco	10.4	10.8	11.0	11.0	11.0	18
Sudan	8.3	8.3	8.3	8.3	8.3	13
Ethiopia	6.4	6.4	6.4	6.4	6.4	10
Tunisia	6.5	6.4	6.0	6.0	6.0	10
Egypt	6.8	6.2	7.3	5.8	6.0	10
Libya	3.6	3.4	3.5	3.5	3.5	6
Zimbabwe	0.5	0.5	0.5	0.5	0.5	1
Mauritius	0.3	0.3	0.3	0.4	0.3	–
Wool growers	**54.4**	**55.5**	**49.1**	**55.6**	**57.9**	**3**
Australia	33.5	35.9	30.6	35.0	35.0	60
New Zealand	10.9	9.6	8.5	10.6	12.7	22
South Africa	9.0	9.0	9.0	9.0	9.2	16
Uruguay	1.0	1.0	1.0	1.0	1.0	2
Balance item	**28.1**	**28.2**	**22.5**	**13.6**	**10.9**	**1**
Global total	**1870**	**1630**	**1808**	**1787**	**1693**	**100**

– Data is less than 0.5%.

* Estimate based on net obverse trade with European Economic Area.

Sources: Foreign Trade Statistics and IWS virgin wool conversion factors

The position was better in Korea and Taiwan, especially for imported wool knitwear and wovenwear from China and Italy, which was encouraging for the industries in both those countries. China was a market which continued to fascinate the international wool industry, and despite warnings of saturation, overheating and lack of effective demand to back up consumer wants, higher quality, fashionable and branded clothing continued to be a major consumer spending priority and sales were up in most segments by 10% between 1994 and 1993, except for the less fashionable wool wovenwear.

In the North American sector of the IWS analysis, the mild weather was also identified as the culprit in lowering wool apparel retail sales although underlying consumer demand remained firm in both the USA and Canada, especially for cheap menswear and the new generation of 'office casualwear' for the new 'casual Fridays'. The volume of chiefly wool imports into the USA rose by 20% in apparel and 32% in carpets in Jan–Sept 1994 compared with 1993 and the trend was continuing to show an improvement. The IWS identified three other emerging countries as having important domestic markets for wool. In India, demand for wool-suiting fabric, wool-poor trouserings and lambswool knitwear is growing as middle class incomes rise. But in Turkey consumption is weak and expected to fall by 10% in 1994, retracing its steps from extremely rapid advances since 1989, and similar results are expected in the CIS/Eastern European states which now consume half of their 1989 levels: Russian wool and yarn production was down by 60% in 1994, consumption was down to just over half its 1989 level, although there are some slight improvements detectable elsewhere in the former Comecon countries, especially in respect of garment making for Western European suppliers. Germany is taking a key role in providing finance for the as yet marginal imports of raw wool into the region. Again, however, the net effect of these relative changes is to shift wool steadily into an 'Asian' from a 'European' commodity.

In terms of the qualitative aspects of consumption, the trend since 1988 has been for the balance between non-wool, all-wool, wool-rich and wool poor garments to evolve highly disparately between garments. Taking the six key countries of France, Germany, Italy, Japan, the UK and USA, for which detailed statistics are available from the IWTO, for mens' outerwear wool's position has barely altered at just over 75%, for mens' suits it has increased from 56% to 68% in a stagnant market, for mens' trousers it has remained at 65% in a reducing market for wool used in trousers (although by 66% for all-wool trousers in the UK), for mens' jackets in a stagnant market it is up from 32% to 37%, for mens' coats in a reducing market a steady percentage of 12–11%, for womens' outerwear down slightly in all categories of wool used in garments, although unchanged for womens' dresses and skirts (in a shrinking market), up slightly in the slowly growing market for womens' suits and steady in the growing market for womens' trousers, and slightly falling for womens' coats and jackets, in two markets respectively falling and growing. There can be little comfort for the wool trade in these figures: many of the apparel markets in which wool is holding its share are either level or declining themselves: mens' sweaters, for instance, where the total market was down 10% between 1988 and 1993 and wool's share fell only from 30% to 27%; or womens' sweaters, where the market was virtually unchanged between 1988 and 1993 and wool's share was unchanged over that period and varied only a couple of percentage points in any one year. Even in adult knitwear, where total consumption has fallen from 348.8m kg (769m lb) to 328.7m kg (723m lb) between 1988 and 1993, wool's share has oscillated and in 1993 was slightly down on its 1988 share.

The position with respect to carpets is better, at least, with the market increasing in size in the eight countries of Belgium, France, Germany, Italy, Japan, the Netherlands, UK and USA by 8% between 1988–93, and up again in 1994 with wool holding its own across all the types of utilisation of wool in carpets, see Table 3.3 and Fig. 3.3.

Within this overall picture, some individual markets are bleaker: use of wool has fallen from 40% to 27% in woven carpets, from 4% to 3% for tufted carpets, and from 93% to 92% for hand-made carpets. Although the second two statistics are probably statistically insignificant, the first is not: especially since the decline appears even across

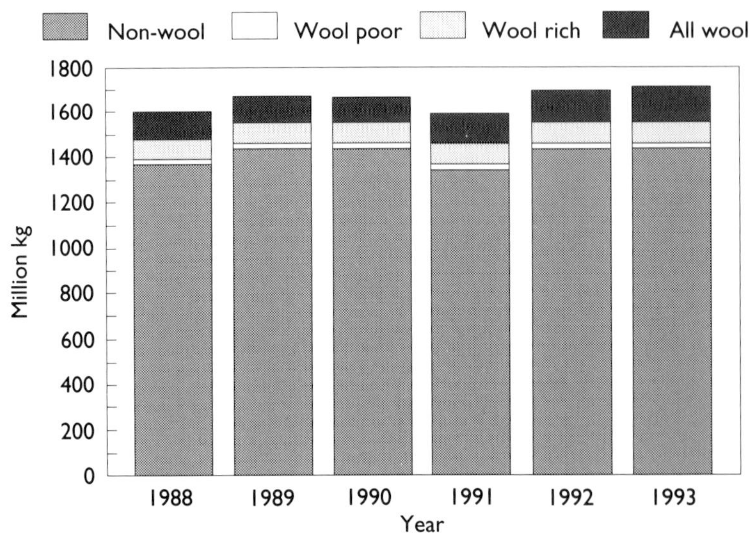

3.3 Consumption of wool in carpets by the eight countries shown in Table 3.3 (source: New Zealand Wool Board).

Table 3.3 Consumption of carpets†, m kg

	1988	1989	1990	1991	1992	1993
Belgium						
All-wool	9.6	9.5	9.4	8.9	8.5	8.3
Wool rich	0.5	0.6	0.5	0.5	0.6	0.5
Wool poor	0.4	0.3	0.2	0.2	0.2	0.2
Non-wool	15.2	16.9	18.8	17.5	17.1	17.2
Total	25.7	27.3	28.9	27.1	26.4	26.2
France						
All-wool	9.1	10.0	9.3	9.2	9.0	9.5
Wool rich	0.7	0.8	0.7	0.7	0.7	0.7
Wool poor	5.5	5.8	6.0	6.2	3.9	2.6
Non-wool	64.5	67.4	67.0	64.9	62.7	60.3
Total	79.8	84.0	83.0	81.0	76.3	73.1
Germany#						
All-wool	52.2	51.1	49.2	53.5	54.2	59.9
Wool rich	2.7	2.7	2.9	2.5	2.2	2.2
Wool poor	1.6	1.6	1.0	1.6	1.3	1.3
Non-wool	153.8	159.3	192.5	210.8	211.1	203.1
Total	210.3	214.7	245.6	268.4	268.8	266.5
Italy						
All-wool	6.0	5.9	7.2	8.9	8.2	9.0
Wool rich	0.4	0.4	0.5	0.4	0.2	0.2
Wool poor	0.1	0.1	0.1	0.1	0.0	0.0
Non-wool	14.8	15.7	15.3	16.0	14.5	14.1
Total	21.3	22.1	23.1	25.4	22.9	23.3
Japan						
All-wool	18.4	17.8	17.7	16.5	15.0	17.2
Wool rich	2.3	2.4	2.8	2.7	2.3	1.9
Wool poor	0.5	0.6	0.7	0.8	0.7	0.6
Non-wool	115.8	122.8	127.2	129.1	126.0	122.1
Total	137.0	143.6	148.4	149.1	144.0	141.8
Netherlands						
All-wool	10.1	9.5	9.5	8.7	6.8	6.7
Wool rich	0.6	0.7	0.5	0.4	2.2	2.2
Wool poor	2.1	1.7	0.4	0.4	0.4	0.3
Non-wool	23.1	24.3	24.9	25.1	25.0	25.2
Total	35.9	36.2	35.3	34.6	34.4	34.4
United Kingdom						
All-wool	8.5	9.5	10.0	9.0	9.5	9.9
Wool rich	48.8	47.7	42.9	38.4	38.5	40.5
Wool poor	1.8	1.2	2.6	3.0	1.9	2.2
Non-wool	118.4	122.9	123.5	112.9	117.0	120.4
Total	177.5	181.3	179.0	163.3	166.9	173.0

*United States**						
All-wool	28.6	32.3	28.8	27.2	32.7	33.9
Wool rich	5.2	7.2	6.1	4.6	4.7	5.0
Wool poor	0.2	0.6	1.0	0.9	0.9	1.0
Non-wool	877.9	925.1	895.0	812.1	926.4	946.1
Total	911.9	965.2	930.9	844.8	964.7	986.0
Total – 8 countries						
All-wool	142.5	145.6	141.1	141.9	143.9	154.4
Wool rich	61.2	62.5	56.9	50.2	51.4	53.2
Wool poor	12.2	11.9	12.0	13.2	9.3	8.2
Non-wool	1383.5	1454.4	1464.2	1388.4	1499.8	1508.5
Total	1599.4	1674.4	1674.2	1593.7	1704.4	1724.3
Total (percentages)						
All-wool	9	9	8	9	8	9
Wool rich	4	4	3	3	3	3
Wool poor	1	1	1	1	1	0
Non-wool	87	87	87	87	88	87
Total	100	100	100	100	100	100

* Please note, break in time series 1989 onwards
† Comprises: woven, tufted, needled, knotted and other construction types
# United Germany after 1990

virtually all countries, except for Germany, where unification has kept the same level between 1988 and 1993. The market for woven carpets in these countries has grown by 26% between 1988 and 1993, however, so the overall use of chiefly wool woven carpets has actually shown a much less dramatic decline than the percentage figure – from 42.5m m^2 to 36.6m m^2.

The economics of wool consumption

Table 3.4 shows mill consumption figures for nine major wool textile manufacturing countries and Table 3.5 shows consumption of virgin wool.

In 1992 there were 22 carpet mills in the former Soviet Union and the NZWB were optimistically considering the increase of exports of New Zealand wool to Russian mills such as Luberetskie for the production of Woolmark carpets. Little progress has been made in this area due to Russian shortages of hard currency and the accompanying steady deterioration of the Russian economy.

In 1994 the BWMB published data on the contribution made by raw wool prices to the finished product – an Axminster carpet. This was in response to questions from producers as to why woollen

Table 3.4 Mill consumption of fibres at the carding stage in nine major wool textile manufacturing countries, '000 tonnes

	1989	1990	1991	1992	1993	1993 Q2	1994 Q1	1994 Q2	Jan–June 1993	Jan–June 1994	% change: Q2 '94 over Q2 '93	% change: Q2 '94 over Q1 '94	% change: Jan–June 94 over Jan–June 93
(i) Virgin wool (clean basis)													
Australia	33.7	32.3	42.9	48.5	48.9	12.2	12.5	14.5	24.1	26.9	+19	+16	+12
Belgium	37.5	31.9	30.3	31.8	27.5	5.9	–	–	14.6	–	–	–	–
France	96.3	83.1	91.0	96.3	77.6	19.7	–	–	41.2	–	–	–	–
Italy	136.6	140.6	158.3	167.4	158.6	45.6	47.8	53.4	91.1	101.1	+17	+12	+11
Japan a	109.4	94.0	96.6	96.4	74.2	18.3	18.9	19.2	39.8	38.1	+5	+2	−4
South Korea	18.1	14.3	17.6	17.4	12.5	3.2	3.6	4.8	6.1	8.4	+52	+34	+38
South Africa	28.4	24.6	26.1	26.6	22.0	5.5	6.3	5.6	11.3	11.9	+2	−11	+5
United Kingdom	94.3	90.3	85.3	89.6	86.7	22.6	22.9	20.3	46.8	43.2	−10	−11	−8
United States a b	64.7	63.8	72.4	72.0	74.8	19.2	19.4	18.6	38.2	38.0	−3	−4	−1
Total	619.0	574.9	620.4	646.1	582.8	114.3f	114.8f	121.9f	233.3f	240.7f	+7f	+3f	+3f
(ii) Other materials c (actual weight)													
Belgium	42.4	36.7	36.6	33.5	32.4	8.1	–	–	18.8	–	–	–	–
France	69.1	60.4	54.2	56.6	50.2	13.3	–	–	27.5	–	–	–	–
Italy	460.8	426.8	420.0	437.6	431.8	119.2	118.0	126.9	231.7	244.9	+6	+8	+6
Japan d	145.6	139.9	132.2	118.0	93.1	24.5	22.5	24.1	47.4	46.6	−2	+7	−2
South Korea	186.3	161.7	131.7	111.1	103.7	25.2	20.9	21.4	54.5	42.3	−15	+2	−22
South Africa	36.6	34.1	27.3	33.2	33.5	8.3	5.9	6.0	17.0	11.9	−28	+2	−30
United Kingdom	61.2	52.9	48.9	47.2	48.2	11.5	12.7	12.3	24.1	25.0	+7	−3	+3
United States	275.9	307.9	310.8	351.6	386.2	96.2	102.5	103.9	190.4	206.4	+8	+1	+8
Total e	1278.0	1220.4	1161.7	1188.7	1179.0	285.0f	282.6f	294.6f	565.1f	577.1f	+3f	+4f	+21

	1989	1990	1991	1992	1993	1993 Q2	1994 Q1	1994 Q2	Jan–June 1993	Jan–June 1994	% change Q2 '94 over Q2 '93	% change Q2 '94 over Q1 '94	% change Jan–June 94 over Jan–June 93
(iii) Total materials													
Belgium	79.9	68.6	66.9	65.3	60.2	14.1	–	–	33.4	–	–	–	–
France	165.4	143.5	145.1	152.8	127.8	33.0	–	–	68.8	–	–	–	–
Italy	597.4	567.4	578.3	605.0	590.4	164.8	165.8	180.3	322.8	346.0	+9	+9	+7
Japan	255.0	233.8	228.9	214.4	167.3	42.8	41.3	43.3	87.2	84.7	+1	+5	−3
South Korea	204.4	176.1	149.3	128.5	116.1	28.4	24.5	26.2	60.6	50.7	−8	+7	−16
South Africa	65.0	58.7	53.4	59.8	55.9	13.8	12.2	11.6	28.3	23.8	−16	−5	−16
United Kingdom	155.5	143.2	134.1	136.8	134.9	34.2	35.5	32.6	70.9	68.2	−4	−8	−4
United States	340.6	371.7	383.1	423.7	460.9	115.4	121.9	122.5	228.6	244.4	+6	–	+7
Total e	1863.3	1763.0	1739.2	1786.3	1713.6	399.3f	401.3f	416.5f	798.4f	817.8f	+4f	+4f	+2f

a Scoured basis.
b Including consumption on cotton and other spinning systems.
c Covering noils, waste, broken tops, recovered and re-used wool, man-made fibres, hair, cotton, silk, etc.
d Based on estimated data provided by the International Wool Secretariat.
e Excluding Australia.
f Excluding Belgium and France.

Table 3.5 Consumption of virgin wool by the wool textile industry at the spinning stage, tonnes clean

	1989	1990	1991	1992	1993
Afghanistan	8 022	6 055	4 790	7 192	7 450
Algeria	21 877	22 351	22 347	22 529	22 695
Afghanistan a	27 414	24 378	39 544	31 946	37 371
Australia	17 974	17 087	16 870	16 379	17 041
* Austria	6 109	5 755	6 438	5 897	5 388
* Belgium	39 000	35 400	33 800	29 500	26 000
Bolivia	4 960	4 755	4 551	4 613	4 652
* Brazil	7 007	7 486	6 936	7 308	6 437
Bulgaria	13 806	14 166	10 025	6 998	4 876
* Canada	6 575	4 338	6 728	4 838	5 495
Chile	8 054	6 740	7 186	9 004	9 565
China	255 525	171 227	273 150	319 609	352 062
Colombia	2 804	2 884	3 190	3 202	3 178
Czechoslovakia	22 389	20 408	16 080	9 854	10 758
Denmark	3 743	2 824	2 995	3 324	1 967
Ecuador	800	824	573	647	703
* Egypt	3 785	4 033	6 173	5 376	3 144
* Finland	1 024	543	567	829	668
* France	28 155	23 617	23 777	23 508	18 444
* East Germany	22 942	18 378 }			
* West Germany	56 913	53 975 }	60 569	61 244	50 523
Greece	13 084	14 479	12 431	9 811	6 038
* Hong Kong	5 162	4 255	6 638	7 056	3 478
* Hungary	4 238	2 264	1 943	1 099	1 409
Iceland	631	467	531	462	501
* India	39 300	38 300	48 810	49 980	54 490
Iran	24 851	22 116	22 958	25 230	24 340
Iraq	4 648	4 384	5 780	4 378	4 378
Irish Republic	9 094	9 176	8 168	6 936	7 092
* Israel	891	678	1 104	1 486	1 395
* Italy	133 598	137 649	155 090	164 438	155 608
* Japan	121 839	110 208	116 719	113 120	84 811
Jordan	1 444	1 531	2 578	1 898	1 952
Kenya	936	1 074	1 094	2 777	1 950
* Korea (South)	64 139	48 416	58 939	67 817	53 445
Libya	1 633	1 587	2 221	2 052	1 937
Macao	1 900	954	1 860	1 940	788
Malaysia	1 391	1 264	2 000	1 824	1 392
Mauritius	2 639	2 904	3 222	2 195	2 873
Mexico	5 546	5 476	6 235	5 638	6 474
Mongolia	7 925	5 130	6 560	7 120	6 840
Morocco	17 628	16 042	16 587	17 209	16 081
Nepal	4 237	4 233	12 952	20 055	18 822
* Netherlands	4 400	4 300	4 500	4 300	4 100
* New Zealand	20 394	17 982	17 127	19 061	19 783
Norway	1 783	1 847	1 967	2 741	2 166

	1989	1990	1991	1992	1993
Pakistan	26 202	25 021	29 707	29 872	26 271
Peru	4 718	4 626	4 159	3 196	4 149
* Poland	21 487	13 243	11 489	8 067	8 841
* Portugal	12 677	11 842	14 315	15 625	12 334
Romania	17 522	19 826	15 592	13 768	15 209
Saudi Arabia	892	897	1 467	674	840
* South Africa	12 168	11 127	3 692	6 704	4 489
Former Soviet Union	224 700	254 000	246 900	185 600	184 500
* Spain	14 048	20 642	17 450	19 162	15 600
* Sweden	479	482	395	576	612
* Switzerland	11 547	11 785	11 621	11 413	9 393
Syria	13 827	13 362	13 757	14 081	15 415
Taiwan	20 917	8 969	30 360	20 749	24 858
Tunisia	5 667	5 895	6 050	6 471	6 706
* Turkey	53 701	65 573	63 499	63 682	79 277
* United Kingdom	80 667	79 739	71 268	79 571	76 956
* United States	56 517	51 344	69 906	61 279	68 418
Uruguay	5 600	6 207	9 045	6 452	8 035
Venezuela	346	386	742	944	580
* Yugoslavia	15 091	13 986	10 674	12 417	6 711
TOTAL of countries shown	1 739 932	1 522 931	1 675 391	1 664 336	1 621 704
Of which EC (The Twelve)...	418 321	412 021	404 363	417 519	374 662
Former Soviet Union, East Europe and China ...	667 592	500 264	561 739	552 115	584 495
28 countries * above ...	833 843	797 379	817 167	835 463	769 249

a Seasonal years ending 30 September of year shown.

NOTE: This table attempts to measure the wool textile industry's intake of raw wool at the spinning stage in the countries listed. That is considered the best point for making comparisons with man-made fibres and at the same time best indicates the size of the wool textile industry in a particular country. Wherever possible the statistics shown have been provided by national statisticians. In the absence of official data, the figures represent net available supplies at the spinning stage as computed by the IWTO from official production and trade data and in consequence do not take account of stock changes.
The asterisked countries are those for which some indication is available of the wool textile industry's intake of both virgin wool and other (competing) materials.
(The statistics for China are based on official production and trade data converted to clean by the IWTO.)

Source: IWTO

products continue to be 'so expensive in the shops compared with the price of raw wool'. Table 3.6 shows the estimated cost of an Axminster carpet. Table 3.7 shows the estimated cost of a knitted garment.

Interestingly, these figures do not quite match those provided by various sources to the *Wool into the 21st Century* report, which suggest that greasy wool constituted some 22% of the cost of

Table 3.6 Estimated cost of one square metre of Axminster woven carpet – 100% wool or 80% wool/20% nylon

Raw wool ex-auction		95 p/kg
Blending	8 p/kg	
Scouring including mothproofing and dyeing (yield 68%)	28 p/kg	
Scoured blend price		192 p/kg
Dyed yarn including carding, spinning, twisting and reeling	300 p/kg	492 p/kg
Carpet manufacturing costs including creeling or beaming, weaving, QC inspection, mending, finishing, jute backing and wastage	900p/m^2	1392p/m^2
Approximate woven Axminster price		£13.92/m^2
Retail mark-up calculated at 100% minimum		£13.92/m^2
Final retail price inc VAT at 17.5%		£32.71/m^2
of which raw wool constitutes around 3%.		

Source: British Wool Marketing Board

Table 3.7 Estimated cost of men's heavy knitted sweaters, cut and sewn and/ or coloured jacquard design

Raw wool ex-auction		105 p/kg
Scouring (yield 61%)	20 p/kg	
Scoured wool price		205 p/kg
Combing (yield 95%)	70 p/kg	
Combing top price		289 p/kg
Dyeing and re-gilling	120 p/kg	
Dyed top price		409 p/kg
Yarn – Dyeing, spinning and winding	223 p/kg	
Dyed yarn price		632 p/kg
Knitting costs	800p/garment	
includes knitting, making up, finishing and wastage		1432 p/garment
Approximate finished garment price		£14.32 per garment
Retail mark-up calculated at 100% minimum		£14.32
Finished retail price per knitted garment incl VAT at 17.5%		£33.65
of which raw wool constitutes around 3%		

Source: British Wool Marketing Board

Table 3.8 The direct costs of harvesting, marketing and delivering New Zealand's scoured wool from sheep's back to mill, ¢/kg clean

Activity	1989/90	1990/91	1991/92	1992/93	1993/94	% change
Net return to grower	**461.7**	**285.4**	**303.3**	**293.4**	**280.3**	−4
with supplement		348.0				
Shearing and crutching	50.9	54.6	52.8	56.1	54.3	−3
Shed hands and other shed costs	22.8	23.0	22.1	26.4	24.9	−6
Pressing and wool packs	8.5	10.4	9.3	8.1	7.0	−13
Sub-total: Shearing shed	82.3	88.0	84.2	90.5	86.2	−5
Sub-total as % of total costs	28.0	34.5	33.9	36.6	36.8	
Transport to store	5.1	4.6	4.5	4.5	4.5	0
Insurance – sheep's back to store	0.9	0.5	0.6	0.9	0.8	−8
Brokers' charges	13.7	15.1	15.2	14.6	14.1	−3
Pre-sale test certificate	3.6	4.0	3.9	3.8	3.8	0
NZWB levy (not incl levy on supp)	47.3	24.4	25.3	25.1	24.0	−4
Sub-total: Transport/selling	70.6	48.6	49.6	48.9	47.2	−3
Subtotal as % of total costs	24.0	19.0	19.9	19.8	20.2	
Average auction price	**614.5**	**422.0**	**437.1**	**432.8**	**413.8**	−4
Brokers' delivery charge	5.9	6.9	6.9	6.8	6.7	−1
Transport to scour and scouring	45.8	36.8	33.9	30.9	30.9	0
Post-sale testing	1.9	1.9	1.9	1.9	2.1	13
Buyers' commission	16.1	13.1	13.3	13.2	12.4	−6
Dump and pack	8.7	8.8	8.8	8.8	8.5	−4
Delivery from dump to port	2.4	2.5	2.0	2.4	2.0	−17
Ocean freight	18.7	22.6	22.2	21.5	17.8	−17
Marine insurance	1.4	0.9	0.9	0.9	0.8	−8
Cost of finance	14.6	7.5	6.6	5.3	4.5	−15
Stock holding	8.8	4.5	4.0	3.2	2.7	−16
Agents fee	12.2	7.9	8.1	8.0	7.5	−6
Destination delivery cost	4.7	5.2	6.3	5.2	4.7	−10
Sub-total: Scouring and shipping costs	141.2	118.6	114.9	108.1	100.6	−7
Subtotal as % of total costs	48.0	46.5	46.2	43.7	43.0	
Costs paid by growers	**152.9**	**136.6**	**133.8**	**139.4**	**133.5**	−4
Costs paid by exporters	**141.2**	**118.6**	**114.9**	**108.1**	**100.6**	−7
Average cost to mill	**755.7**	**540.6**	**552.0**	**540.9**	**514.4**	−5

Notes:
- Broker fee is a combined fee for the whole country.
- Assumes all wool is scoured and in dumped bales (average container has 16 tonnes).
- Costs are for wool shipped to Bradford, England.
- Prices based on the average auction price paid.

manufacture of a woollen suit in Australia in 1990 which would produce an equivalent of 11% but the cost of scouring was quoted as much less, producing a similar percentage cost element for scoured wool. In 1992/93 the AWC estimated that the wool grower received A$113.96 out of an auction price of A$632 per bale and a mill price of A$690/bale. Similarly the NZWB published figures in 1993 which suggested that in cents per kg clean of production, the net return to growers had fallen dramatically from 546.6 NZ¢/kg in 1988/89 down to 294.8 NZ¢/kg in 1992/93. The average cost to the mill over the same period evolved from 816 ¢/kg to 541.3 ¢/kg. Table 3.8 shows the direct costs of harvesting, marketing and delivering scoured wool.

It obviously depends on which costs are taken into account at which stage, but the general structure of the BWMB costings can be taken as approximately correct for other wools and other garments.

CHAPTER

4

World wool supply

World wool stocks and production

The majority of the world's sheep, and hence wool production, is in the southern hemisphere. Oceania produces more than three times the European total clip. Australia is the world's largest wool producer, and Russia and the other CIS countries taken together the next largest. The wool clip periods are in New Zealand's spring (November/December) and over a longer period in Australia. South America produces more than Europe, where the most significant producer is Turkey, and then the UK, and South Africa produces more than North America. This is in contrast to grain or cotton, for instance. Why is production thus distributed? It is partly because the southern hemisphere is less and more recently settled, and therefore has plenty of space for animal husbandry. Wool is a compact product which stores well and over a long period; it is sufficiently valuable by weight to bear high transport costs. Some of the wool producing areas, moreover, are sub-humid/semi-arid, and simply not suitable for alternative socio-economic uses without substantial irrigation. Sheep, however, especially the fine-woolled Merino, are well suited to these conditions of variable and seasonal forage growth, and can survive well when herbage is sparse in warm dry areas, as well as in high and rough areas. As a result, sheep numbers do not vary as widely as does other crop production (wheat as an alternative to cotton, for example, in California) and world wool production, though on a steady incline, seldom varies more than 5% plus or minus the year before, and very rarely more than 10%.

The world wool supply in 1992/93 was almost 5bn lb (2270m kg),

8% less than 1991/92. The world wool supply comprises two factors: production and stocks. At the start of the 1991/92 season, there were 1.65bn lb (750m kg) in stock worldwide, about 50% of world annual consumption. At the start of the following season, world stocks were 1.3bn lb (589m kg), 21% less. This reflected the determined efforts by the major wool-producing countries to reduce their stocks. World production was 4% less, too, reflecting the decrease in world wool demand and the determination of major wool producing countries to cut production. As a result the world wool clip of 1992/93 was the smallest for a decade and over 26% of supply in 1992/93 came from stocks. The 1992/93 world wool clip was made up of 45% Merino production, 27% cross-bred, and others (mostly carpet wool) 28%.

In 1992 the BWMB identified the reasons for the high stockpiles as 'a dramatic increase in production which followed on from the high prices achieved in 1986, 1987 and 1988, a general reduction in manufacturing activity in the consuming countries, and particularly, the dramatic fall in imports by China and the USSR' (BWMB presentation, I M Hartley, 1992). Figure 4.1 shows national stockpiles, 1991–4.

The supply of world wool in the 1993/94 season was estimated by the United States Department of Agriculture (USDA) in August 1994 to be down 2.3% from the 1992/93 season. Production, at 3.63bn lb (1650m kg) clean (6.27bn lb (2844m kg) greasy) is 2.4% down from the 1992/93 season, reflecting the recent trend of smaller sheep numbers. Carry-in supplies were 1.37bn lb (621m kg), down 2% on

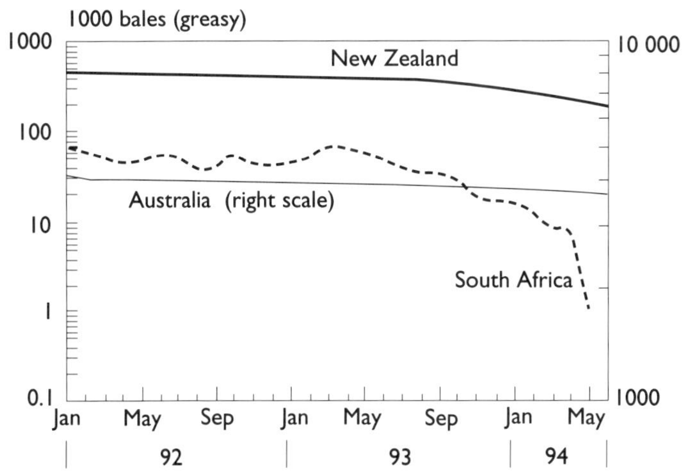

4.1 National stockpiles, 1991–1994 (source: USDA).

Table 4.1 World wool supply and disappearance, 1987/88–1993/94

Year	Sheep population	Production (greasy)	Production (clean)	Consumption (clean)	Exports (greasy)	Beginning stocks (clean)
	million head			million lb		
1987/88	1118	6905	4010	3867	2584	212
1988/89	1013	7105	4134	3976	2441	165
1989/90	1154	7421	4348	3836	2131	291
1990/91	1133	7333	4273	3356	1937	1162
1991/92	1097	6651	3845	3658	2431	1594
1992/93	1069	6442	3724	3646	2140	1393
1993/94	1053	6272	3633	3594	2271	1365

Note: Sheep population during April–June of the second year indicated for most countries. Consumption data are on a calendar year basis for the second year indicated for most countries. Stocks are for countries that are major producers and exporters.

Source: International Wool Textile Organization in succession to the Commonwealth Secretariat

the year before and accounting for almost 27% of world wool supply. Yields were estimated by Wool International as 66%, unchanged, with an unchanged average weight of 177 kg (390 lb). World sheep numbers, production, consumption, exports and stocks are shown in Table 4.1.

The declining sheep yields since the early 1990s have been caused by the decline in CIS countries' effectiveness in production, and also the lack of incentive for farmers to move wool to market in more efficient wool producing countries such as Australia and New Zealand. The major sheep producing countries remain Australia, India and the CIS countries, but together this group constitutes just over one-third of the world's sheep, see Table 4.2. In wool production, however, Australia dominates, producing some 29% of the world's wool in 1992/93. 'Other' countries as a group produced only 26%; the CIS countries were then estimated to produce 13%, New Zealand 10%, China 9%, Argentina 4%, Uruguay 3%, South Africa 2%, and the USA and UK 1% each. Table 4.3 shows production of raw wool by country.

The wool was primarily Merino, although Merino production has been down substantially in the early 1990s as the stockpile is eliminated and increasingly less cross-bred wool is being produced worldwide. World apparel wool production was 1210m kg (2668m lb) clean in 1992 compared with overall production of 1658m kg (3655m lb) (73%); this compares with 1146m kg (2526m lb) and 1667m kg (3675m lb) respectively in 1982 (69%). This reflects the concentration of wool production towards Merino apparel wools, see Fig. 4.2.

Table 4.2 Estimated world woolled sheep population, million

	1959/60	1969/70	1979/80	1987/88	1988/89	1989/90	1990/91	1991/92
Argentina	48.5	44.3	35.2	29.2	29.3	28.6	27.6	25.7
Australia	149.0	174.3	132.7	156.6	165.2	175.2	166.6	150.7
Brazil	19.0	24.4	17.8	19.9	20.1	20.0	20.1	20.3
China	61.0	59.0	102.6	102.7	110.6	113.5	112.8	110.9
CIS	137.1	130.7	143.6	140.8	141.0	138.9	134.6	119.8
India	39.2	42.6	40.0	39.0	39.0	40.0	40.0	40.0
Iran	24.3	22.4	33.7	45.0	45.0	45.0	45.0	45.0
New Zealand	47.1	60.3	68.8	64.6	60.6	57.9	55.2	52.5
South Africa	33.5	32.4	29.1	24.2	25.9	25.6	24.4	23.2
Spain	22.6	18.7	14.5	20.3	23.1	22.7	24.0	24.3
Turkey	33.6	36.4	46.0	48.8	49.0	48.8	47.5	47.3
UK	27.9	26.1	31.4	40.9	43.0	43.8	43.6	44.0
United States	33.2	20.4	12.7	10.9	10.9	11.4	11.2	10.8
Uruguay	21.7	19.9	20.0	24.1	24.9	25.2	25.9	25.6
Other	220.3	240.1	261.6	378.3	385.1	376.1	386.6	383.5
Total	918.0	952.0	989.7	1145.3	1172.7	1172.7	1165.1	1123.6

Source: IWTO in succession to the Commonwealth Secretariat

Table 4.3 World wool production, '000 tonnes

	Average 1980-81/ 1984-85	1987-88	1988-89	1989-90	1990-91	1991-92	1992-93	1993-94
Greasy								
Albania	3	3	3	3	3	2	2	2
Argentina	170	157	164	149	136	121	114	102
Australia	702	916	959	1100	1066	875	869	801
Brazil	30	26	26	26	27	26	25	18
Bulgaria	35	32	31	29	28	23	19	12
Canada	1	1	1	2	2	2	2	2
Chile	20	19	20	20	18	19	19	19
China	160	209	222	237	239	240	238	240
Czechoslovakia	4	6	5	6	5	3	2	3
Falkland Isles	2	2	3	3	3	3	3	3
France	24	24	23	23	23	22	22	22
East Germany	11	17	17	17	21	15	15	15
West Germany	5	6	6	7				
Greece	10	10	10	10	10	10	10	10
Hungary	11	10	10	9	7	6	5	3
India	35	27	30	35	35	35	35	35
Iran	34	32	32	32	32	33	34	34
Iraq	18	17	17	17	17	20	18	18
Irish Republic	8	11	13	15	17	18	19	20
Italy	12	14	14	14	14	15	14	13
Lesotho	2	3	3	3	3	2	2	1
Mongolia	20	18	19	19	20	22	21	21
Morocco	30	34	34	35	35	35	35	35
Namibia	4	2	2	2	1	–	–	–
New Zealand	347	346	339	311	305	296	256	284
Pakistan	37	53	55	59	63	64	66	67
Peru	11	11	12	10	10	10	10	10
Poland	13	17	16	16	15	11	7	5
Portugal	9	9	9	9	9	9	9	8
Romania	36	39	38	35	38	33	32	34
South Africa	105	92	96	99	106	83	75	71

	Average 1980–81/ 1984–85	1987–88	1988–89	1989–90	1990–91	1991–92	1992–93	1993–94
Former Soviet Union	449	461	478	479	475	441	412	401
of which:								
Russian Federation	220	226	227	230	227	204	179	171
Central Asian Republic	197	200	216	214	213	206	205	204
Ukraine and Moldavia	30	33	33	33	33	29	26	24
Baltic States	1	1	1	1	1	1	1	1
Belarus	1	1	1	1	1	1	1	1
Spain	28	33	38	39	42	40	39	38
Turkey	81	85	85	85	83	79	75	75
United Kingdom	49	62	65	70	72	70	71	68
United States	49	39	41	41	41	40	38	36
Uruguay	69	92	85	96	97	87	90	93
Yugoslavia	10	10	10	10	10	9	5	5
Other Africa (a)	87	100	103	106	105	110	111	112
Other America (a)	18	20	19	18	17	16	16	17
Other Asia (a)	58	55	59	59	62	62	63	64
Other Western Europe (a)	10	12	11	11	14	14	14	13
World total of which:	2817	3132	3223	3366	3326	3021	2913	2830
Former Soviet Union, China, Eastern Europe	731	795	822	833	830	781	738	721
of which:								
Merino	1144	1377	1436	1551	1585	1377	1318	1237
Crossbred (c)	810	811	830	863	787	708	711	701
Other (carpet) (c)	863	944	957	952	954	936	884	892

	Clean yield factors	1987–88	1988–89	1989–90	1990–91	1991–92	1992–93	1993–94
Clean								
Albania	50.0	1	1	1	1	1	1	1
Argentina	60.0	94	98	89	82	73	68	61
Australia	65.1	594	626	724	699	569	566	521
Brazil	70.0	18	18	18	19	18	17	13
Bulgaria	43.0	14	13	12	10	10	8	5
Canada	60.0	1	1	1	1	1	1	1
Chile	58.0	11	12	12	10	11	11	11
China	50.0	105	111	119	120	120	119	120
Czechoslovakia	48.0	3	2	3	3	2	1	1
Falkland Isles	64.0	1	2	2	2	2	2	2
France	50.0	13	13	13	13	12	12	11
East Germany	52.0 }	8 }	8 }	8 }	11	7	7	7
West Germany	}	3 }	3 }	4 }				
Greece	55.0	6	6	6	6	6	6	6
Hungary	38.0	4	4	3	3	2	2	1
India	80.0	22	24	28	28	28	28	28
Iran	45.0	14	14	14	14	15	15	15
Iraq	40.0	7	7	7	7	8	7	7
Irish Republic	67.0b	7	9	10	11	13	13	13
Italy	45.0	6	6	6	6	7	6	6
Lesotho	50.4	2	1	1	1	1	1	1
Mongolia	57.0	10	11	11	11	13	12	12

	Clean yield factors	1987–88	1988–89	1989–90	1990–91	1991–92	1992–93	1993–94
Morocco	40.0	14	14	14	14	14	14	14
Namibia	69.7	1	1	1	1	–	–	–
New Zealand	75.5	260	254	233	227	221	193	214
Pakistan	42.0	22	23	25	26	27	28	28
Peru	65.0	7	8	7	7	7	7	7
Poland	54.0	9	9	9	8	6	4	3
Portugal	58.0	5	5	5	5	5	5	5
Romania	45.0	18	17	16	17	15	14	15
South Africa	58.7	54	57	59	63	49	44	41
Former Soviet Union	45.0	207	215	216	214	198	185	180
of which: Russian Federation	45.0	102	102	104	102	92	81	77
Central Asian Republic	45.0	90	97	96	96	93	92	92
Ukraine and Moldavia	45.0	15	15	15	15	13	12	11
Spain	45.0	15	17	18	19	18	18	17
Turkey	50.0	43	43	43	42	40	38	38
United Kingdom	67.0b	42	44	47	48	47	48	45
United States	53.3	21	22	22	22	21	20	19
Uruguay	65.7	63	58	65	64	57	59	61
Yugoslavia	50.0	5	5	5	5	5	3	3
Other Africa (a)		46	48	49	49	51	51	52
Other America (a)		9	9	9	8	8	8	9
Other Asia (a)		27	29	30	31	31	32	32
Other Western Europe (a)		7	7	7	8	8	8	8
World total		1819	1875	1972	1938	1747	1682	1634
of which: Soviet Union, China, Eastern Europe		371	383	390	389	367	346	338
of which:								
Merino (c)		805	846	924	944	813	777	727
Crossbred (c)		473	487	512	459	409	406	401
Other (carpet) (c)		541	542	536	535	525	499	506

(a) For country coverage see footnote to Table 2.1, p 19.
(b) Weighted average factor for shorn and skin wool.
(c) For micron ranges covered see footnote below.

Note:

1) Merino wool covers 24.5 microns and finer
Cross-bred wool covers 24.6 microns to 32.5 microns
Other (carpet) wool covers 32.6 microns and coarser.

2) On the basis of expert advice, a Clean Yields Sub-Committee comprising representatives from the International Wool Textile Organisation, the International Wool Study Group, the International Wool Secretariat and the Commonwealth Secretariat, has revised the country factors used for converting from greasy to clean in the above table. This has necessitated the re-calculation of the world production data back to 1970–71. The individual country factors for the most recent year are shown in the first column in the above table.

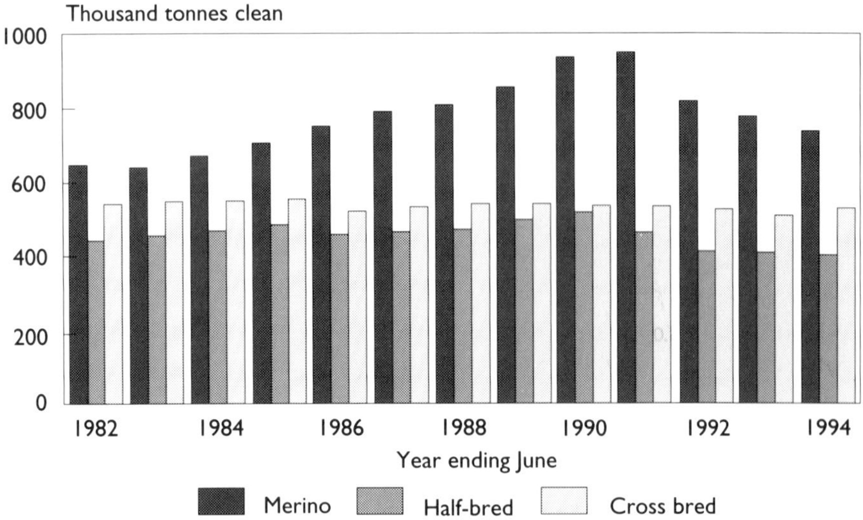

4.2 World wool production by category (source: International Wool Secretariat).

Wool stocks and production by country

Australia

Australia is by far the world's greatest wool-producing country in the world, with almost 15 times as many sheep as people and 60 000 or more wool growers, spread in a continuous crescent from the north of Queensland to the mid-north of Western Australia and including Tasmania and the islands of Bass Strait. Individual flocks range from a few hundred to as many as 100 000 or more, with some three-quarters of all sheep run in flocks of 3000 or more. It was estimated by the Australian Wool Corporation (AWC) in 1992 that over 190 000 people were employed directly on wool growing properties, with a further 150 000 people engaged in full time contract work like the 15 000 shearers, 37 000 registered classers of wool, or those involved in marketing the wool clip. A further third of a million people rely indirectly on the wool industry for a large part of their income in the transport, textile and manufacturing industries as well as in services like insurance and banking. It is difficult to see what could easily take wool's place in Australia – although other crops such as rice and cotton are rising gradually in relative importance.

In 1987, Australian wool stocks were just 17 000 tonnes (37m lb). 1991 saw the deregulation of the wool industry in Australia. In June 1991 Australia started the selling season with a stockpile of 4.766m bales (80% of the then annual clip) at that time equivalent to a sterling value of £120bn. To these stocks had to be added commercial stocks in the hands of growers, who preferred to withdraw their wool from wool auctions because of low prices. At the time, estimates of how long it would take to dispose of the stock were between 15–20 years – a timescale eerily reminiscent of the worries surrounding post-war wool stocks in 1946. The level compared with 3m bales a year before. The effect was to turn the AWC's bank balance from a cash surplus of A$1.8bn to a debt of A$2.7bn, on which the interest alone was A$160–170m. Lynne Johnston, President of the Wool Marketing Reform Group of Australia, commented that the AWC had spent A$5.9bn to acquire a stock worth A$1.4bn. The position of the AWC became untenable; the Australian government refused their request for support as they did not have an acceptable plan to reduce the stockpile. On 11 February 1991, therefore, auction sales were suspended. The floor price scheme was stopped; it had been 870¢, was then 700¢ and finished at 440–450¢. Wool sales resumed under the free market on February 25th. The AWC was subsequently broken up into three organisations (see Chapter 8, pp 173–4).

Only 120 000 bales were sold from the stockpile during the 1992/93 season, partly because of the Federal government's decision to sell from the stockpile before 1 July. Australia then tried hard to cut production, aided by drought; output in 1992/93, the worst seen in the world wool markct for many years, was 1.8bn lb (800m tonnes), 4.3% less than the previous season. The Australian Wool Realisation Committee (AWRC) said that production would be even lower with much lower returns for the remaining producers, suggesting that there would eventually have to be a reduction of some 30–35m sheep. But by 2 September 1994 the stocks held by Wool International (WI) were down to 3.475m bales, almost 10% below the 1992/93 season's ending level and a quarter below the January 1991 peak. Even at this rate the stockpile would have been exhausted within nine years. Figure 4.3 shows the composition of the Australian stockpile in May 1994. The Garnaut Committee deliberated between destroying the stock and selling it off, and decided eventually on a fixed sales schedule which 'would make everyone certain about the quantity of wool coming on to the market' thereby creating an incentive for traders to hold stocks and removing the luxury from wool processors of having the old AWRC stockpile and its release policy there to ensure supplies and keep down prices whilst hopefully avoiding the

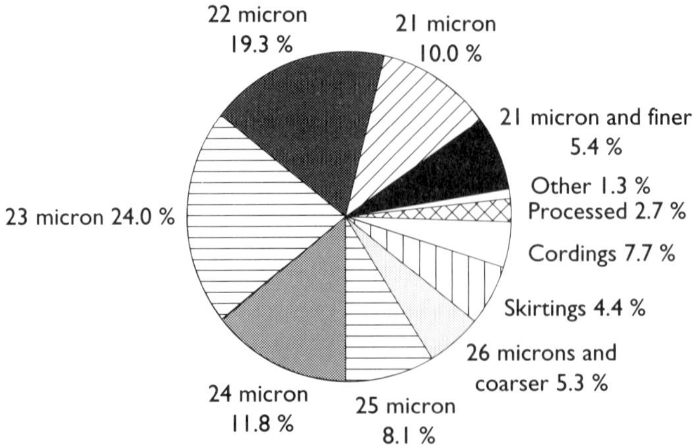

4.3 Composition of Australian stockpile holdings on 27/5/94 (source: National Council of Wool Selling Brokers of Australia).

quite understandable suspicion from traders that WI would have a privileged position in the international marketplace. Under the legislation, WI had to sell 28 000 bales per month between July and December 1994 and 187 000 bales per quarter from January 1995 until privatisation, using a mixture of selling methods including spot sales by private treaty, forward selling up to nine months ahead, private tenders for deferred delivery and auction selling.

The latest Australian estimate for the 1993/94 season reported by the USDA in August 1994 placed the number of sheep on 3 March 1994 at 132m, 5.7% below the previous season, see Table 4.4. Wool production was forecast for the season to be 1.79bn lb (812m kg), greasy, 6.3% below the 1992/93 season. Shorn wool production was 1.68bn lb (762m kg) and pulled wool 0.011bn lb (4.9m kg). The Australian Wool Production Forecasting Committee, in August 1994, forecast Australian shorn wool production for the 1994/95 season at 1.65bn lb (748m kg), down 3.5% from the 1993/94 season, but still reaching in the order of $4.3bn as it has averaged over the last five years and still, of course, by far Australia's largest agricultural product. The prospect of the unseasonably dry weather that occurred in the summer and autumn of 1994 was a key factor in the forecast. The high level of uncertainty attached to weather predictions caused the committee to forecast production within a 66m lb (30m kg) range. The Committee stated that the major impact from dry weather would be felt in the latter part of the 1994/95 season and on into 1995/96.

In greasy wool equivalent, Australia reached its peak production in the 1989/90 season with 1100m kg (2425m lb), declining to 801m

Table 4.4 IWTO/Commonwealth Secretariat estimates of Australian wool output

	1988/89	1989/90	1990/91	1991/92	1992/93	1993/94
Sheep numbers, million	165	175	163	148	140	132
Wool production, m lb clean	1380	1596	1541	1254	1248	1168
Output per sheep, lb/head	8.36	9.12	9.45	8.47	8.91	8.85

Source: IWTO in succession to the Commonwealth Secretariat

kg (1766m lb) – levels akin to the early 1980s – by 1994/95, according to the Australian Wool Production Forecast Committee (AWPFC). Production of shorn wool continues to increase its share of overall production, almost 94% at the time of writing. In terms of the states of Australia, New South Wales continues to dominate production with 276m kg (608m lb) (greasy) from 46.9m sheep, compared with Western Australia's 199m kg (439m lb) from 32.7m sheep, Victoria's 150m kg (330m lb) from 23.4m sheep, South Australia's 97m kg (214m lb) from 15m sheep, Queensland's 62m kg (137m lb) from 11.4m sheep and Tasmania's 18m kg (40m lb) from 4.3m sheep (AWPFC, 1994 estimate) with the other states effectively now producing nothing from a negligible number of sheep.

The state distribution of production (see Table 4.5) shows a decline since 1989/90, the year of peak production, in the share of New South Wales, from 35.8% to 34.4%; Tasmania's production is also falling quite consistently and all the other states have shown increases in their share. This suggests that sheep production in New South Wales is the leading edge of Australian wool production and it is most likely to show a more rapid increase as demand picks up in the mid-1990s. Tasmania's decline, however, along with sheepbreeding in the other states, may be a longer term trend.

In terms of the average weight of fleece shorn from sheep and lambs, Southern Australia produces the heaviest at 4.92 kg/head (10.85 lb/head), followed by Western Australia at 4.51, NSW at 4.32, Victoria at 4.3 and Queensland at 4.29. Tasmania comes last at 3.81 kg. These figures have all shown substantial declines since 1989/90, when they peaked throughout Australia. Even the somewhat reduced levels of the mid-1990s, however, are above those achieved before the mid-1980s except for 1974/75 and the overall trend is to heavier fleeces.

Table 4.5 Australian total wool production (a), m kg greasy

	NSW	VIC	QLD	SA	WA	TAS	NT & ACT	Shorn wool including crutchings	Dead and fellmongered	Wool exported on skins	Total
1945–46	195.7	69.1	78.6	33.4	39.5	7.4	1.0	369.4	29.9	25.3	424.7
1946–47	196.2	89.4	65.7	42.2	40.9	7.5	1.0				443.0
1947–48	191.5	90.5	69.7	52.8	43.3	7.0	0.9				455.8
1948–49	210.1	92.6	71.1	52.1	45.1	7.6	1.0				479.6
1949–50	233.6	102.2	73.6	55.0	44.8	7.7	1.1				518.0
1950–51	223.2	99.0	70.2	56.9	48.7	7.8	1.1	466.9	20.6	19.5	506.9
1951–52	198.6	102.0	62.9	61.5	54.6	9.3	0.9				489.8
1952–53	252.4	114.4	74.0	72.0	58.1	9.0	1.2				581.0
1953–54	247.2	101.4	79.1	66.0	61.0	9.1	1.1				564.9
1954–55	245.4	114.9	80.1	70.6	58.8	10.8	1.1				581.7
1955–56	269.3	124.0	88.0	78.8	70.9	10.6	1.3				642.9
1956–57	299.5	135.9	103.3	85.6	70.9	13.0	1.3				709.5
1957–58	252.8	134.5	92.7	84.3	71.8	13.2	1.1				650.4
1958–59	310.3	135.6	99.4	84.8	75.5	14.8	1.2				721.5
1959–60	324.5	146.5	107.1	90.0	77.3	15.2	1.4				762.0
1960–61	301.3	146.1	106.9	80.5	86.8	14.5	1.2	677.7	17.0	52.4	737.3
1961–62	318.0	150.0	104.5	80.5	87.2	15.6	1.6				757.4
1962–63	314.7	143.6	106.0	93.9	83.5	15.7	1.1				758.5
1963–64	331.7	151.6	115.8	94.1	98.2	15.4	1.2				808.0
1964–65	320.3	163.9	114.0	95.5	93.9	18.0	1.5				807.1
1965–66	262.8	166.4	87.4	105.4	112.3	19.0	1.3	682.0	11.1	61.2	754.6
1966–67	282.5	171.6	92.4	108.5	112.3	19.6	1.5				788.4
1967–68	295.0	150.8	102.9	99.3	136.2	17.4	1.4				803.0
1968–69	305.5	165.3	112.0	108.0	170.4	21.3	1.4				884.0
1969–70	340.1	193.8	89.1	124.7	152.6	21.9	1.7	837.4	9.8	78.6	923.9
1970–71	314.3	195.4	76.6	117.5	158.9	21.7	1.5	800.6	8.0	81.8	885.9
1971–72	281.8	197.5	83.2	119.2	178.2	21.1	1.2	681.5	72.8		882.2
1972–73	226.2	172.3	70.2	100.9	146.9	18.2	0.7	623.9	78.8		735.4
1974–75	254.3	165.5	66.3	108.0	180.0	18.9	0.5	605.5	71.5		793.5

1975–76	240.3	137.9	66.3	105.6	183.6	20.0	0.6	642.4	66.1	754.3
1976–77	232.9	126.1	64.4	94.3	166.4	18.1	0.5	637.9	63.3	702.7
1977–78	231.0	131.6	59.3	86.3	149.4	18.9	0.5	660.9	56.3	677.0
1978–79	239.7	138.7	63.8	87.4	155.1	19.1	0.5	641.5	60.2	704.3
1979–80	232.5	147.4	59.0	97.9	151.3	20.0	0.4	671.2	56.4	708.5
1980–81	220.6	146.3	46.5	102.8	164.5	20.1	0.4	752.7	61.1	701.2
1981–82	234.9	146.7	60.7	103.7	148.9	21.8	0.4	762.1	67.4	717.1
1982–83	238.7	132.1	54.1	103.0	151.4	21.7	0.4	813.7	76.6	701.4
1983–84	248.7	142.1	65.6	108.7	141.3	22.0	0.4	843.0	73.4	728.8
1984–85	275.1	170.4	67.8	108.4	170.0	21.9	0.5	898.9	60.5	814.1
1985–86	280.6	171.0	65.5	112.3	175.8	25.0	0.5	1029.4	70.9	830.7
1986–87	287.4	196.6	75.0	115.8	188.7	26.3	0.5	989.6	76.6	890.3
1987–88	307.7	194.9	78.2	122.4	188.5	23.5	1.5	801.0	74.0	916.7
1988–89	339.2	197.7	76.3	118.9	203.2	22.3	1.8	815.1	54.3	959.4
1989–90	394.5	216.1	90.5	134.2	236.1	27.0	1.9	762.0	52.0	1100.3
1990–91	403.6	190.6	105.9	118.6	222.3	23.3	2.0	750.0	51.0	1066.2
1991–92	305.1	169.0	80.8	109.5	189.0	19.9	1.7			875.0
1992–93(P)	294.1	168.0	64.0	117.8	205.5	19.5	0.5			869.4
1993–94(F)	274.0	152.0	60.0	103.0	206.0	19.0	0.0			814.0
1994–95(F)	276.0	150.0	62.0	97.0	199.0	18.0	0.0			801.0

Note: Totals may not add due to rounding.
(a) Includes shorn wool, fellmongered and other wool.
(P) Provisional (F)Forecast

Source: Australian Bureau of Statistics: Wool Production and Utilisation (1945/46–1992/93), Australian Wool Production Forecasting Committee (1993/94–1994/95)

Merino sheep continue to constitute over 70% of the Australian sheep population, with Merino cross-breeds taking about another 10%, Corriedale 2%, Polwarth 1% and other breeds 14%. Yields have been relatively consistent, increasing only slightly in the late 1980s and remaining at the 65%+ mark in the early 1990s.

Australia produces 98% of world apparel wool in the mid-1990s, compared to 90% a decade ago. Specialisation in international wool production has advanced still further and this has reinforced Australia's position. Wool continues to contribute more than $A3bn to export revenue.

New Zealand

About half of New Zealand's 27m ha land area is occupied for farming. Sheep grazing takes 11m ha across some 27 000 farms, divided into high, hill and low country (see Table 4.6) and averaging 400 ha each, of which over 50% run 500+ sheep. There were, in 1992, 19 328 sheep farms on North Island with 24.7m sheep, compared to 36 185 sheep farms on South Island with 27.8m sheep. The key regions for sheep grazing are Canterbury, Otago, Southland, Manawatu-Wanganui and to a lesser extent Waikato. Sheep graze all year but there is usually a need for some supplementary feeding. Generally, New Zealand farms are owned and worked by one farming family, with major farm work, such as shearing or fencing, often being done by contract labour. New Zealand sheep tend to be of many different breeds, most descended from the Romney Marsh breed, but dual purpose: meat and wool; the share of wool and meat in total revenues varies depending on relative prices; in the mid-1990s wool has recovered to become the major earner again.

The New Zealand share of world wool production has fallen gradually, from 16% in 1985 to less than 14% in 1993/94. Raw wool production declined at an average annual rate of 3.3% between the record production levels of 1984/85 and 1991 where production levels resembled those of the 1950s, whilst world wool production increased by 2.05%, see Table 4.7.

Even with this decline in production, the New Zealand stockpile increased, being at the start of the 1991/92 season 655 000 bales (over 100m kg (220m lb) greasy), equivalent to 35% of the annual clip. It has been steadily sold off, mainly to wool exporters but some to the CIS states and at auction, with the NZWB concentrating on out-of-season types to avoid competition with growers' sales of new wool. The NZWB estimated that the cost of holding the stock in 1992/93 was

Table 4.6 New Zealand farming systems

Farm type	% of farms	Size (ha)	Sheep	Cattle (per farm)	Wool (kg per ha)	*Meat	Main breeds
High hill country							
South Island high country	1	10 000	8700	320	4	6	Merino Half-bred Corriedale
Hill country							
South Island hill country	4	2000	4900	270	13	33	Half-bred Corriedale
North Island hard hill country	8	800	4500	400	30	79	Perendale Romney
North Island hill country	24	400	3300	250	46	123	Perendale Romney
Low country							
North Island intensive fattening	21	200	2000	150	59	177	Romney Coopworth Perendale
South Island fattening/ breeding	20	360	3100	65	24	102	Romney Corriedale Coopworth Half-bred
South Island intensive fattening	18	200	2600	25	79	182	Romney Coopworth
South Island mixed cropping/ fattening	4	230	1600	10	35	185	Romney Coopworth Corriedale Half-bred

Source: New Zealand Wool Board

NZ$11.194m, made up of NZ$3.028m storage costs and the remainder interest costs.

Sheep numbers have fallen throughout the 1990s, due to economic restructuring throughout New Zealand, combined with bad weather and farm economics which caused stock slaughter and a switch into cattle production, especially on North Island. Cross-bred production is the most important for New Zealand, and in this category production fell 18% between 1985–91. There are many different breeds of sheep; the Romney used to account for some 75% of numbers in the 1960s, but now accounts for less than half. By contrast New Zealand produces only about 10 000 tonnes of Merino annually, about 5% of production, although it does command a large premium at auction and nearly all is sold. There is one shearing a year with availability peaking in October/November of each year.

Table 4.7 New Zealand wool production, 1946–94

Season	Sheep numbers, million(1)	Wool production, '000 tonnes greasy	clean(2)	Clip per head(3), greasy kg	Average yield(4), %	Average bale weight, greasy kg
1946/47		166	120			
1947/48	32.7	164	118	5.0		
1948/49	32.5	166	120	5.1		
1949/50	32.9	177	127	5.4		
1950/51	33.9	177	127	5.2		
1951/52	34.8	185	133	5.3		
1952/53	35.4	190	137	5.4		
1953/54	36.2	193	139	5.3		
1954/55	38.0	206	148	5.4		
1955/56	39.1	210	151	5.4		
1956/57	40.3	223	161	5.5		
1957/58	42.4	225	162	5.3		
1958/59	46.0	245	176	5.3		
1959/60	46.9	262	189	5.6		
1960/61	47.1	267	190	5.7	71.3	
1961/62	48.5	266	188	5.5	70.8	152.0
1962/63	49.0	281	202	5.7	71.9	153.8
1963/64	50.2	279	202	5.6	72.5	151.9
1964/65	51.3	283	205	5.5	72.3	153.2
1965/66	53.8	315	228	5.9	72.3	155.7
1966/67	57.3	322	231	5.6	71.7	155.1
1967/68	60.0	330	240	5.5	72.6	155.8
1968/69	60.5	332	244	5.5	73.4	155.1
1969/70	59.9	328	237	5.5	72.4	156.0
1970/71	60.3	334	244	5.5	73.1	157.4
1971/72	58.9	322	234	5.5	72.7	156.9
1972/73	60.9	309	223	5.1	72.1	154.8
1973/74	56.7	285	205	5.0	71.9	154.3
1974/75	55.9	294	211	5.3	71.8	156.5
1975/76	55.3	312	227	5.6	72.8	153.7
1976/77	56.4	303	219	5.4	72.3	152.9
1977/78	59.1	311	226	5.3	72.6	149.8
1978/79	62.2	321	235	5.2	73.2	151.0
1979/80	63.5	357	256	5.6	71.7	151.2
1980/81	68.8	381	272	5.5	71.3	151.7
1981/82	69.9	363	261	5.2	72.0	150.7
1982/83	70.3	371	274	5.3	73.8	152.2
1983/84	70.3	364	271	5.2	74.5	153.9
1984/85	69.7	373	277	5.4	74.3	156.0
1985/86	67.9	357	265	5.3	74.2	160.6
1986/87	67.5	348	260	5.2	74.8	160.0
1987/88	64.2	346	260	5.4	75.1	162.3
1988/89	64.6	339	254	5.2	75.0	161.4
1989/90	60.6	311	233	5.1	74.9	162.9
1990/91	57.9	305	227	5.3	74.8	163.1

Season	Sheep numbers, million(1)	Wool production, '000 tonnes greasy	clean(2)	Clip per head(3), greasy kg	Average yield(4), %	Average bale weight, greasy kg
1991/92	55.2	296	221	5.4	74.9	163.4
1992/93	52.6	256	193	4.9	75.5	163.9
1993/94	50.3	284	214	5.6	75.5	165.8

1 Sheep numbers as at the beginning of the season.
2 Converted from greasy production using average yield figures. Prior to 1960/61 an assumed average yield of 72% was used. This is the average for the period 1960/61 to 1969/70. Revised for 1985/6 onwards.
3 Greasy production divided by sheep numbers.
4 For the period 1960/61 to 1976/77 average assessed yield; since 1977/78 averaged tested yield.

In common with other wool producing countries, and as these figures suggest, New Zealand had an exceptionally difficult time in the early 1990s. There were difficulties in marketing the product and in obtaining satisfactory returns. Some growers were driven out of the industry altogether, whilst others accepted losses in 1991 and 1992 in the hope that trading conditions would improve in 1993, which they did. In New Zealand the knock-on effect of poor trading conditions was felt by brokers, scourers, exporters and private merchants. Although the price support scheme was abolished in 1991 it took several years before rational price policies were established and the groundwork for a recovery was properly laid.

New Zealand wool production in the 1993/94 season was 481m lb (218m kg) clean (637m lb (289m kg) greasy). This was as a result of good growing conditions and 13% above the previous season, see Table 4.8. Despite a rather static sheep population, the higher wool output was caused by an increase in the yield of wool per sheep to a 15-year high. At the end of the 1993/94 season it was 173 030 bales, 50% of the year before, 73% below the recent high in January 1994 and only just over a quarter of the level in early 1992. Approximately 86% of the clip comes from live sheep.

Table 4.8 IWTO/Commonwealth Secretariat estimates of New Zealand wool output

	1988/89	1989/90	1990/91	1991/92	1992/93	1993/94
Sheep numbers, million	61	58	55	53	50	51
Wool production, m lb	560	514	500	487	425	481
Output per sheep, lb/head	9.18	8.86	9.09	9.2	8.5	9.43

China

Table 4.9 shows estimates of Chinese wool output. Statistics on Chinese wool output are not necessarily very reliable. The general unmistakeable trend, however, is towards a steady increase in the number of sheep, although by less than even the much reduced levels of population increase that China is experiencing in the 1990s. It may not be easy to generalise, however, about Chinese yields, despite a series of increases since the late 1980s except for 1993/94.

Table 4.9 IWTO/Commonwealth Secretariat estimates of Chinese wool output

	1988/89	1989/90	1990/91	1991/92	1992/93	1993/94
Sheep numbers, million	111	114	113	111	110	116
Wool production, m lb	245	262	265	265	273	265
Output per sheep, lb/head	2.2	2.3	2.35	2.39	2.48	2.28

Argentina

As the statistics show, Argentina is another country where the profitability of wool production has been insufficient to prevent a long term decline in production, see Table 4.10. First estimates for Argentine wool production in 1993/94 were 92 000 tonnes, 11% down on the previous season (103 000 tonnes). Federacion Lanera Argentina stated that low wool prices had resulted in reduced flocks as farmers in all regions turned to alternative production.

Table 4.10 IWTO/Commonwealth Secretariat estimates of Argentinian wool output

	1988/89	1989/90	1990/91	1991/92	1992/93	1993/94
Sheep numbers, million	29	29	27	24	22	20
Wool production, m lb	216	196	181	161	150	134
Output per sheep, lb/head	7.45	6.76	6.7	6.71	6.82	6.7

Table 4.11 shows raw wool production by type and production areas. The areas are shown in Fig. 4.4.

Table 4.11 Argentinian raw wool production and balance sheet, '000 tonnes greasy

	1985/86	1986/87	1987/88	1988/89	1989/90	1990/91	1991/92	1992/93	1993/94
Raw wool production									
Shorn and skin wool	140.0	138.0	145.0	152.0	138.6	125.0	110.0	103.0	92.0
Wool content of domestic sheepskins	12.2	12.2	12.2	12.2	10.6	10.6	10.6	10.6	9.8
Total	152.2	150.2	157.2	164.2	149.2	135.6	120.6	113.6	101.8
Breakdown by type									
of which									
Merino	56.1	52.6	52.6	51.4	46.3	42.2	39.4	44.0	39.0
fine cross-bred	54.2	68.8	73.3	80.3	74.0	64.7	57.8	49.1	44.8
medium cross-bred	23.8	15.7	18.2	19.4	17.6	14.7	12.4	11.1	10.2
coarse cross-bred (including Criolia types	18.9	13.1	13.1	13.1	11.3	14.0	11.0	9.4	7.8
Breakdown of shorn wool by production areas									
Corrientes	9.2	9.7	10.0	11.5	10.0	10.0	9.0	7.0	6.5
Entre Rios	5.6	5.0	5.6	6.2	6.0	6.0	5.0	4.0	3.7
Buenos Aires	42.0	40.0	46.0	49.5	45.0	33.1	22.8	18.0	15.6
La Pampa	3.0	2.0	2.0	2.1	2.0	3.5	3.2	2.5	2.1
Neuquen	3.5	3.5	3.5	3.7	3.0	3.3	3.0	3.0	2.8
Rio Negro	13.4	14.0	14.0	13.5	11.0	11.0	10.0	10.5	10.0
Chubut	25.0	26.3	26.3	26.0	24.0	22.0	20.0	27.0	22.6
Santa Cruz	26.6	25.0	25.1	25.5	23.0	21.0	22.0	15.0	14.0
Tierra del Fuego	3.5	3.5	3.5	3.5	3.5	2.9	2.8	2.8	2.8
Jujuy }	8.2	} 9.0	} 9.0	} 10.5	2.1	2.7	2.7	2.8	10.4
Other }		}	}	}	9.0	9.5	9.5	2.8	9.1
Total	140.0	138.0	145.0	152.0	138.6	125.0	110.0	103.0	92.0
Balance sheet (a)									
Opening stocks	79.8	65.8	58.5	63.5	105.3	125.2	132.5	132.5	123.5
Production	140.0	138.0	145.0	152.0	138.6	125.0	110.0	103.0	92.0
Total supplies	*219.8*	*203.8*	*203.5*	*215.5*	*243.9*	*250.2*	*242.5*	*235.5*	*215.5*
Consumed locally	36.0	34.0	27.0	26.0	23.0	28.0	33.0	28.0	24.0
Exported	118.0	111.3	113.0	84.2	95.7	89.7	77.0	84.0 }	
Closing stocks	65.8	58.5	63.5	105.3	125.2	132.5	123.5	123.5 }	191.5

(a) Excluding the wool content of domestic sheepskins.

Source: Argentine Wool Federation

4.4 ***Argentina.***

Uruguay

By contrast to its South America neighbour, Uruguay has been steadily increasing its wool production, largely through improvements in yield, see Table 4.12. Comparison with other wool producing countries, however, suggests that Uruguay has yet some way to go.

Table 4.12 IWTO/Commonwealth Secretariat estimates of Uruguayan wool output

	1988/89	1989/90	1990/91	1991/92	1992/93	1993/94
Sheep numbers, million	25	25	26	26	24	23
Wool production, m lb	128	143	141	126	130	134
Output per sheep, lb/head	5.12	5.72	5.42	4.85	5.42	5.83

South Africa

Wool is produced in varying amounts in most parts of South Africa under a range of conditions. There were about 25 000 woolgrowers in South Africa in the early 1990s but their numbers are falling. The history of South African wool production shows that peak output was reached in the mid-1960s, and there has been a steady decline since, see Table 4.13. South African wool production fell dramatically in the 1992–94 period due to the usual reasons of low international wool prices, combined with a devastating drought experienced in most wool producing areas and farmers switching over to mutton breeds to improve cash flow at a time of high South African mutton prices. South Africa used to produce around 100m kg (220m lb) per annum in the early 1980s, down to 69m kg (152m lb) in the 1992–93 season and with further falls in the 1993–94 season, see Table 4.14. South Africa is sliding out of the premier league of international wool producers, at least for the 1990s.

The South African wool clip was estimated by the USDA in August 1994 to be 0.09bn lb (41m kg), clean, 0.16bn lb (73m kg) greasy, down a further 5% from the season before and reflecting the factors noted above. SAWB stocks were down to 30 000 bales as early as late 1993.

The clip is divided into Merino (80% of the clip in the 1992/93 season compared with 69% in 1980/81), other white wool (11% –

Table 4.13 Mass and value of wool production in South Africa

Season	Greasy, m kg	Value, m R	Greasy price, ¢/kg	Average yield	Clean price, ¢/kg
1945/46	95.1	21.1			
1946/47	95.8	29.4	30.72		
1947/48	93.7	45.2	48.31		
1948/49	99.3	62.8	63.26		
1949/50	98.7	77.1	78.09		
1950/51	103.2	181.6	175.99		
1951/52	111.0	98.1	88.45		
1952/53	116.5	121.0	103.89		
1953/54	121.7	128.4	105.54		
1954/55	131.5	117.7	89.45		
1955/56	134.5	105.7	78.59	51.63	152.21
1956/57	137.1	144.6	105.40	52.95	199.06
1957/58	128.1	103.7	80.94	53.03	152.62
1958/59	133.5	80.7	60.48	49.28	122.72
1959/60	134.0	100.7	75.10	52.45	143.18
1960/61	134.0	90.1	67.25	52.97	126.96
1961/62	142.3	98.4	69.12	51.49	134.24
1962/63	136.3	104.4	76.60	52.66	145.46
1963/64	138.8	127.9	92.14	54.30	169.69
1964/65	134.1	100.2	74.68	53.24	140.28
1965/66	148.3	115.6	78.00	53.34	146.24
1966/67	135.5	98.0	72.28	51.43	140.54
1967/68	140.2	96.8	69.07	52.26	132.16
1968/69	145.9	106.5	73.01	52.26	139.70
1969/70	147.3	93.9	63.73	51.18	124.53
1970/71	118.6	54.2	45.67	51.25	89.12
1971/72	111.7	60.6	54.22	53.94	100.52
1972/73	103.3	161.1	155.94	55.02	283.43
1973/74	104.1	157.2	150.99	55.12	273.94
1974/75	103.9	106.3	102.30	56.10	182.35
1975/76	102.8	141.3	137.50	57.55	238.92
1976/77	99.6	161.5	162.09	57.96	279.65
1977/78	102.9	169.7	164.96	57.35	287.64
1978/79	98.8	181.4	183.58	57.36	320.05
1979/80	99.8	205.6	206.00	57.82	356.29
1980/81	101.8	209.0	205.41	56.47	363.74
1981/82	105.7	277.2	262.12	57.13	458.82
1982/83	107.3	265.9	247.92	57.40	431.91
1983/84	101.6	290.5	285.87	56.73	503.92
1984/85	98.2	402.8	410.30	57.29	716.19
1985/86	92.7	426.7	460.06	56.62	812.54
1986/87	86.1	417.9	485.33	57.58	842.88
1987/88	87.5	739.4	844.87	58.31	1448.92
1988/89	93.2	983.2	1054.86	59.13	1783.96
1989/90	96.9	858.2	885.67	59.26	1494.55

Season	Greasy, m kg	Value, m R	Greasy price, ¢/kg	Average yield	Clean price, ¢/kg
1990/91	101.7	618.9	608.61	59.20	1028.06
1991/92	77.8	534.6	687.13	59.50	1154.84
1992/93	69.6	406.5	584.27	58.91	991.80

Conversion: Pound to kilogram = 1lb × 0.45359291
Pound to rand = £ x 2

Notes:
(1) The above figures exclude wool on skins.
(2) Details of seasons 1946/47 to 1951/52 based on SAWDO – *Summaries of Statistics.*
(3) Details for the seasons 1952/53 to 1971/72 based on the mass and value of wool sold at auctions.
(4) Details for seasons since 1972/73 based on mass and realization value of wool delivered to the SAWB.
(5) During the 1972/73 season 1 425 044 kg of Karakul wool has been sold privately, which resulted in a total production of 105 232 412 kg for the season. This private sale was not included in the mass and value of the season's clip.

Table 4.14 IWTO/Commonwealth Secretariat estimates of South African wool output

	1988/89	1989/90	1990/91	1991/92	1992/93	1993/94
Sheep numbers, million	26	26	26	26	24	23
Wool production, m lb	126	130	139	108	97	90
Output per sheep, lb/head	4.85	5	5.35	4.15	4.04	3.91

unchanged), Basuto (3%/unchanged), Ciskei and Transkei (2%/3.5%), coarse and coloured (3%/7%), Karakul (zero compared to 6.5%) and dead wool (less than 1% in both cases). Clearly what this signifies is that South African wool production has concentrated more on Merinos at the expense of other breeds.

The United States

Total US production now amounts to somewhat under 40m lb (18m kg) clean. Contrary to preconceptions and against opportunity, US wool production shows a consistent downward trend since the 1970s, falling 15% even in 1994. Sheep inventories are less than a fifth of their 1942 level of 49m. Fleece weight is also falling as is the return in dollars, now under half that at the beginning of the 1970s. This is a matter of considerable concern to US wool interests and is accounted for by differential production costs and the continued emphasis on lamb and mutton production for US sheep, although even there consumption has proved difficult to boost. Most of the statistics provided by the American Sheep Industry are on lamb and mutton prices, for example. The Wool Quality Improvement Programme was launched in 1990 with the aim of bringing US grown wool into line with international standards in respect to preparation, packaging and marketing.

Tables 4.15 and 4.16 show US wool production and Fig. 4.5 shows production by state.

Table 4.15 US wool production, clean m lb

	1990	1991	1992	1993	1994
Production	46.8	46.7	44.1	41.2	35

Source: USDA

Table 4.16 US wool production and value

Mktg year	Shorn wool production m lb	Support price[1], cents per lb	Average market price received by producers[2], cents per lb	Shorn wool payment rate[3], %	Value of shorn wool produced, m $	Government payments[4], m $
1955	241.3	62	42.8	44.9	103.0	57.6
1956	242.2	62	44.3	40.0	107.2	51.9
1957	239.1	62	53.7	15.5	127.8	16.1
1958	243.7	62	36.4	70.3	88.6	85.1
1959	259.9	62	43.3	43.2	112.3	53.9
1960	265.3	62	42.0	47.6	111.4	59.5
1961	259.2	62	42.9	44.5	111.4	56.9
1962	246.6	62	47.7	30.0	117.6	39.2
1963	232.4	62	48.5	27.8	112.4	27.2
1964	212.3	62	53.2	16.5	112.9	20.2
1965	201.5	62	47.1	31.6	95.0	34.2
1966	195.1	65	52.1	24.8	101.2	26.2
1967	189.0	66	39.8	65.8	75.2	57.9
1968	177.4	67	40.5	65.4	71.8	54.4
1969	165.7	69	41.8	65.1	69.5	50.7
1970	161.6	72	35.5	102.8	57.2	64.0
1971	160.2	72	19.4	271.1	31.4	102.8
1972	158.5	72	35.0	105.7	55.5	68.0
1973	143.7	72	82.7	*	118.8	*
1974	131.4	72	59.1	21.8	77.8	14.7

Mktg year	Shorn wool production m lb	Support price[1], cents per lb	Average market price received by producers[2], cents per lb	Shorn wool payment rate[3], %	Value of shorn wool produced, m $	Government payments[4], m $
1975	119.5	72	44.7	61.1	53.5	41.6
1976	111.1	72	65.7	9.6	73.3	7.0
1977	107.3	99	72.0	37.5	77.3	28.8
1978	102.9	108	74.5	45.0	76.7	36.1
1979	104.9	115	86.3	33.3	90.5	31.0
1980	105.4	123	88.1	39.6	92.8	37.6
1981	109.8	135	94.5	42.9	103.7	47.0
1982	106.1	137	68.4	100.3	72.8	71.5
1983	102.9	153	61.3	149.6	63.0	116.8
1984	95.7	165	79.5	107.5	76.0	92.3
1985	88.1	165[5]	63.3	160.7	55.7	103.9
1986	84.4	178	66.8	166.5	56.3	102.4
1987	84.5	181	91.7	97.4	77.0	91.6
1988	89.5	178	138.0	29.0	125.0	39.4
1989	89.2	177	124.0	42.7	110.5	45.5
1990	88.0	182	80.0	127.5	69.5	105.4
1991	87.7	188	55.0	241.8	47.2	134.4
1992	82.8	197	74.0	166.2	60.1	116.0
1993	77.3	204	51.0	300.0	39.0	121.7
1994		209				

1 Support prices and payments are for the marketing years beginning 1 April for 1955–1962, the nine months 1 April – 31 December for 1963, and calendar years for 1964 and forward.
2 Prices for 1955, 1956, and 1964 and forward are calendar year prices; prices for 1957–1962 are for April–March marketing years; price for 1963 is for the period April–December.
3 Payment rate for shorn wool is expressed as a percentage and is applied to each producer's return from the sale of wool.
4 Includes unshorn lamb payments, promotion deductions and marketing assessments. May include late payments from previous marketing years. Excludes administrative expenses. Preliminary for 1992 and 1993.
5 Altered to comply with Gramm-Rudmann.
* No payments were required on 1973 marketings because the national average wool price exceeded the support level.

Source: Wool, USDA

Estimated total shorn wool production 70 353

4.5 1994 estimated US wool production, thousand lb (source: American Sheep Industry Market Information Services).

Table 4.17 IWTO/Commonwealth Secretariat estimates of Soviet/CIS wool output

	1988/89	1989/90	1990/91	1991/92	1992/93	1993/94
Sheep numbers, million	141	139	135	130	123	116
Wool production, m lb	474	476	472	437	408	397
Output per sheep, lb/head	3.36	3.42	3.5	3.36	3.32	3.42

Europe

The Commonwealth of Independent States

The figures in Table 4.17 show the dismal story of the decline in wool production in Russia and the other CIS states since the collapse of the former Soviet Union and indeed before. Most of these estimates of decline subsequently prove to be underestimates, and when taken together with the decline in imports due to foreign exchange shortages, there must be adjudged to be real under-supply of wool to meet consumer needs in these countries. Information on wool production in the former CIS countries is at present scarce; an analysis of the latest statistics, for 1993/94, suggest however that the rate of decline, at least, is slowing and the share of world population has stabilised.

The United Kingdom

The UK produces about 2.5% of world output, some 50m kg (110m lb) annually out of 35m sheep. About 20m sheep are shorn annually. The forty or so British breeds and many half-breeds, hybrids and crosses produce mainly coarser quality wool (see Chapter 7). British sheep can be divided into three main groups: short wool and down, long wool and lustre, and mountain and hill. Hill and lowland sheep are complementary; the flocks on hill and upland grazing, comprising three-quarters of the UK land mass, provide lambs for fattening in the lowlands and cross-bred ewes to produce future lambs (see Fig. 4.6) Revenue to the approximately 90 000 UK producers – the largest, though steadily falling, number of small producers of any textile in

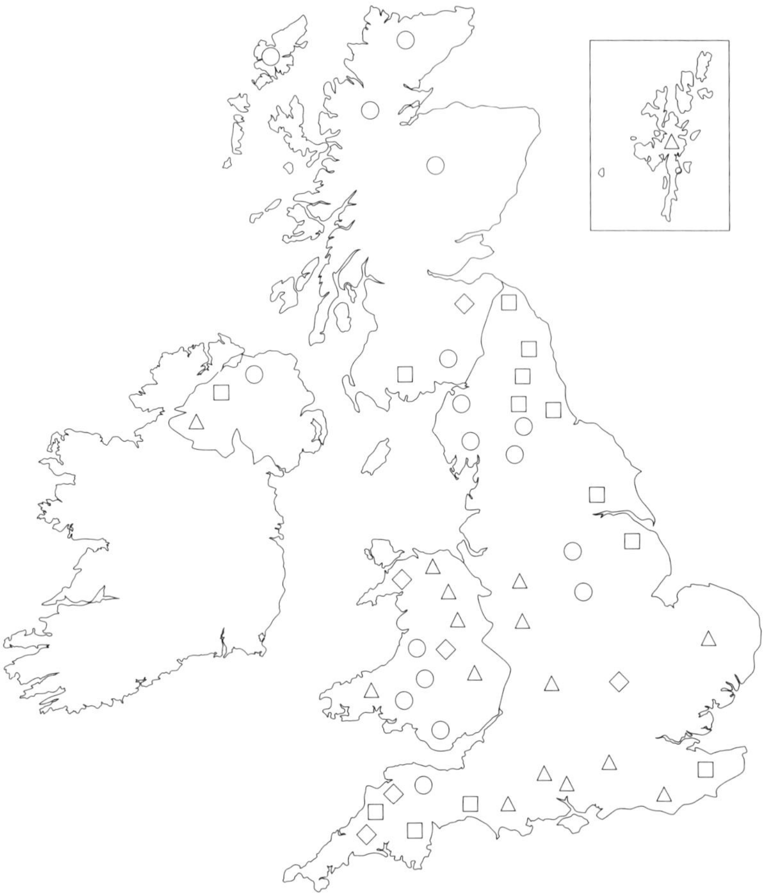

△	Short wool and down	5 500 000 kg
◇	Medium wools	10 000 000 kg
□	Longwool and lustre	16 750 000 kg
○	Mountain and hill	21 750 000 kg
		54 000 000 kg

Wool production by country	
England	27 000 000 kg
Scotland	12 000 000 kg
Wales	11 500, 000 kg
Northern Ireland	3 500 000 kg
	54 000 000 kg

4.6 Geographical distribution of British sheep breeds in the 1990s (source: British Wool Marketing Board).

Europe – is directly affected by the world market situation and the trends in the major producing countries are reflected in British wool.

In the 1991/92 season the delayed payment system was continued by the BWMB, which started the 1992 selling season with 38 800 bales, equivalent to 9m bales greasy, 17% of the UK annual clip. This placed the UK in a better situation than most countries but still at an unacceptably high level. There were the usual reasons for the stockpile: high production levels in 1989/90 flowing from the high prices of 1986–88, the worldwide recession and the collapse in demand from the CIS countries and China. Wool production did not fall in the UK despite this because the demand for sheepmeat is the controlling production factor, not wool, although pressure from the meat trade has to be resisted to control wool quality. As the then BWMB Managing Director, Maurice Grass, said in 1992, 'British wool production is governed by the viability of the sheep meat market'.

Despite these problems, the stockpile was cut to 6m kg (13m lb) by April 1993 and the BWMB reported in November 1993 that the stockpile would be eliminated by the April 1994 carryover, which it was. The impact of the ending of the price support scheme had not been as fierce as feared. Wool production anyway makes up a small portion of UK farm revenue, some 4% on average. Moreover, lamb prices were exceptionally high during the 1993/94 season and EU and government grants did become available for farmers specialising in wool production. Production continued at a high level in the 1994/95 season as did concerns that potential quality improvements were not all being made.

CHAPTER

5

Wool prices

Measurement of wool prices

Each wool producing country has its own domestic prices for wool, and these depend on national production constraints and costs, and international availability of competitive wool from the major producers. It is inevitable, therefore, that wool prices are said to be 'led' by the major world producers, and in particular, those obtainable for Merino wool in Australia. Prices for coarse wool in the UK and New Zealand, and Merino wools in other countries, can vary in their proportions to Australian wool, but only within reasonably predictable levels. Discussion of international wool prices, therefore, centres around prices in the major production centres, and on those prices which have gained international credibility as benchmarks: principally those in Australia, New Zealand and to a lesser extent in the UK.

Australia

Wool International has changed the way that Australian wool market quotes and the market indicator is established. The old Australian Wool Corporation Indicator was the price of an average of lots at Sydney wool auctions, covering 13 types and 11 grades of wool, from 19 to 30 microns in diameter, quoted in Australian cents/kg on a clean basis. Now there is no longer a national indicator. An eastern market indicator is calculated from prices at the eight eastern centres. A western market indicator relates only to Fremantle sales and covers

21–25 micron wools and Merino cardings. The eastern market indicator comprises, as before, 13 categories with 11 representative types from each, reported for 19 to 31 micron wools and Merino and cross-bred cardings. But the mix of types has been changed and the weighting factors have been revised, and are now based on the average composition of wool production over the past two seasons. The two indicators' respective category indicators are not comparable because of the use of different types and weights. However the eastern market indicator has now become the international industry standard price measure.

New Zealand

The New Zealand Wool Board Strong Segment Indicator, which is used for the New Zealand Wool Futures Contract, is a price index for cross-bred wool representing 70% of the New Zealand clip. It comprises wool types between 32-41 microns of first and second shear fleeces and oddments. It is calculated at every wool sale and is intended to measure the average price of a composition of cross-bred wool from one sale to another. Only wool sold during official sessions of wool auctions is calculated in the indicator.

The United Kingdom

The BWMB also produces an indicator based on a combination of British wool prices, as does the South African Wool Board. The BWMB states that its indicator is calculated in respect of each wool sale by taking a weighted average sale price of 43 grades of wool which is representative of the whole clip. The same grades are used throughout the season. The weights applied to particular grades are fixed for the whole season and are arrived at from production figures for those grades from the previous season.

In the USDA weekly publication *Wool* there is a full price quotation list, an example of which (from 11 August 1994) is reproduced as Table 5.1.

Wool tops' prices tend to move in line with greasy wool prices.

Table 5.1 Domestic wool and mohair quotations, week ending 11 August 1994*

GRADED TERRITORY WOOL[1]

USDA Grade	Clean Delivered	%	Grease Equivalents[2]	%	
64s	$2.10–2.50	52	1.09–1.30	48	1.01–1.20
(20.60–22.04 microns) 2 3/4" and up		44	.92–1.10	38	.80–.95
62s	1.70–2.10	47	.80–.99	43	.73–.90
(22.05–23.49 microns) 3" and up					
60s	1.50–1.70	47	.70–.80	43	.64–.73
(23.50–24.94 microns) 3" and up					
58s	1.35–1.50	52	.70-.78	46	.62–.69
(24.95–26.39 microns) 3 1/4" and up					
56s	1.20–1.35	52	.62–.70	46	.55–.62
(26.40–27.84 microns) 3 1/4" and up					
54s	1,15–1.25	53	.61–.66	47	.54–.59
(27.85–29.29 microns) 3 1/2" and up					
GRADED FLEECE WOOL[3]*					
54s	1.15–1.25	54	.62–.68	47	.54–.59
(27.85–29.29 microns) 3 1/2" and up					
ORIGINAL BAG WOOL					
		Texas Wool[4]			
64s	2.10–2.50	54	1.13–1.35	50	1.05–1.25
(20.60–22.04 microns) 2 3/4" and up		46	.97–1.15	38	.80–.95
		Territory Wool[1]*			
64s	2.00–2.35	53	1.06–1.25	48	.96–1.13
(20.60–22.04 microns) 2 3/4" and up		43	.86–1.01	39	.78–.92

ORIGINAL BAG TEXAS MOHAIR**

Adult – $2.15 Yearling/Young Goat – Kid –

AUSTRALIAN WOOL CORPORATION+

In Bond Type	Charleston, SC 08-04-04 Micron	US Grade	Clean
60	19	80s	427
61	20	70s	371
62	21	64/70s	323
63	22	64s	246
64	23	62s	199
64A	24	60/62s	192
433	25	58s	190
433A	26	56/58s	185
434	27	56s	184
434A	28	54s	183
435	29	50/54s	180
435/30	30	50s	174

+ Quotes reflect auction on floor values converted to ex Charleston USC/lb.

Exchange Rate: $.7292=$1.00A
Eastern Market Indicator: 680A cents per kilo clean.

* Clean prices based on actual sales of whiteface wools when available, otherwise nominal.
** Grease basis, FOB warehouse.
1 Wool grown in the range areas of Washington, Oregon, the Intermountain States, including Arizona and New Mexico, and parts of the Dakotas, Nebraska, Kansas and Oklahoma. This wool covers a wide range in shrinkage and colour.
2 In order to assist in estimated grease wool prices, delivered to mill clean basis market prices have been converted to grease basis equivalents using the various yields quoted. Prices determined in this manner are largely nominal and not necessarily those received by individual growers, as allowances for freight, handling, etc., must be considered.
3 Most wool grown in the farm areas of the Dakotas, Nebraska, Kansas, Oklahoma, and parts of Minnesota, Wisconsin, Iowa and Missouri is somewhat dark in colour and of moderately heavy shrinkage. Most of that grown in the states east of the Mississippi River and in parts of Minnesota, Iowa and Missouri is bright in colour and of relatively light shrinkage.
4 Wool grown in the range areas of Texas, mostly bright in colour and moderate in shrinkage, except in the panhandle, where it is considerably darker in colour and heavier in shrinkage.
5 Imported wools are subject to the following duties: Grade 46s and finer grease wool at 10 cents clean content basis, scoured wool at 11 cents clean content basis, and carbonized wool at 13 cents net weight basis. Grade 44s grease wool at 3 cents, scoured at 4 cents, and carbonized at 6 cents. Grade 40s and coarser grease wool at 2.5 cents, scoured at 3 cents, and carbonized at 5 cents.

Source: USDA

History of wool prices

It is interesting to note fluctuations in wool prices in the UK between the two world wars. Taking 1914 as 100, the wholesale price index was 198 in 1924, 116 in 1929, 56 in 1932, 113 in 1937 and 80 in 1838. Taking the years 1934–38 as 100, the wholesale price of wool in the UK was 170 in 1946, 200 in 1947, 261 in 1948, 320 in 1949 and 671 in 1950. During World War II prices were controlled and supplies managed so that it was only after the war, with the exhaustion of surplus wartime stocks and a wave of panic buying that wool prices soared. They reached their peak in March 1951, when the index figure was 1476. At the same time, spurred by the Korean War, there was a wool price boom in Australia, see Table 5.2. In 1950–51 the average greasy wool auction price leapt from A$0.76/lb to A$1.7302. Prices during the mid-1950s were significantly lower but in 1964 prices reached £1.44/lb for superfine Merino wool. Prices of carpet wools lagged behind those for apparel types – partly this was caused by financial exchange problems but also because demand was relatively less, in particular for the Argentine grades. Competition from man-made fibres became an important factor in keeping prices down. In general, however, relatively inelastic demand for wool is combined with considerable fluctuations in demand, with the result that wool prices have always been and continue to be quite volatile, especially at times of war and international tension.

Table 5.2 Average annual wool prices, A¢/kg clean

	Nominal prices		Nominal prices		Nominal prices
1945/46	49	1961/62	169	1977/78	303
1946/47	76	1962/63	184	1978/79	328
1947/48	123	1963/64	217	1979/80	390
1948/49	150	1964/65	179	1980/81	411
1949/50	197	1965/66	187	1981/82	423
1950/51	449	1966/67	177	1982/83	434
1951/52	226	1967/68	156	1983/84	467
1952/53	255	1968/69	167	1984/85	498
1953/54	254	1969/70	140	1985/86	538
1954/55	221	1970/71	109	1986/87	614
1955/56	191	1971/72	126	1987/88	975
1956/57	248	1972/73	314	1988/89	991
1957/58	194	1973/74	299	1989/90	843
1958/59	151	1974/75	203	1990/91	631
1959/60	180	1975/76	229	1991/92	551
1960/61	162	1976/77	302	1992/93	475

Source: National Council of Wool Selling Brokers

After 1988, wool prices moved swiftly and apparently relentlessly downwards. In the last quarter of the 1991/92 season the Australian Market Indicator (AMI) averaged A$5.78/kg. Domestic prices for fine grade Australian wool in November 1992 had fallen substantially from the beginning of the season: 80s were down 10%, 70s down 11%, 64s down 9%, 62s down 7%, 58s and 56s down 4%. The AMI's lowest figure during the 1992/93 season's first half was A$4.96, and it finished the year at $A5.09, well off the unimpressive high of AS$5.39. The Australian Wool Realisation Committee pointed out in November 1992 that wool prices in Australia were 'at their lowest level this century in real terms'. The 1992/93 season had started by a continued downward spiral for Australian wool prices: by mid-1993, the AMI stood at A$4.41, well below the estimated cost of production at A$6.00. Wool sold at an average of A$4.88 during the season as a whole.

Traders were surprised and farmers appalled at the steady continuation of price falls throughout the first half of the 1993/94 season, see Table 5.3. But these falls masked the fact that the global demand for wool had increased each quarter during the 1992/93 season, and as a result the national indicators all rose in the following season (see Fig. 5.1 and Table 5.4). The AMI (a weighted-average indicator of 15 categories) average for the first quarter of the season was A$4.29/kg, A$4.76 in the second quarter (up 11%), A$5.28 in the third quarter (up another 11%) and A$6 in the final quarter (up a

Table 5.3 International wool prices

	Australia		New Zealand		South Africa
Year	**Market indicator 1/**	**Minimum floor price 2/**	**Market indicator 1/**	**Minimum floor price**	**Market indicator 1/**
	A cents/kg, clean		NZ cents/kg, clean		SA cents/kg, clean
1987/88	1003	645	600	476	1664
1988/89	990	870	672	500	2093
1989/90	870	870	589	525	1790
1990/91	627	3/	423	3/	1268
1991/92	557	3/	435	3/	1277
1992/93					
July	539		471		NS
August	537		479		NS
September	538		461		1109
October	514		460		1067
November	516		443		1070
December	517		440		1103
January	504		438		1066
February	467		415		1026
March	438		414		1008
April	393		387		959
May	440		382		975
June	449		379		1008
Season	488		431		1039
1993/94					
July	448		385		NS
August	428		380		NS
September	426		384		983
October	462		407		1013
November	491		423		1159
December	474		401		1066
January	497		401		1187
February	531		417		1331
March	548		468		1378
April	570		464		1458
May	605		474		1540
June	626		467		1695
Season	514		424		1210
1993/94					
July	681 4/		487		NS

NS = No sales.

1/ Weighted average of all types offered. 2/ The guaranteed minimum floor price was reduced to A 700 cents per kg for the last 4 weeks of 1989/90 season. 3/ The minimum floor price was eliminated. 4/ New updated method of calculation; on a comparable basis; the July 1993 average would be A477 cents per kilogram, clean.

Source: International Wool Textile Organization in succession to the Commonwealth Secretariat

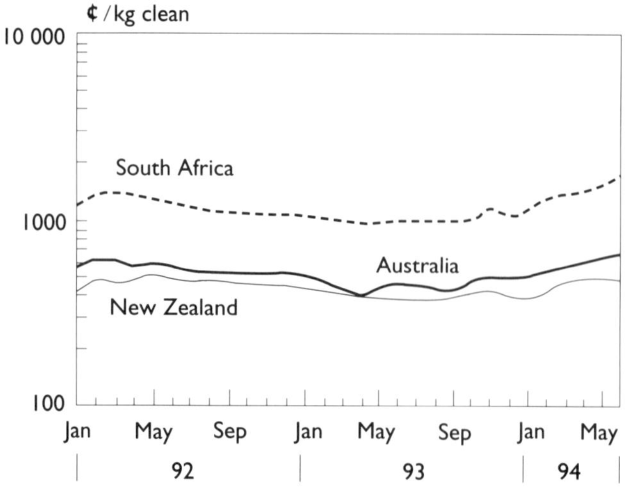

5.1 Wool indicator prices, 1991–94 (source: USDA).

further 14%). The market indicator average for June 1994, A$6.26, was the highest monthly average since the A$7.06 recorded in June 1991. This upturn reflected a strong demand by wool interests in the Far East and Europe.

At the beginning of the 1992/93 season, in August 1992, New Zealand wool prices were 3% below the average of the fourth quarter of 1991/92. In September 1992, the New Zealand market indicator fell 4% more from the August average to reach NZ$4.6/kg and by mid-November 1992 it had fallen to NZ$4.35, Historically, however, the price was on a par with the 1991 average of NZ$4.39 and 5% higher than the 1990 season average of NZ$4.13. New Zealand wool markets experienced a slower growth than the Australian wool market during the 1993/94 season. The New Zealand average market indicator for the second quarter, NZ$4.1, rose 7% above the first quarter. The third quarter average, NZ$4.28, was 4.45 above the second. The fourth quarter average, NZ$4.67, was 9% above the third and the highest in four years.

South African wool prices also fell, falling to SA1043¢/kg in October 1992 before reviving slightly in November 1992 to reach SA1050¢/kg. The strong demand for South African wool during the 1993/94 season was reflected in the growth of the South African indicator, which averaged SA1080¢ in the second quarter, up 10% from the first, SA1292¢ in the third, up 20% and SA1538¢ in the last quarter, 19% above the third. During June 1994 the indicator rose to SA1695¢, the highest weekly level in four years.

US prices of clean mill-delivered raw wool fell 5–20% during 1992. The simple average price received by producers for greasy wool

Table 5.4 Australian clean on floor average quotations, A¢/kg clean

	Combing average style														Carding
Season averages	**19M**	**20M**	**21M**	**22M**	**23M**	**24M**	**25M**	**26M**	**27M**	**28M**	**29M**	**30M**	**31M**	**MI**	**Merino**	**Cross-bred**
1974/75	282	270	256	246	232	221	206	–	195	–	–	151	–	–	122	96
1975/76	284	274	262	254	244	236	224	–	209	–	–	183	–	233	161	142
1976/77	341	334	329	323	316	311	303	–	283	–	–	257	–	300	230	218
1977/78	349	344	337	327	320	315	304	–	277	–	–	247	–	303	324	216
1978/79	394	386	372	358	343	336	326	–	309	–	–	289	–	335	276	257
1979/80	534	492	460	427	395	381	366	–	351	–	–	329	–	395	302	276
1980/81	540	484	470	456	436	418	394	–	357	–	–	299	–	411	337	256
1981/82	547	522	506	489	464	446	426	–	379	–	–	294	–	432	318	239
1982/83	589	545	521	504	484	464	442	–	372	–	–	297	–	445	317	240
1983/84	697	586	555	533	514	500	479	450	409	365	–	327	–	485*	356	297
1984/85	985	723	620	564	537	501	467	424	395	362	–	331	–	526	364	319
1985/86	812	700	635	583	550	508	471	425	404	389	–	375	–	534	399	352
1986/87	902	802	742	699	635	561	512	488	484	484	–	478	–	626	504	434
1987/88	1998	1633	1277	1083	929	799	716	672	658	655	–	616	–	1003	763	599
1988/89	1881	1536	1235	1064	958	361	779	710	677	663	–	596	–	980	616	519
1989/90	1706	1313	1059	953	872	772	713	649	614	592	–	530	–	870	576	451
1990/91	1281	1340	1009	673	594	532	494	458	434	420	–	391	–	628	383	304
1991/92	801	681	630	588	544	507	478	460	445	438	421	400	380	557	415	295
1992/93	680	598	507	458	419	392	380	372	383	385	385	362	340	444	347	227
1993/94 End of month prices																
July	706	590	502	468	433	414	397	392	394	395	398	394	376	448	327	197
Aug	654	536	465	430	398	378	364	361	368	361	361	352	349	413	307	195
Sept	672	531	476	448	417	404	393	384	382	385	390	386	383	434	349	257
Oct	790	625	546	512	466	440	426	414	411	414	414	408	395	492	406	287
Nov	772	597	520	478	433	412	402	396	401	404	403	398	394	465	371	302
Dec	748	598	529	493	448	432	419	411	409	412	409	403	398	472	356	296
Jan	869	699	618	561	481	450	430	417	410	408	405	397	395	522	375	284
Feb	913	724	604	533	456	446	433	422	417	416	411	404	403	516	382	301
Mar	949	775	657	569	506	500	488	463	445	442	443	440	433	558	400	310
Apr	978	804	682	580	512	508	492	474	462	462	454	448	432	568	379	319

* NOTE: Prior to 1983/84 season, market indicator based on 11 categories each comprising 11 representative types. From 1983/84 season through 1990/1991 season, market indicator based on weighted average across 13 categories each comprising 11 representative types. From 1991/92 on, market indicator based on weighted average across 15 categories each comprising 11 representative types.

Source: Australian Wool Corporation

was \$0.625 in October 1992, compared with \$0.695 in 1991. Early season US 1994/95 prices for the finer grades of Australian raw wool, reflecting the increases in the Australian market, rose from the Apr–Jun average in the second quarter of 1994. The 80s, at \$4.27/lb, were up 8%. The 70s, at \$3.71, were up 5%. The 64s were \$2.43, the 62s were \$1.99, the 58s were \$1.9 and the 56s were \$1.84.

US prices for clean, mill-delivered territory raw wool, finer grades, 64s and 62s, increased by 5–8% by mid-August 1994 from the Apr–Jun average in line with the overall increase in world prices. In contrast, prices of the 60s and medium grades were unchanged, bearing out the Todhunter thesis that high grade wools sustain and direct international wool prices. The 64s rose to \$2.3/lb from an average of \$2.19, the 62s were \$1.9, up from \$1.85, the 60s were unchanged at \$1.6, whilst 56s and 58s remained at \$1.28 and \$1.43 respectively.

The NZWB and BWMB indicators moved together downwards in 1991 and thereafter - so did the AWC indicator which was on the revised floor price from Jan–Feb 1991 when it was abandoned. The Bradford indicator price fell to 58p/kg in 1991 and finished 1992 at 62p/kg, having been lower during the year, which the BWMB said was 'very low in historical terms'. In 1993 prices rose slightly, reaching 67p/kg towards the end of the year. The main fluctuation in prices came at the end of 1993, when very strong competition and excellent clearances increased British wool prices, for example, to 102p/kg by March 1994, the highest point for three years. The BWMB described this as a steeper and more dramatic increase than they would have liked, probably caused in their assessment by buyers, realising that stocks were reducing, buying to cover orders. Other origin wools rose similarly and parities were not unduly changed by the rapid rise. It was September 1994 before the various market indicators across the world began to settle back as these same buyers began to reassess the risks to overseas demand in the light of such rapid price increases. So the Eastern Market Indicator in Australia fell back from its peak of A\$0.835 to A\$0.754 and continued to fluctuate around that level. The price falls in September tended to be concentrated in the finer micron wools, especially in superfine where stocks had been low and which was affected by drought in Australia.

Certainly the price of wool since the demise of the Australian wool reserve price scheme in January 1991 has become a very responsive and volatile market. Many worldwide factors play a major role in the determination of wool prices, including currencies, the state of different economies, the stocks of yarn and tops available, fashion trends, retail conditions, world climatic conditions (in the medium term at least) the quality and quantity of the wool available in the stockpile and the price differential between wool and other textile products such as cotton or synthetics. Certainly the wool price recovery in 1993–94, when it came, paralleled other price rises for commodities, the *Economist* commodity price index, for instance, rising 40% in the year to September 1994. Increased demand was an important factor in all cases, but as with wool, supply contractions were the most important factor.

Forecasting the market

An assessment of likely price movements is a central component of decision-making by wool producers, traders, governments, hedgers and speculators on futures markets, and it is the lifeblood of the trading companies such as Cargill and Chargeurs. Trading companies will only buy or sell (including sell short – i.e. sell what they have yet to buy) stocks of wool if they have a firm view of what is going to happen to prices. Although hedgers are risk averse, they may choose not to hedge substantial components of their portfolio if they believe that prices are set to rise, if they are holding stocks of wool.

Most wool traders rely on their own experience to trade wool. Experienced wool traders made a great deal of money, for instance, when Australian wool prices fell during mid-1992 as stocks were unloaded on to world markets. In the wool trade an appreciation of not just the direction of price movement but its extent and likely duration, is knowledge which is at a great commercial premium, as there are relatively few experienced physical wool traders with the necessary judgement, contacts, experience and courage to take a position, for example whether to enter into a forward contract for Australian wool which could be worth up to $1m.

Assessing likely price movements is a central element of decision-making for both hedgers and speculators in the Japanese and Australian wool futures markets. Speculators will only adopt a trading position if they take a view of what prices are likely to do, and hedgers' degree of participation in a futures market likewise in practice depends on their perception of future prices especially when balancing risks and rewards and deciding the precise time of entering a trade and closing it out. Apart from this experience and personal contacts, there are two basic methods which are used, especially in the futures markets where there is an available track record of prices and a forecasting, or at least a prediction, culture. These methods are all less important for raw wool than for the Japanese domestic yarn market because of the low volumes recorded on the Australasian markets compared with Tokyo and Nagoya. This in turn reflects the attitude of wool producers that they are price-takers who are powerless to avoid wide fluctuations in their incomes from year to year, and that there is therefore little point in discovering in advance a situation that they are unable to alter. The absence of an effective hedging mechanism generates the absence of real interest in forecasting.

Fundamental forecasts

Fundamental analysis relates price movements to changes in supply and demand conditions; it is therefore the kind of price analysis with which economists are familiar. Because long-term prices always relate to supply and demand conditions, fundamental analysis is always advisable for participants in futures markets and cash markets. For example, wool traders will always pay close attention to the weather conditions in Australia, because this may determine the availability and quality of the next season's level of Australian production. The amount of rain that falls during a season is crucial in determining the annual production level; sheep-rearing areas in Australia, New Zealand and South Africa frequently experience serious droughts.

Demand tends to fluctuate seasonally throughout the year, high prior to shearing and lower thereafter - not so much because of the availability of wool but because of certainty; the stocks and their disposal will also affect future prices. To the extent that these seasonal patterns conform to market expectations, there will be no substantial market response. There are also longer-term considerations, such as growth in real incomes, national populations, area available for wool production, yields, consumer tastes and foreign exchange reserves, which have an impact on wool prices. Traders always pay close attention to all weather factors, although to the extent that changes in supply follow already anticipated patterns, the price will not change. Carryover stocks are also important contributors to price levels, because they affect import demand and hence price levels. The absolute size, disposal policy, the location of stocks between countries and organisations also affects price levels - more so with wool than most other commodities. International organisations and national policies, especially of Japan, the USA, Australia and the EU, in respect of imports and the Australians, New Zealanders and South Africans for export policy are major determinants of world wool prices. The quality and timeliness of information provided explains why wool traders are very concerned to secure access to the International Wool Secretariat (IWS) and USDA data and analysis - the accuracy of information collected through the analysis of economic and political factors is essential for the prediction of the future direction of prices and a successful trading strategy, whether as a physical wool trader or a futures market player.

Traders and analysts' analysis of the supply and demand conditions for wool is comprehensive and thorough, though usually unaccompanied directly by any formal econometric model. Part of the reason for not adopting complex econometric models is the difficulty of incorporating unpredictable climatic factors. Another problem specific to wool is the need to construct segmented models, perhaps one for each type of wool or even every export destination. Where does one market stop and another begin? There is little doubt that fundamental analysis is worthwhile: droughts, late rains, gradually increasing populations, relative prices for substitute goods such as synthetics and other factors such as the income elasticity of demand for woollen products are what determine wool prices in the long term.

The forecasting work undertaken by ABARE is outlined in the quarterly publication *Australian Commodities*. Short-term forecasts for wool are provided three times annually and a medium term forecast once a year. ABARE also conducts the OUTLOOK conference on an annual basis. Wool forecasts are also undertaken by the IWS and by the USDA.

The measure of information dispersion and the lack of significance attached to accurate forecasts within the major organisations of the wool industry is illustrated by the reluctance of the BWMB to concede its own status as a forecasting organisation or to provide details on others; in fact the Board makes its own forecasts: late in 1993 the BWMB forecast that the price of British wool would rise to 80-85p/kg by the end of the marketing year and that there would be longer-term expectations of a rise to 105p/kg by mid-1994 - at the time those in the industry were more cautious, not expecting a significant rise in wool prices until 1995, although in practice these prices were greatly exceeded by early 1995 as the wool market entered a prolonged bull phase.

The Japan Wool Importers' Association, supported by the fact that yarn is sold on a long-term forward basis in Japan, does not publish official forecasts, although they note that each company forecasts price movements including the raw wool price in Australia.

The problem with fundamental analysis is to translate the general principle that demand and supply conditions are the determinants of prices into short-term trading instructions. This problem is exacerbated in a market such as wool where the degree of accuracy of the futures market in interpreting short-term trading signals is relatively small, except for the Japanese yarn market. Wool traders are sceptical of the statistical techniques which can be used to quantify the impact of administrative changes - but some argue that they work better in predicting long-term changes. Indeed, for long-term forecasting, there is no alternative to statistical methods. But long-term modelling is no use if short-term prices work against the trader, or if the specific deal the trader intends in a physical market does not work because of loading problems, quality failure on inspection or - worst of all - default.

For short-term analysis it is virtually impossible to build a model that is sensitive to changes in supply and demand conditions which depend on market sensitivities often on the other side of the world. Wool traders use econometric models, if at all, to provide background analysis of long-term trends, and mostly at second hand by reading ABARE, USDA, IWS or other market forecasts. All traders are sceptical of economic forecasting.

Technical analysis

The alternative, which is certainly used by some participants on the Japanese markets and which is closely followed by wool analysts in the major US trading companies, although not apparently by any in the Australasian or European physical wool markets, is 'technical' analysis, based on the evaluation of prices themselves independent of their alleged causes - akin to time series analysis in econometrics.

This type of analysis is more commonly used for short-term trading; technical analysts analyse whatever trends can be detected to try to establish what is likely to happen next, assuming that prices follow patterns that do not require external economic considerations to understand and predict, at least in the short term. But technical traders also use other data from the markets, such as trading volume, open interest, price spreads between contract months and the equivalent data from options contracts where they exist.

The key difficulty is always to establish that the patterns can be validated which is why experienced technical traders usually put in stops (sell or buy orders cancelling out their original positions) at crucial price points which would invalidate their reasoning. Technical traders contend that all fundamental factors have already been incorporated into the current price of the commodity, and that changes are instantly discounted.

The relatively high liquidity of the wool futures markets in Tokyo and Nagoya are an incentive for Japanese technical traders, as it provides an incentive for speculators to become involved, and technical analysts place great store by liquidity itself as it smooths out price distortions caused by individual orders which may be irrational. So far as the Tokyo and Nagoya markets are concerned, there can be little doubt that the price interacts with the spot market price: Tokyo and Nagoya prices, as with Australian, British, New Zealand and South African auction prices, respond to all three sets of stimuli: fundamentals impacting the physical market, what one might call 'quasi-fundamental factors' - reports and analyses commenting on the market which quickly become incorporated into short-term market psychology, and technical factors.

Exchanges publish market volume and open interest statistics (number of contracts still to be closed out) on a daily basis. Although there are in theory a virtually limitless number of traders in any one market, in practice this data provides some guide as to why prices are moving in the way they are; for example if both price and volume move up together, this is probably due to fresh long positions in the market, so a fall in volume will probably herald a fall in price. Again, the higher the open interest the more vulnerable a market becomes to sudden changes, especially given that because of the relatively high volumes involved in the market, occasionally individual contract months on the Tokyo and Nagoya Exchanges can become subject to squeezes where there appears to be insufficient yarn to meet the necessary implicit deliveries in the exercise of the warrants.

Other technical indicators are essentially ways of following trends and changes in trends. Identifying a trend can simply be a matter of looking at a bar, point or figure chart and relying on visual inspection. A more complex way is to calculate moving averages (averaging the sum of a predetermined number of daily closing prices - as a new closing price is added, the first is subtracted), which reduce the extent of variation caused by a single day's trading: these can be taken across different time periods, for example over nine or fifteen days, with the problem that the longer the period taken, the less distortion but also the less information that is likely to emerge from the analysis. Similarly, the momentum indicators can also be used.

Chart analysis is perhaps the most commonly used method, however. Chart analysis involves graphing prices on a bar chart, where each day's highs and lows are written, with a line connecting them and a horizontal line showing the day's closing price. These charts clearly show the evolution of prices over time, and changes in trend – identifying support and resistance levels – are often thought to be signalled by characteristic chart patterns. Charts are studied going back decades to establish significant trends in the market; most traders study long-term charts on a monthly or weekly basis, so they are able to spot potential longer-term price reversals before analysts looking only at daily prices can. Considerable scepticism attends all these contentions, mainly from those who believe that the wool market, like any other, follows, albeit imperfectly, the basic fundamentals of the underlying cash market and the fundamental factors that determine that. Hence technical patterns reflect just a process of adjustment by the market to changes in outside conditions. That is not to say that individual traders on the Tokyo or Nagoya markets cannot make substantial profits out of this lack of correlation: they can and do.

The problem for technical analysis is to tell the difference between a change in price due to daily fluctuations, and a change due to a trend. The many aspects of technical analysis can be combined into a trading system, i.e. a number of rules which are used by traders and fund managers. There are many successful trading systems, but they are not publicly available, and the suspicion must be that a measure of competent intuition is allowed to disrupt rigorous technical analysis from time to time. Comparing technical and fundamental analysis as trading tools, it is clear that fundamental analysis is very limited in advising the initiation of trades and is weak in being able to predict the effect of sudden shocks. Technical analysis, by comparison, can reveal something of market psychology, but can generate a host of conflicting signals. It is worth noting that technical analysis has had an especially long history in Japan, home of wool futures for the foreseeable future, and in some cases the signs and signals that Japanese technical analysts look for in trading may make Japanese commodity markets function differently from those in the West. That, and the fact that the Japanese woollen markets are for yarn, and related to specifically Japanese conditions, are sufficient to make them difficult to forecast for Western analysts. For more information on wool futures markets see Chapter 7.

There can be no doubt that forecasts can be inaccurate, and

perhaps it may seem unduly savage to examine any track record at all. However, a forecasting organisation does a good job insofar as it makes the right predictions in exactly the same way that a car is a good one if it goes faultlessly from A to B, whatever the institutional reasons may be for buying consistently inaccurate forecasts or unreliable cars. Forecasts also change themselves. Celebrated examples of inaccurate wool forecasts, as with other commodities, tend to come when institutional factors change, and the 1990s has seen a surfeit of such changes in the wool trade. At ABARE's 1990 Conference it was predicted that 'the AWC will continue to accumulate stocks throughout 1990 but the rate of purchase will decline due to improving demand'. This relative optimism about the international demand for commodities was held in common with a number of different forecasting organisations, largely in turn based on World Bank optimism, proved wholly unfounded, as to the development of the world economy in 1990–91. So for example in January 1989, ABARE predicted that 1993/94 production would be 1090, downsized to 975 by January 1990. Stocks in 1993/94 were predicted to be 20 000 bales in January 1989, whereas by January 1990 the forecast had changed to 3 060 000 bales (not too far off) whilst the price indicator forecast was changed from 1130 to 880 ¢/kg. As the history of all three factors from previous chapters has demonstrated, none of these forecasts – from possibly the most professional organisation in the business, and certainly the one closest to the production action – was accurate.

In ABARE's defence, these were the worst possible years in which to make medium-term forecasts, and their forecasting accuracy has improved subsequently. There does seem a definite tendency on the part of wool organisations to oscillate between extreme pessimism and sustained over-optimism. For example in the aftermath of the suspension of the Reserve Price Scheme, John O'Connor of the AWC said that: 'The fall in wool prices means that wool is now more price competitive than it has been at any time since the 1960s ... it will be at least a year and possibly two before the full extent of the boost in market share is realised' (*Wool Australia, The Official Record 1990–91*, p15). The expected increase in market share did not happen.

Again in 1990 the AWC believed that 'It is anticipated that processed wool could represent 30% of total wool exports by the early 1990s' which they did not, unless scoured wool is counted as processed. Such medium-term forecasts are to be distinguished from short-term IWS production forecasts, as previously carried out by the AWC, which are based on wool grower surveys and which, following a recent review by the Wool Council of Australia, are to continue despite the fact that they are prone to, perhaps inevitable, relatively slight revisions: for example at the meeting of the AWPFC on 26 May 1994 the estimate for 1993/94 was raised 1.5%, and for 1994/95 by 2%. There is a strong case for centralising and analysing wool forecasts within an independent organisation, or at least for an organisation to monitor all forecasts.

It is also worth noting that although for the international wool trade itself, price and volume forecasts are what matters, the extent of these in turn depend on final demand, and both the extent and the structure of this is also forecast. The former IWS, for example, produced a Trend Collection, forecasting colour and design trends two years ahead for carpets - now a responsibility of Wools of New Zealand - and also a Fashion Forecast for apparel.

CHAPTER

6

The wool trade

The international picture

Approximately 40% of world wool production is traded, which makes it an important traded commodity in its own right - substantially different from a primarily domestic crop such as rice or potatoes, but the high percentage traded is something shared with cotton and silk. International trade data for wool are available from several sources: mainly the International Wool Textile Organisation (IWTO), the International Wool Secretariat (IWS), working in succession to the Commonwealth Secretariat, the USDA, and the UN, which although two years in arrears provides information by value as well as by volume. Wool moves promptly to local, national and international markets. The major southern hemisphere producers use only a small fraction of their output domestically. World wool exports increased from 1.19m tonnes in 1980 to a peak of 1.46m tonnes in 1987. The 1980s were characterised by the dominance of the international market by Australia and New Zealand - not even competitors - followed by the EC.

However, the rise in wool prices and - it is held - some discontent from importers in respect of quality standards, in 1988 *inter alia* curtailed demand and caused exports to fall to 1.03m tonnes by 1990. In 1991 there were some improvements, mainly caused by the liberalisation of the wool market in Australia. This lowered wool prices relative to other competing fibres. Wool stocks rose in Japan, a small increase in European imports occurred, and China relaxed its self-imposed wool import quota. The medium term effect of the changes was to cut the scope of the international wool trade, creating a depressed international trading environment which endured until prices revived in 1993/94.

Analysts widely concur in their view that the former Australian Wool Corporation must take some of the blame for the slump in the international wool trade after 1988, along with the more usual explanations of the collapse of the Comecon bloc - Russia has remained absent from the international market since 1992 and Japan has also cut imports drastically, leaving China as the only major export source for Australian wool - and the world recession. Now once again the world trade in wool has resumed its long term growth path, one which has been followed since 1945, albeit with occasional retreats. The major wool exporters are Australia, New Zealand and the EU (see Table 6.1), although they are far from direct competitors to one another because of the different types and qualities of wool that they export. Argentina follows and South Africa and Uruguay are the next largest exporters. The share of all the other wool exporting countries, which include Mongolia, Chile, the CIS countries, Pakistan, India, Norway, the Falklands and Ireland rose from nearly 6% in 1980 to 8% in 1990 and is continuing to rise.

World exports of wool oscillated after 1988/89 as exporting nations struggled to dispose of their immense stockpiles. '1993 was an extremely difficult year for everybody involved in the international wool industry - farmers, raw wool traders, combers, spinners, weavers and knitwear producers - and in many cases it brought heavy losses' as the German textile giant BWK stated in its Annual Report. Raw wool purchasing activity began to accelerate towards the end of 1993 and this continued into 1994. Exports of Australian wool to the three major trade areas of Western Europe, Japan and China increased significantly in mid-1994, especially to China during May. Figure 6.1 shows world wool exports.

The main apparel wool importers are the EU, followed by East Asia, China and then, a long way behind and still falling, the CIS countries and Eastern Europe. Amongst the East Asian countries, Taiwan, South Korea and Hong Kong have all increased their import levels in comparison with Japan, increasing from 27.5% in value in 1978 and 28.4% in 1988 and well over 30% in the 1990s. These three countries increased their share of world wool imports very substantially during these decades. The international recession of the late 1980s/early 1990s hit them less hard than the European countries; their wool import share rises have largely been caused by a slower rate of decline rather than an actual increase. The USA is, by contrast, a relatively small importer of wool due mainly to a restrictive tariff (pre-Marrakesh World Trade Organisation deal), of 22 ¢/micron for greasy

Table 6.1 Wool export data for Australia, New Zealand, South Africa, Argentina and Uruguay

	Exports of raw wool (actual weight)						Exports of raw wool (clean equivalent)					
	Australia	**New Zealand**	**South Africa**	**Argentina**	**Uruguay**	**Total 5 actual wt**	**Australia**	**New Zealand**	**South Africa**	**Argentina**	**Uruguay**	**Total 5 clean equiv**
Units:	mkg	mkg	mkg	mkg	mkg	mkg	mkg	mkg	mkg	mkg	mkg	mkg
Period:	Jul–Jun	Jul–Jun	Jul–Jun	Oct–Sep	Oct–Sep		Jul–Jun	Jul–Jun	Jul–Jun	Oct–Sep	Oct–Sep	
Source:	WS	WS	WS	WS	WS	WS	WS	WS	WS	WS	WS	WS
1963	662					1131	405					737
1964	641					1151	392					745
1965	636					1234	389					801
1966	652					1131	397					731
1967	673	263	109	123	50	1219	412	205	62	87	33	797
1968	706	309	118	113	44	1289	430	242	67	80	30	848
1969	755	303	112	96	40	1306	460	240	64	67	26	857
1970	684	295	77	81	47	1183	415	236	45	58	31	784
1971	731	315	111	74	78	1259	446	254	63	54	19	836
1972	702	288	81	81	24	1176	424	233	47	55	17	776
1973	515	214	74	36	27	865	313	173	43	26	18	572
1974	495	219	62	63	42	881	305	181	36	44	29	595
1975	629	272	76	84	25	1085	386	223	44	59	17	730
1976	729	253	78	81	24	1164	448	209	45	56	16	774
1977	540	243	74	99	33	988	334	209	43	68	23	669
1978	626	259	57	78	23	1043	390	217	34	54	16	711
1979	567	285	56	80	26	1014	355	240	34	55	18	702
1980	601	280	63	101	49	1094	378	235	37	70	33	752
1981	561	284	57	80	42	1025	353	239	33	57	28	709
1982	543	322	46	65	42	1017	339	269	27	46	29	711
1983	564	308	62	75	38	1048	356	259	37	55	26	732
1984	630	317	58	60	25	1090	397	268	36	44	17	763
1985	699	281	45	70	35	1129	443	241	27	50	25	785
1986	782	300	37	60	43	1222	497	259	23	45	30	854
1987	769	276	35	60	33	1172	490	236	21	46	23	816

	Exports of raw wool (actual weight)						Exports of raw wool (clean equivalent)					
	Australia	New Zealand	South Africa	Argentina	Uruguay	Total 5 actual wt	Australia	New Zealand	South Africa	Argentina	Uruguay	Total 5 clean equiv
Units:	mkg	mkg	mkg	mkg	mkg	mkg	mkg	mkg	mkg	mkg	mkg	mkg
Period:	Jul–Jun	Jul–Jun	Jul–Jun	Oct–Sep	Oct–Sep		Jul–Jun	Jul–Jun	Jul–Jun	Oct–Sep	Oct–Sep	
Source:	WS	WS	WS	WS	WS	WS	WS	WS	WS	WS	WS	WS
1988	722	275	41	43	27	1107	497	238	26	37	20	815
1989	621	210	51	46	39	966	430	184	29	38	29	710
1990	555	204	48	44	27	879	390	182	31	33	21	657
1991	754	246	41	35	26	1103	531	217	28	27	21	823
1992	n/a	n/a	n/a	n/a	n/a	n/a	n/a	n/a	n/a	n/a	n/a	n/a

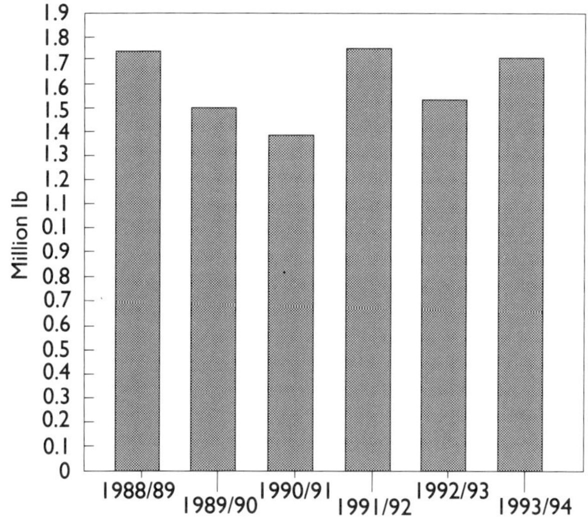

6.1 *World wool exports, m lb clean, 1988/89–1993/94.*

wool and stiffer still charges for finished wool goods.

Wool top and hair tops (included carded sliver) ought to show, if the Todhunter thesis (see Chapter 2 and Chapter 10) is correct, increases in top exports from Australia being counterbalanced by a decrease in wool top exports from most European countries. EU wool top imports had carried, pre-Marrakesh, a tariff of 2.5% for some time. The statistics bear out this thesis, see Table 6.2.

Exports of wool by country

Australia

Australian wool exports are shown in Tables 6.3 and 6.4 and Fig. 6.2. Australian exports represented a 61% share of world wool exports in 1988/89 and the same share in the 1993/94 season. This represented a levelling off after an increase from 45% to 55% between 1978–87 and a low point in 1990. Top exports have almost doubled from 1988, rising from 18 360 tonnes to 32 934 tonnes. Australian wool is exported to all the major wool importing countries of the world, with the EU constituting its major and most stable market, taking nearly one-third of Australia's wool exports.

Australian wool has been having a progressively tougher time in East Asian markets. Its export share to Japan, Taiwan, South Korea and

Table 6.2 Trade in wool and hair tops, including carded sliver, tonnes (a)

	1988	1989	1990	1991	Jan–Sept 1992	Jan–Sept 1993	Jan–Dec 1992	Jan–Dec 1993
Exports								
Argentina	11 071	8 552	11 755	12 549	8 316	9 382	11 257	12 429
Australia	18 360	16 915	15 520	24 662	16 717	18 865	22 307	32 934
Belgium	14 207	15 585	14 114	13 142	10 764	13 153(e)	17 559	–
France	58 324	58 072	55 406	57 699	45 709	38 783	57 861	52 375
Germany (West)	17 695	15 175	15 130	22 677	21 715	21 936(e)	28 939	27 979(e)
Italy	2 811	4 015	3 201	3 992	3 040	2 324	4 060	3 296(f)
Malaysia	5 665	4 647	4 567	4 639	2 553	3 860	3 542	5 147(g)
South Africa	21 547	14 540	12 224	20 884	13 950	10 567	18 597	15 291
Switzerland	1 730	1 502	1 646	1 907	1 401	1 083	1 814	1 467
Taiwan	5 413	6 001	6 641	9 850	9 270	7 375	11 449	9 109(h)
United Kingdom	19 698	20 624	19 647	21 322	16 077	16 984	21 569	21 800(f)
United States	7 391	6 295	7 550	8 968	6 392	4 185	8 670	6 091
Uruguay	35 716	27 273	42 910	48 051	34 692	29 187	47 274	43 663
Total	219 628	196 196	210 311	250 342	190 196	177 144	237 319(d)	231 581(d)
Imports								
Austria	4 268	3 886	3 837	4 239	3 235	2 440	4 035	3 326
Belgium	10 384	11 662	11 390	9 906	5 913	6 174(c)	7 258	–
Canada	3 339	3 649	1 990	2 931	1 798	1 559	2 178	1 899
China	34 104	39 572	24 246	53 812	31 021(a)	45 836(a)	53 600(a)	64 936(a)
France	6 042	5 773	7 231	7 049	4 761	3 950	6 222	5 910
Germany (West)	24 578	24 860	26 932	26 234	22 041	18 487(e)	29 686	23 965(e)
Hong Kong	8 384	9 850	6 411	14 027	12 448	14 780	17 639	19 358
Italy	46 160	43 421	50 362	51 282	45 224	42 685	59 078	56 078(f)
Japan	30 243	30 060	25 459	31 566	29 724	21 016	35 275	25 481
South Korea	10 674	12 109	11 459	18 692	14 663	13 493	18 232	18 132
Portugal	1 260	1 544	1 761	3 749	3 930	4 176	5 468	4 255(h)
Spain	1 477	1 828	2 118	2 213	2 213	2 538	2 726	2 769(f)
Switzerland	10 451	11 319	10 981	11 285	8 797	7 237	12 102	8 902

Taiwan	9 528	7 639	5 021	12 349	9 857	8 891	11 915	10 669(h)
United Kingdom	9 267	7 861	7 596	8 256	6 355	8 936	8 793	9 225(f)
Total	210 199	215 033	196 794	257 500	209 980	202 198	266 949(b)	253 965(b)

(a) Calculated from the trade returns of supplying countries
(b) Excluding Belgium
(c) Estimate based on data for six months
(d) Excluding Belgium
(e) Estimate based on data for eight months
(f) Estimate based on date for eleven months
(g) Estimate based on data for nine months
(h) Estimate based on data for ten months

Source: IWTO

Table 6.3 Australian exports of wool, m lb

Year	Clean	Greasy equivalent
1988/89	1095	
1989/90	948	1369
1990/91	860	1224
1991/92	1171	1663
1992/93	1069	1511
1993/94	1076	

Source: IWTO/Commonwealth Secretariat

Table 6.4 Exports of wool from Australia

	Greasy	Scoured	Carbon-ised	Tops	Noils	Waste	Skins with wool
Quantity, m kg							
1950/51	411.6	40.3	11.8	1.2	1.2	3.3	10.2
1955/56	482.4	34.1	5.9	5.0	2.0	4.9	45.9
1956/57	547.3	36.0	6.3	6.8	2.1	8.7	45.1
1957/58	490.2	34.3	6.4	7.7	1.5	3.0	55.9
1958/59	537.8	34.7	7.0	9.2	2.0	5.5	61.6
1959/60	586.7	38.8	7.2	10.3	1.8	4.0	76.1
1960/61	570.6	37.9	6.9	7.6	2.0	2.4	78.1
1961/62	603.0	37.7	7.6	9.7	1.8	2.1	79.1
1962/63	579.5	38.7	8.2	9.8	2.2	2.9	83.0
1963/64	626.4	34.2	6.6	11.8	2.3	2.8	84.3
1964/65	605.2	33.9	6.7	8.7	1.9	2.3	86.0
1965/66	599.9	33.5	7.5	10.5	1.7	2.5	91.7
1966/67	619.9	29.6	7.3	10.9	1.9	1.2	90.1
1967/68	630.6	33.6	8.8	10.3	1.8	1.3	93.7
1968/69	665.8	32.2	7.6	10.9	1.5	1.0	99.2
1969/70	713.0	33.3	8.2	10.0	1.2	1.0	112.2
1970/71	650.5	25.5	7.7	8.9	1.3	1.6	117.5
1971/72	688.1	35.7	7.6	10.0	1.5	2.6	132.3
1972/73	665.1	26.8	8.7	9.1	1.2	2.1	124.3
1973/74	487.6	20.2	6.8	5.8	1.0	1.3	73.6
1974/75	456.7	31.5	6.9	5.0	0.7	1.0	74.5
1975/76	583.3	36.1	9.1	8.5	0.9	1.2	83.5
1976/77	675.4	41.2	12.1	11.7	1.1	1.7	90.0
1977/78	493.6	35.4	10.5	10.0	1.2	1.4	76.4
1978/79	565.9	48.4	12.0	11.0	1.7	1.4	73.1
1979/80	504.0	50.7	12.0	12.5	1.1	2.1	88.8
1980/81	529.4	55.6	13.8	13.2	0.9	1.7	71.4
1981/82	497.3	52.3	11.3	13.5	1.5	1.7	66.4
1982/83	488.8	46.0	9.5	16.2	1.0	2.9	60.9
1983/84	497.3	53.1	13.1	13.8	1.5	1.4	61.2
1984/85	554.4	56.8	18.4	15.1	1.7	1.1	69.7
1985/86	607.8	70.6	20.2	16.9	2.2	1.8	91.2
1986/87	676.9	84.2	20.8	16.3	2.0	2.3	110.5
1987/88	662.8	84.1	21.2	17.5	1.7	2.4	105.8
1988/89	628.1	72.1	19.4	19.0	1.2	1.6	80.5
1989/90	539.9	60.5	19.0	15.0	2.3	1.7	95.9
1990/91	460.8	76.7	17.9	20.0	2.4	1.1	77.9
1991/92	621.6	105.8	26.1	23.7	3.8	1.6	81.1

	Greasy	Scoured	Carbon-ised	Tops	Noils	Waste	Skins with wool	Total
FOB value, $m								
1950/51	1097.8	122.6	32.8	5.2	3.0	5.2	41.6	1308.2
1955/56	587.6	54.8	10.4	12.0	3.6	6.6	30.6	705.6
1956/57	851.4	66.4	12.0	18.6	3.8	15.2	38.8	1006.2
1957/58	651.0	58.4	11.0	21.6	1.8	3.0	40.4	787.2
1958/59	528.4	41.0	8.4	19.6	2.4	4.6	29.6	634.0
1959/60	674.2	57.4	10.0	24.6	2.4	3.6	46.4	818.6
1960/61	592.4	48.0	8.6	16.2	2.0	1.6	42.8	711.6
1961/62	661.0	49.8	9.2	21.4	2.0	1.6	48.4	793.4
1962/63	671.4	51.4	10.0	21.5	2.2	2.2	55.5	814.2
1963/64	859.4	56.0	10.8	29.4	2.8	2.4	73.8	1034.6
1964/65	721.3	49.7	9.7	21.1	2.3	1.8	60.6	866.5
1965/66	699.8	45.8	10.8	24.0	2.1	2.1	64.2	848.8
1966/67	726.3	40.4	10.4	26.4	1.9	1.1	63.0	869.5
1967/68	643.3	39.2	10.2	20.3	1.8	0.7	46.3	761.8
1968/69	717.0	43.1	10.0	22.6	1.7	0.7	56.4	51.4
1969/70	684.6	44.1	10.5	20.6	1.1	0.8	63.7	825.4
1970/71	493.1	24.7	7.8	16.2	1.1	0.6	49.2	592.7
1971/72	524.5	32.3	6.8	16.7	1.0	0.9	50.9	633.1
1972/73	1064.2	45.8	17.3	24.1	1.4	1.7	107.4	1261.9
1973/74	1062.3	52.3	16.6	22.3	1.7	1.3	91.4	1247.9
1974/75	663.9	59.6	12.2	16.3	0.8	0.8	61.1	814.7
1975/76	842.3	73.3	19.0	25.3	1.1	1.0	69.6	1031.6
1976/77	1276.6	118.2	35.9	43.6	1.5	1.6	109.5	1586.9
1977/78	993.5	112.6	34.0	39.8	1.7	1.4	106.4	1289.4
1978/79	1227.0	157.5	43.1	49.5	3.7	1.9	109.9	1592.6
1979/80	1287.6	188.8	48.0	63.9	2.7	3.2	149.2	1743.4
1980/81	1455.6	240.7	64.8	72.6	2.1	1.6	89.9	1935.2
1981/82	1469.8	236.9	50.3	78.4	2.5	1.7	76.6	1916.2
1982/83	1469.4	205.4	37.3	98.0	1.5	3.7	69.5	1884.8
1983/84	1573.4	252.5	61.3	77.5	3.7	1.9	80.4	2050.7
1984/85	1956.1	289.6	88.8	91.8	4.7	1.5	117.3	2549.8
1985/86	2285.3	395.3	118.6	124.2	6.1	3.0	177.4	3109.9
1986/87	2837.4	525.0	132.5	127.5	5.7	3.3	263.1	3894.5
1987/88	4270.1	747.5	195.1	175.1	6.1	3.5	327.5	5724.8
1988/89	4581.2	753.9	169.3	232.3	6.0	2.9	203.2	5948.8
1989/90	3344.6	549.1	146.2	159.9	8.8	3.0	186.4	4398.2
1990/91	2136.5	524.0	109.2	170.6	7.6	1.2	106.1	3055.2
1991/92	2558.0	711.5	171.2	164.9	10.9	2.1	115.6	3734.1

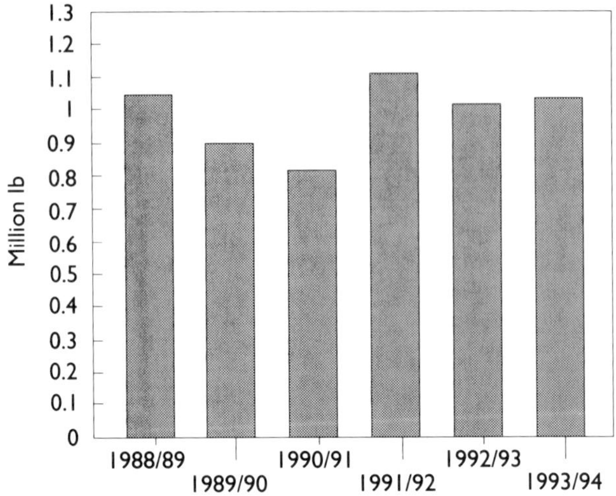

6.2 Australian wool exports, m lb clean, 1988/89–1993/94.

Hong Kong fell from 34.1% in 1978 to 29.1% in 1988. The main fall was occasioned by the collapse in the Australian share of the Japanese wool market, which in 1978 took 27% of Australian wool but which by the 1990s was taking less than 10%. The share taken by the former Comecon countries has slumped too, from a peak of 24% to less than half that. Shipments to the USA have, by contrast, held up well. The slack has been intermittently taken up by China, which took a tiny fraction of Australian wool exports in 1978 but this area as with so many other commodities has now assumed an increasingly dominant role.

The current export destinations for Australian wool are shown in Tables 6.5 and 6.6a and b.

The value of Australian wool exports also fell during the wool recession of the early 1990s, but can now be expected to be mounting at a rate in excess of 15% per annum. The value of Australian wool exports was A$2953 in 1990/91, A$3622 in 1991/92, A$3208 in 1992/93 and A$3198 in 1993/94. In the first months of 1994, exports began to rise again to all destinations and this was expected to continue throughout the 1994/95 season. Table 6.7 demonstrates the considerable importance that China now has in Australian wool exports as well as the total collapse in exports to the CIS countries and the downward trend in the value of exports to Europe. China now takes 22% of Australian exports and is just one country, as compared with Western Europe as a whole taking 34%. The long term trends are heavily against Europe. Europe cannot expect to be treated with deference by Australian wool exporters, if its demand continues to fall as a

Table 6.5 Australian wool exports, m kg greasy equivalent

Destination	**Jul 93 to May 94**	**Change, %**
Belgium	3.186	−75.6
China	166.158	9.3
Columbia	0.323	−59.6
Czech Republic	4.727	46.0
France	67.465	23.1
Germany	48.963	3.3
Greece	2.412	−38.5
Hong Kong	17.437	−26.1
India	23.503	8.1
Iran	1.078	0.8
Italy	111.370	20.8
Japan	93.787	−8.9
Malaysia	18.168	2.5
Mexico	2.589	−30.7
Nepal	0.000	0.0
Netherlands	1.929	−46.2
Pakistan	1.233	36.2
Russian Fed.	2.365	–
South Korea	52.622	27.3
Spain	9.546	−11.6
Taiwan	45.113	−10.4
Thailand	9.133	97.9
Turkey	9.399	−17.2
UK	21.916	−6.4
USA	43.634	10.0
Others	15.682	−13.9
Total*	773.737	4.1

* Totals may not sum due to rounding.

Source: Australian Bureau of Statistics; includes greasy, scoured, carbonised, tops, noils and waste.

Table 6.6a) Australian annual exports of greasy wool, scoured wool and wool tops, m kg

	Greasy			Scoured			Tops		
Country	**1990/91**	**1991/92**	**1992/93**	**1990/91**	**1991/92**	**1992/93**	**1990/91**	**1991/92**	**1992/93**
China, P R	24.084	68.535	123.391	6.232	11.318	10.995	5.627	6.292	9.274
Japan	72.360	73.528	51.998	31.809	38.579	33.569	6.341	5.925	4.591
Italy	77.621	88.006	63.039	10.812	14.959	15.069	0.605	0.467	1.719
France	59.286	71.942	56.854	0.713	0.941	1.003	0.108	0.000	0.031
Taiwan	31.429	59.322	49.266	0.508	1.951	1.161	0.980	1.478	1.388
Germany	40.722	47.445	47.385	1.610	1.578	1.407	0.051	2.379	0.107
USA	26.937	28.034	28.658	6.138	8.674	8.286	0.165	0.723	0.616
Korea, Rep	21.757	21.867	18.642	5.970	9.322	7.502	3.265	2.105	2.812
United Kingdom	9.838	15.182	19.009	2.405	3.579	3.586	0.096	0.030	0.237
India	17.242	18.117	18.983	1.115	1.937	2.918	0.249	0.067	0.088
Hong Kong	0.000	5.342	11.860	0.397	2.343	1.323	1.637	1.549	3.584
Malaysia	9.403	9.283	8.534	1.995	3.647	5.824	0.019	0.090	0.420
Belgium/ Luxembourg	8.185	26.905	12.264	0.043	0.039	0.215	0.000	0.032	0.000
Turkey	3.589	3.542	10.037	0.172	0.325	1.909	0.012	0.074	0.378
Spain	10.470	11.327	7.531	0.487	0.586	2.368	0.000	0.010	0.068
Czech Republic	3.037	2.652	4.087	0.006	0.073	0.013	0.000	0.263	0.028
Mexico	2.533	3.125	3.907	0.011	0.012	0.193	0.000	0.000	0.000
Netherlands	7.007	9.713	3.733	0.010	0.047	0.064	0.000	0.000	0.000
Greece	2.466	4.533	3.306	0.155	0.290	0.348	0.012	0.051	0.032
Israel	1.619	4.891	3.390	0.000	0.000	0.058	0.000	0.000	0.000
Other	30.582	48.316	10.800	5.973	5.562	6.097	0.805	2.212	1.798
Total	460.167	621.607	556.674	76.561	105.762	103.908	19.972	23.747	27.171

Note: Table shows the top twenty importing countries 1992/93.

Source: Australian Bureau of Statistics

Table 6.6b) Australian annual exports of greasy wool, scoured wool and wool tops, A$m

Country	Greasy			Scoured			Tops			Carbon-ised	Noils	Waste	Woolled sheep skins
	1990/91	1991/92	1992/93	1990/91	1991/92	1992/93	1990/91	1991/92	1992/93	1992/93			
China, P R	85.164	267.088	498.409	28.180	65.529	64.341	46.092	40.371	73.307	39.101	0.000	0.096	12.917
Japan	420.722	377.713	235.423	249.912	281.436	226.523	50.286	46.673	35.264	12.813	0.235	0.056	5.533
Italy	425.202	378.606	238.154	67.052	91.672	92.844	6.101	4.142	16.175	32.901	4.657	0.115	2.107
Germany	185.037	202.986	181.143	8.916	9.105	8.244	0.459	7.757	0.861	1.187	1.913	0.328	44.146
France	213.604	253.974	184.719	4.183	4.814	5.024	1.108	0.000	0.305	55.964	0.000	0.000	9.943
Taiwan	97.340	185.662	160.286	2.182	14.454	7.259	7.470	10.223	10.420	0.442	0.053	0.000	3.314
USA	137.262	119.151	108.893	32.612	41.841	46.302	1.544	5.611	4.890	2.565	0.000	0.000	0.093
Korea, Rep	107.194	100.047	77.687	46.870	72.616	54.033	35.245	17.307	24.803	1.117	0.174	0.115	0.339
United Kingdom	35.032	57.714	71.445	14.697	25.894	23.523	0.721	0.233	1.500	28.266	0.117	0.009	1.374
India	57.562	62.954	64.332	5.716	13.199	18.579	2.469	0.580	0.492	0.303	0.327	0.085	1.015
Malaysia	43.699	37.140	36.690	16.159	29.405	42.372	0.155	0.943	3.864	0.148	0.010	0.170	0.234
Hong Kong	0.000	22.549	45.650	1.978	16.173	9.093	11.920	10.368	27.474	0.051	0.000	0.000	0.037
Turkey	19.172	18.170	43.902	0.790	1.692	10.150	0.121	0.581	3.136	0.553	0.000	0.000	7.387
Belgium/ Luxembourg	42.511	115.295	46.666	0.176	0.168	0.776	0.000	0.192	0.000	0.000	0.255	0.420	1.254
Spain	32.153	33.646	20.988	2.584	3.021	7.060	0.000	0.040	0.534	0.611	0.000	0.000	3.330
Mexico	17.899	20.381	20.574	0.120	0.077	0.709	0.000	0.000	0.000	3.206	0.000	0.000	2.839
Thailand	0.677	0.957	0.258	28.592	25.383	20.830	0.661	1.400	0.152	0.000	0.000	0.000	0.078
Czech Republic	16.303	12.802	17.789	0.038	0.378	0.754	0.000	1.505	0.160	0.000	0.000	0.000	0.054
Greece	12.296	20.120	13.942	0.744	1.707	2.592	0.039	0.375	0.227	0.105	0.017	0.008	0.017
Netherlands	33.963	45.357	14.551	0.067	0.202	0.289	0.000	0.000	0.000	0.000	0.000	0.000	0.313
Other	157.080	225.640	57.266	12.761	12.645	19.115	6.169	16.598	14.626	2.472	0.107	0.022	19.396
Total	2139.872	2557.952	2138.767	524.329	711.511	660.412	170.56	164.899	218.190	181.805	7.865	1.424	115.720

Note: Table shows the top twenty importing countries for 1992/93.

Source: Australian Bureau of Statistics

Table 6.7 Australian wool exports by trade area, m kg greasy equivalents

Trade area	1993/94 season	1992/93 season	% change over previous season
Western Europe	286	273	6
Eastern Europe	11	8	55
China, P R	187	166	9
Japan	106	116	−9
Other Asian	189	180	4
North America	50	47	7
Total	852	817	4

percentage of total output – especially given high transport costs and administrative inconvenience, let alone dealing with many European languages and as many sets of regulations.

New Zealand

The wool and wool sector export trade is particularly important to the New Zealand economy. For most of the 1980s the sector contributed about 15% of total merchandise exports annually, falling to 10.7% in 1990 and 7.6% in 1992 before once again reviving as wool prices increased thereafter. Sheepmeat exports contributed about 10% over the same period. Wool and sheepmeat combined form New Zealand's largest export industry: wool on its own is the fourth largest. Of the nine exporting ports, the main one is Auckland, followed by Port Chalmers of which the share fell in the early 1990s, Napier and then Wellington.

New Zealand's wool exports peaked at over 325m tonnes in 1983, then fell to 201.4m tonnes in 1990. New Zealand's share of the world wool market is declining although New Zealand wool is still exported to over 50 countries. The EU is, as with Australian wool, the main export market, taking some 70% although as with every commodity Europe's relative, if not absolute, importance is declining. In 1978 the EC took 54% of New Zealand's exports, but now takes somewhat less than half of that percentage. The former Comecon countries took almost 19% of New Zealand wool at their peak, but now take less than 10% all told and the amount is still falling. Exports to Japan have also fallen dramatically. The NZWB states that 'developing markets in the Indian Sub-continent, the Persian Gulf and East Asia are becoming increasingly important destinations' (*Annual Report*, 1994).

The USA, Iran, India, Nepal and Turkey continue to be small

export destinations - in the past the USA took some 15% - but New Zealand exports of its wool for hand-knotted carpets have been reduced by cheap wool exports from Russia and the southern CIS countries. These countries have exported wool to Pakistan, India, Turkey and Iran as the export component of barter deals or as a way of getting scarce foreign currency. Russian farmers have sold direct to these countries, despite Russian regulations that say they must sell directly only to their own textile mills: the temptation of hard currency and higher prices has proved too great. Germany remains a vital destination for wools finer than 28 microns, with China dominating the 29-34 micron range for use in hand-knitting yarns. Slipe wool is exported to over 30 countries with the UK traditionally being the largest customer, taking over half. China is increasingly important in this market too, rising from having taken only 3% of New Zealand wool in 1978 to 26% more recently. Table 6.8 shows wool fibre exports and 6.9 shows the mirror profile of exports in 1993/94.

New Zealand is the biggest producer (30%) and exporter of cross-bred wools worldwide. New Zealand cross-bred wools enjoy a quality advantage, but this has not been successful in preventing other countries, notably China, Spain, the UK and Ireland from competing successfully against New Zealand, mainly on price. As a result New Zealand's market share has fallen from 70% to 60% in the last decade. The vast majority of New Zealand's Merino production is shipped abroad as greasy wool for high quality apparel but some is used domestically by New Zealand garment manufacturers.

New Zealand wool exports broken down into wool fibre, sheepskins, waste, intermediate products and final products are shown in Table 6.10. Some 30% of New Zealand carpet yarn was exported in 1992-93, earning $52m, mainly to Australia but also to the USA, Hong Kong and the UK. What the current figures suggest is that recovery is bringing the market back to a previous equilibrium, and in particular that New Zealand is returning to its previous position in the wool export market. Wool fibre exports from New Zealand rose by 25% to 226 000 tonnes in the 1993/94 season. Scoured wool exports remained the major form of wool export, taking 80% of wool fibre exports compared with 53% six years before. Strong demand from China, a gradual recovery in Western Europe and India's return to the buying levels of two years before were responsible for the recovery in exports. China was the largest export customer, at 60 300 tonnes, up 65% from a year ago and with exports to Hong Kong a further 11 900 tonnes on top of that. The UK became the second largest export destination, testimony to the effectiveness of New Zealand wool marketing.

Table 6.8 New Zealand wool fibre exports, 1962–94, '000 tonnes clean

Season	UK & Eire	Western Europe*	Japan	USSR/ CIS	China and Hong Kong	India, Iran Nepal and Pakistan	USA	Other	Total wool fibre exports (all countries)
1962–63	49.2	78.0	12.0	–	1.4	1.5	33.6	2.8	191.7
1963–64	54.1	74.7	11.4	1.2	2.3	0.1	28.3	7.1	192.4
1964–65	43.4	69.1	11.6	1.9	2.0	0.1	28.1	12.1	178.2
1965–66	47.7	77.9	23.6	5.0	3.6	0.3	31.8	8.0	209.7
1966–67	38.8	55.1	20.6	8.2	6.6	0.3	25.3	10.3	173.9
1967–68	48.6	76.8	13.8	7.7	5.4	0.3	28.1	9.3	204.0
1968–69	52.8	92.3	24.8	11.8	2.3	0.5	28.8	10.2	238.6
1969–70	49.8	81.4	27.3	15.0	3.4	1.6	26.3	18.0	237.5
1970–71	43.7	83.1	23.5	17.0	1.7	1.0	25.0	26.6	231.9
1971–72	51.0	85.2	18.9	22.2	2.0	1.2	22.8	35.1	246.9
1972–73	40.5	72.1	28.4	13.9	4.0	3.5	16.4	32.3	218.5
1973–74	27.9	53.7	12.6	17.9	8.2	3.4	7.6	28.8	166.5
1974–75	34.2	59.5	15.3	18.3	11.1	8.0	5.3	23.3	181.2
1975–76	29.9	81.7	20.7	22.6	9.2	6.7	6.8	40.1	226.5
1976–77	38.6	72.6	15.7	18.6	6.1	7.4	8.3	39.6	213.9
1977–78	42.5	67.0	17.8	19.1	7.1	7.6	7.1	34.5	210.2
1978–79	33.6	69.3	30.0	25.0	11.4	6.3	8.1	30.1	226.1
1979–80	27.2	72.9	25.2	32.2	15.0	17.5	9.3	40.6	253.8
1980–81	26.9	64.8	21.1	21.9	29.2	22.8	9.1	38.7	245.5
1981–82	29.9	63.3	32.9	28.6	22.8	12.5	8.1	39.0	248.5
1982–83	36.5	64.0	30.2	26.3	35.0	27.6	8.2	41.7	278.6
1983–84	33.4	68.5	34.1	24.7	22.7	18.1	14.9	39.3	267.9
1984–85	38.6	76.0	37.0	17.7	39.0	5.9	12.5	38.9	278.1
1985–86	34.5	60.7	25.1	24.8	32.0	11.3	11.7	39.6	249.8
1986–87	32.8	56.6	25.1	25.1	56.3	11.3	13.2	40.8	269.5
1987–88	24.4	50.8	21.0	22.0	55.4	16.7	11.9	38.6	246.7
1988–89	21.8	45.8	19.4	24.1	66.6	17.2	12.9	30.6	244.2
1989–90	17.3	42.6	21.4	26.7	18.3	22.8	9.9	31.7	190.7
1990–91	20.3	39.0	24.6	7.8	22.2	32.6	7.5	34.9	188.8
1991–92	21.2	41.5	19.7	4.7	57.4	35.9	9.2	34.8	224.3
1992–93	17.7	29.5	15.6	1.6	45.4	36.3	8.4	26.0	180.5
1993–94	24.8	35.4	14.9	2.1	72.2	35.9	8.4	32.4	226.0

* France, Germany, Belgium, Italy and Netherlands.

Table 6.9 Micron profile of New Zealand shorn wool exports, 1993/94, clean tonnes

Destination	28 microns and finer	29 to 34 microns	35 to 41 microns	Total
United Kingdom/Eire	1 120	8 468	12 614	22 202
West Europe	5 335	7 156	14 910	27 401
East Europe	122	1 400	908	2 430
West Mediterranean	4 073	2 255	1 897	8 225
East Mediterranean	349	1 969	5 533	7 851
Scandinavia	96	366	329	791
Indian Ocean/Persian Gulf	535	8 310	26 998	35 843
East Asia	4 084	17 888	13 504	35 476
China	1 179	35 102	22 698	58 979
Americas	588	3 696	4 428	8 712
Africa	306	1 766	163	2 235
Australia and Pacific Isands	135	1 432	8 996	10 563
Grand total	17 922	89 808	112 978	220 708

Totals may not add owing to countries with less than 4 tonnes not being displayed.
Source: Compiled by NZWB from copies of export entries

Table 6.10 New Zealand wool sector exports, $NZ m FOB

Year ending June	1992	1993(r)	1994(p)
Wool fibre			
Greasy	307.9	196.7	217.1
Scoured	744.8	680.4	814.1
Slipe	28.7	23.7	22.9
Total	1 081.3	900.8	1 054.1
Sheepskins			
Raw	6.2	5.7	3.0
Processed	23.0	30.3	37.9
Final products	22.3	30.9	32.2
Total	51.5	66.9	73.1
Wool waste	**0.9**	**1.7**	**2.4**
Intermediate products			
Carpet yarn	58.5	52.2	46.0
Other yarn	17.0	19.3	17.3
Tops, sliver	16.9	13.6	11.6
Total	92.4	85.1	74.9
Final products			
Carpet, rugs	66.7	66.0	63.8
Travel rugs, blankets	1.2	1.7	1.3
Knitted apparel	7.5	8.3	3.5
Woven apparel	7.2	10.7	7.5
Fabrics	4.1	4.2	5.2
Total	86.7	90.9	81.2
Total wool sector	1 312.9	1 145.4	1 285.6

Year ending June	1992	1993(r)	1994(p)
Total merchandise exports	17 205.9	18 240.4	19 150.1
Wool sector as percentage of total merchandise exports	8%	6%	7%

r revised p provisional
Source: Statistics New Zealand

Germany was the premier export destination for wool fibre between 29 and 34 microns, followed by Italy and Japan. It is an old German tradition dating from the nineteeth century to create monopsony situations in minority commodities and one must question whether there is a wholly economic justification for this concentration on more expensive New Zealand fine quality wools. China continued to be the main customer for wool fibre of 29–34 microns, taking 35 100 tonnes – 40% of exports in this range – and also of wool more than 35 microns, 22 700 tonnes. Western Europe as a whole reduced its imports of New Zealand wool by 14%, Eastern Europe by 24%. Interestingly, Wools of New Zealand now places Italy out of Europe in its categorisation, in 'West Mediterranean'. Greece goes into 'East Mediterranean'. Italy and Greece were the only EU countries apart from the UK to show an increase in imports of New Zealand wool in the 1993/94 season. Exports to East Asia were up 19%, however. Thailand, Vietnam, Indonesia, the Philippines and Taiwan all showed strong growth. New Zealand now exports more wool to East Asia than to Western Europe (excluding Italy) and by the end of the century, it can be expected that China and East Asia between them will take over half of New Zealand wool production. In terms of export ports Port Chalmers and Lyttleton are becoming increasingly important as an export port by comparison to Auckland, which however remains – just – the leading export port.

Carpet yarn exports, on the other hand, were virtually unchanged between 1993 and 1994, but other yarn exports actually fell. Carpets themselves showed an increase in exports from 2 070 000 m^2 in March 1993 to 2 456 000 m^2 in March 1994. Figures for the second and third quarters of 1994 ought to show similar increases and so the worrying figures depicted in the following paragraph ought to show reversals in the data for 1994/95.

In terms of product value, New Zealand wool sector exports have risen by 12%, reaching NZ$1286m in 1993/94, during a period when total merchandise exports also rose 12%. Wool fibre exports constituted $1055m of this total, and the average FOB value rose from $4.91/kg in 1992/93 to $4.67/kg in 1993/94. The value of wool fibre exports rose 17% (of which greasy wool was 10% and scoured 20% with slipe continuing to decline, by 3%) sheepskin exports increased by 9% (concealing a large readjustment with the raw sheepskin exports falling by 47% but processed exports rising by 25%) but the value of yarn, top and sliver fell by 12%, relatively evenly distributed, and - most worrying for the New Zealand industry - the value of final products exported fell by 11% - a serious drop. The largest fall in export value was in knitted apparel, down 58%, followed by woven apparel down 30%, fabrics down 27%, then travel rugs and blankets down 25% and finally carpet rugs down 3%. Industry sources, however, are not concerned, as they point to a recovery already under way.

The current export destinations for New Zealand wool are shown in Table 6.11.

Table 6.11 New Zealand wool exports, m kg greasy equivalent

Destination	Jul 93 to May 94	Change %
Australia	13.786	45.0
Belgium	16.620	11.4
China	72.159	59.5
Columbia	0.000	0.0
Czech Republic	0.286	0.0
France	2.592	0.0
Germany	16.118	27.7
Greece	2.351	−28.5
Hong Kong	14.974	36.3
India	21.927	60.0
Iran	5.524	3.8
Italy	10.326	29.6
Japan	18.651	−3.4
Malaysia	0.134	–
Mexico	0.132	−14.0
Nepal	15.541	−33.1
Netherlands	0.131	−72.5
Pakistan	3.099	−23.9
Russian Fed	2.831	–
South Korea	2.303	90.0
Spain	0.415	18.5
Taiwan	5.685	67.5
Thailand	1.418	38.9
Turkey	5.291	−24.3
UK	27.655	37.6
USA	10.299	0.3
Others	11.622	36.3
Total*	281.870	23.8

* Totals may not sum due to rounding.

Source: New Zealand Wool Board; includes greasy, slipe and scoured

Europe

In 1978, the EC accounted for less than 10% of world wool exports, shipping mainly coarse wool. The share fluctuated somewhat during the 1980s, being 8.5% in 1990. In the late 1970s over three-quarters of EC wool exports went to other EC member states, but ten years later this proportion had fallen to nearly 2–3%, while exports to Japan, China and other Eastern European countries had increased. The EU still takes 45% of British wool exports, in particular Benelux countries, which in turn produce carpets that are exported in large measure back to the UK. In the mid-1990s the BWMB believed that China was a growth market for EU (which meant primarily UK) exports, and maintained an office in Japan. The USA is taking a steadily increasing share of EU wool exports.

UK wool exports are certainly bringing in more money - £672m in 1989, £500m in 1991, £540m in 1992 and over £600m the following year with wool price rises in 1994 certain to raise that figure still further. The effect of sterling's exit from the exchange rate mechanism in September 1992 had a rapid effect on the competitiveness of UK wool exports. This was partly accounted for by direct exchange rate considerations and partly in dealing with some Arab countries and NICs which habitually price their international trading contracts in dollars. The timing was good in terms of the selling season, coming just before the main London and Paris trade fairs. Sales to Europe rose 19% over 1991 in the period Jan–Jul 1992 and to the rest of the world by 1%. This occurred despite the slowness with which expected Middle East buying resumed after the Gulf War and despite recession in Europe. Although some raw materials became more expensive towards the end of 1992, stocks were still high and the industry, which in the UK normally works some 6–12 months in advance, was able to pass these on to consumers.

Argentina

Argentina is the fourth largest wool exporting country. It accounted for 6.8% of global trade in 1980, but its share fell to 3.2% in 1989, increasing to 5.4% in 1990 as exports from the Australasian countries fell. Argentina's major markets are the CIS countries, the EU, China and the USA - the usual destinations. In 1978, 40% of Argentina's exports went to the EC, followed by the Soviet Union with just over 35%, the USA with almost 4% and China with a tiny fraction, less than 0.2%. By 1988 China had become Argentina's largest market, taking 38% followed by 27% for the Soviet Union, the EC with 26% and the USA with 2.6%, having stood as high as 7.5% before the Falklands War.

Argentinian wool exports, as shown in Table 6.12, represent a share of world exports of 4.2% in 1988/89 up to 5.7% in 1993/94. In 1992/93 Argentine wool was exported to 34 countries. Greasy wool exports comprised 31% of the total. The current export destinations for Argentinian wool are shown in Table 6.13.

Table 6.12 Argentinian wool exports, m lb

1988/89	75
1989/90	83
1990/91	73
1991/92	59
1992/93	69
1993/94	101

Source: IWTO/Commonwealth Secretariat

Table 6.13 Argentinian wool exports, m kg greasy equivalent

Destination	Oct 1992 to Sep 93	Change, %
Australia	0.000	–
Belgium	1.644	–27.4
China	5.509	–29.3
Columbia	0.163	–68.8
Czech Republic	0.141	213.3
France	2.202	66.4
Germany	16.949	30.0
Greece	0.252	60.5
Hong Kong	9.221	124.9
India	7.604	102.0
Iran	1.173	9.1
Italy	7.600	22.2
Japan	3.865	–34.8
Malaysia	0.000	0.0
Mexico	2.280	41.9
Nepal	0.000	–
Netherlands	16.612	10.7
Pakistan	0.000	–
Russian,Fed	0.010	–
South,Korea	0.896	–36.3
Spain	1.587	–17.6
Taiwan	2.829	–40.3
Thailand	0.331	0.0
Turkey	1.131	46.9
UK	1.404	2.9
USA	0.852	–35.3
Others	5.509	–8.8
Total*	89.764	11.2

*Totals may not sum due to rounding.

Source: Federacion Lanera Argentina; includes greasy, scoured, slipe, carbonised, tops and noils

South Africa

South Africa is the world's fifth largest wool exporter. About 95% of the South African wool clip is exported, according to the SAWB; some 60% of the clip is exported in semi-processed form (scoured and combed). Some 70% of exports are fine Merino wool for apparel. South African wool exports are shown in Table 6.14 and represent a share of world exports of 3.3% in 1988/89 down to 2.7% in 1993/94. These figures are substantially lower than figures from 1980 (62 000 tonnes in 1980 compared with 50 000 tonnes in 1990, reaching a low point of 33 000 tonnes in 1987). The EU is the largest single market, accounting for 93% of all recorded exports in 1978, three-quarters of which was taken by the UK, France, Germany and Italy. Then the share fell to 77% as exports to the USA increased from virtually nothing in 1978 to 12% in 1983. In 1987 economic sanctions were imposed on South Africa which caused US imports again to fall away. In the EC countries sanctions did not work as effectively, and South African wool exports to Europe actually increased in volume. The EC took 94.6% of South Africa's wool in 1988. Exports to Japan fell from a 10% share in 1980, the highest, to 2% in 1988. Exports to Taiwan have ranged from 1–2% and the proportion going to Hong Kong and South Korea is even smaller. Table 6.15 shows South African wool exports by class and Table 6.16 shows exports by country of destination.

Table 6.14 South African wool exports, m lb

1988/89	58
1989/90	65
1990/91	67
1991/92	61
1992/93	42
1993/94	47

Source: IWTO/Commonwealth Secretariat

Table 6.15 South African wool exports by class, 1992/93

Class of wool	Net mass, 1 000 kg	FOB value, R1 000,	Average FOB price, ¢/kg
Greasy	22 202	148 379	668.31
Scoured	6 621	73 150	1 104.82
Top	17 107	290 388	1 697.48
Noil	1 510	11 262	745.83
Waste	492	1 443	293.29
Total	47 931	524 622	1 094.54

Source: South African Wool Board.

Table 6.16 South African wool exports by country of destination, 1000 kg and R1 000, 1992/1993

Country		Grease	Scoured	Top	Noil	Waste	Total	% of total
France	R	32 256	4 399	3 478	574	240	40 947	7.81
	Kg	5 059	356	185	83	108	5 791	
Germany	R	52 764	13 363	32 410	127	36	98 700	18.81
	Kg	7 257	1 360	2 435	21	18	11 091	
Italy	R	17 101	22 080	29 966	4 314	36	73 497	14.01
	Kg	2 150	2 162	1 733	592	10	6 647	
UK	R	22 070	4 271	20 058	1 144	226	47 769	9.11
	Kg	4 220	401	1 252	39	39	5 951	
Hong Kong	R	99	5 059	41 025	0	0	46 183	8.80
	Kg	14	328	2 346	0	0	2 688	
Japan	R	2 777	1 273	32 362	3 035	0	39 447	7.52
	Kg	343	102	1 980	361	0	2 786	
South Korea	R	0	1 722	50 219	0	0	51 941	9.90
	Kg	0	104	2 637	0	0	2 741	
Taiwan	R	10 145	2 958	49 630	0	0	62 733	11.96
	Kg	1 382	200	2 789	0	0	4 371	
Other countries	R	11 167	18 025	31 240	2 068	905	63 405	12.09
	Kg	1 777	1 608	1 750	414	317	5 865	
Totals	R	148 379	73 150	290 388	11 262	1 443	524 622	100.00
	Kg	22 202	6 621	17 107	1 510	492	47 931	

Source: South African Wool Board.

Uruguay

Uruguay is the sixth largest wool exporter in the world. Its share fell to 1.9% in 1985 but recovered to 3.6% in 1990. In 1978, the major markets for Uruguayan wool were the EC with 43%, the Soviet Union with 25.8% and the rest of Eastern Europe with 17.4%. In 1988 Uruguay shipped 37.7% of its wool exports to the Soviet Union, 12.2% to other Eastern European countries and 28.5% to the EC. China's share rose from nothing in 1978 to 8.3% a decade later. By contrast the USA has taken progressively less Uruguayan wool, the share falling from 7.6% in 1984 to 3.6% in 1988.

Uruguayan wool exports, as shown in Table 6.17, represent a share of world exports of 2.4% in 1988/89 recovering after a series of low exporting years to 3.8% in 1993/94. The current export destinations for Uruguayan wool are shown in Table 6.18.

The United States

Table 6.19 shows US wool exports in recent years. Raw wool exports in the second quarter of 1994 were 1m lb (454 tonnes), 33% above the

Table 6.17 Uruguayan wool exports, m lb

1988/89	44
1989/90	64
1990/91	47
1991/92	46
1992/93	35
1993/94	67

Source: ITWO/Commonwealth Secretariat

Table 6.18 Uruguayan wool exports, m kg greasy equivalent

Destination	Oct 1992 to Mar 93	Change, %
Australia	0.000	–
Belgium	0.151	−74.9
China	12.949	−22.3
Columbia	1.254	76.5
Czech Republic	0.068	100.0
France	0.088	−63.2
Germany	6.153	32.7
Greece	0.103	−56.6
Hong Kong	5.637	−3.6
India	0.307	−15.9
Iran	0.000	–
Italy	4.221	−24.9
Japan	0.526	−65.7
Malaysia	0.000	–
Mexico	0.205	42.6
Nepal	0.000	–
Netherlands	1.517	−24.5
Pakistan	0.000	–
Russian Fed	0.000	–
South Korea	0.213	−67.4
Spain	0.345	−46.1
Taiwan	0.023	−88.0
Thailand	0.000	–
Turkey	0.074	−53.3
UK	2.683	−44.9
USA	1.623	83.2
Others	4.623	32.0
Total*	42.760	−14.2

* Totals may not sum due to rounding.

Source: Secretariado Uruguayo de la Lana; includes greasy, scoured, tops and noils

Table 6.19 US wool exports, m lb

1990	2.7
1991	3.9
1992	3.4
1993	2.5
1994 est	3.0

Source: USDA

first quarter and 31% above 1993. Overseas shipments of shorn wool amounted to 0.67m lb (304 tonnes). About 36% went to Mexico, 30% to Korea, and 24% to Japan. Exports of pulled raw wool (not shorn) were 0.12m lb (54 tonnes). About 52% went to Canada and 27% went to Mexico. Exports of carbonised wool were 0.22m lb (99 tonnes); about 44% went to the Italian wool industry and 25% to Korea. In 1993 Japan was the main export destination for US raw wool, followed by Germany, Canada and then India. Export destinations for US wool shift substantially from one year to the next, see Table 6.20.

Table 6.20 US raw wool exports by country of destination, clean yield, '000 lb

	Shorn wool				Unshorn wool				Carbonised wool			
Country	**1991**	**1992**	**1993**	**Jan-Jun 1994**	**1991**	**1992**	**1993**	**Jan-Jun 1994**	**1991**	**1992**	**1993**	**Jan-Jun 1994**
Australia	–	–	8.4	–	–	–	–	–	–	–	–	–
Canada	58.0	75.7	112.3	59.6	157.0	113.9	152.7	87.0	–	4.8	20.2	–
Belgium	172.3	100.4	60.0	–	–	45.9	11.2	–	–	–	36.6	35.2
Czechoslovakia	–	–	–	–	–	–	–	–	–	4.6	–	–
China M	–	–	–	–	–	30.4	122.4	–	–	–	–	224.0
Dominican Rep	–	181.1	–	–	–	15.4	–	–	–	–	–	–
Guatemala	–	–	–	–	–	26.0	–	–	–	–	–	–
Hong Kong	–	29.1	–	–	100.0	111.5	123.5	–	43.2	–	–	–
India	206.4	77.1	105.2	–	–	49.2	48.5	–	–	–	–	–
Iraq	–	–	–	–	–	–	–	–	–	–	–	–
Italy	36.4	–	–	32.8	79.2	44.3	–	–	–	11.8	173.1	190.8
Japan	511.7	581.4	480.0	190.7	71.2	75.2	–	–	6.9	–	116.2	–
Kiribati	–	–	–	–	–	6.7	–	–	–	–	–	–
Korea	185.5	–	–	202.4	–	–	–	24.2	2.2	–	–	54.9
Luxembourg	–	–	–	–	–	31.3	–	–	–	–	–	–
Mexico	195.3	182.4	–	363.0	67.1	4.2	3.7	33.4	–	–	4.8	–
New Zealand	–	7.7	–	–	–	–	–	–	–	–	–	–
Pakistan	–	–	30.6	–	–	–	–	–	–	–	–	–
Portugal	–	27.7	–	–	–	–	–	–	–	–	–	–
Singapore	–	–	–	–	–	–	–	–	–	9.7	–	–
Spain	50.3	–	–	–	14.6	13.2	–	–	–	–	43.0	–
Taiwan	61.0	97.8	–	–	243.1	–	–	–	2.6	–	–	–
Thailand	–	–	–	–	96.5	–	3.9	–	–	–	–	–
United Kingdom	314.2	301.5	30.3	–	201.4	175.8	41.6	73.2	9.0	4.3	485.6	74.2
West Germany	873.5	724.6	272.8	137.7	135.0	283.9	–	2.1	–	–	–	–
Other	14.4	0.0	10.7	0.0	22.9	0.0	31.9	–	40.9	0.1	0.0	0.0
Total	2679.0	2386.5	1110.3	986.2	1188.0	1026.9	539.4	219.9	104.8	35.3	879.5	579.1

– = No exports

Source: US Bureau of the Census

Exports of wool tops in the second quarter of 1994 were 3.7m lb (1.7m kg), 99% above the first quarter and 63% more than 1993. Three countries took more than 93% - Korea 51%, China 39% and Hong Kong, 3%. In 1993 the main source for these exports was China, followed by Korea. Export shares for different countries vary less substantially than for raw wool, see Table 6.21.

Table 6.21 US exports of wool tops, 1990–94, m lb

Country	1990	1991	1992	1993	Jan–Jun 1994
Argentina	–	3.2	–	3.3	–
Australia	199.1	–	–	–	–
Belgium	46.3	–	–	–	–
Brazil	–	–	–	–	–
Canada	651.4	565.8	349.5	349.8	121.7
Chile	–	–	–	–	–
China	1 782.6	7 707.5	5 394.1	5 637.7	1 578.6
Columbia	–	–	42.2	–	42.5
Ecuador	–	–	–	–	–
France	154.9	26.7	–	–	–
Hong Kong	213.9	546.9	933.6	213.9	106.4
India	–	–	472.7	–	–
Ireland	–	–	167.3	–	–
Israel	–	–	–	–	–
Italy	110.7	175.3	290.8	74.8	–
Japan	4 472.4	1 909.6	859.9	28.5	73.5
Mexico	44.1	1.4	8.6	11.7	1.4
Netherlands	6.0	–	–	–	11.0
New Zealand	–	–	–	–	–
Peru	–	–	–	–	–
Singapore	–	–	–	2.2	–
South Africa	–	–	–	–	–
South Korea	1 341.0	3 380.7	4 910.5	3 285.6	3 376.0
Taiwan	636.5	1 354.0	843.9	360.6	173.8
Turkey	299.5	–	–	–	–
United Kingdom	43.1	228.2	1.9	–	–
Uruguay	–	8.5	–	–	–
Venezuela	262.1	856.1	976.0	373.7	114.6
West Germany	43.9	62.5	479.0	110.9	–
Other	0.6	1.5	0.0	1.1	0.1
Total	10 308.1	16 824.7	15 730.0	10 453.9	5 599.6

– = no imports or exports

Source: US Bureau of the Census

Imports of wool by region

The two main wool importing countries of the world are in Asia, China - which has risen from insignificance at the start of the 1980s to the world's largest importer in 1993, and Japan. The four next largest importing countries - Italy, France, the UK and Germany - are however in Europe, which accounts for the continuing importance of Europe in the international wool trade. Total wool imports slumped in the early 1990s, but are now showing a considerable rate of increase and are currently estimated by the IWS on the complex basis of national foreign trade statistics to be exactly the same in 1993 as in 1980. Table 6.22 gives imports of virgin wool country by country.

Table 6.22 Imports of virgin wool, actual weight, m kg

	1980	1989	1990	1991	1992	1993p
Australia (a)	9.9	12.9	9.5	9.6	11.2	11.3
Austria	5.0	2.3	1.9	2.2	2.0	2.2
Belgium	42.2	69.1	54.3	52.3	54.6	37.6
Brazil	2.4	1.2	0.2	0.2	1.7	0.8
Canada	4.3	1.5	1.3	1.0	1.0	1.2
China (c)	29.1	101.4	31.9	103.8	154.0	185.2
Former Czechoslovakia	26.0	20.4	18.0	13.6	7.8	9.3
Denmark	3.9	4.2	3.0	3.2	3.7	2.1
France	117.2	126.0	99.3	127.1	122.0	91.7
Germany (b)	92.7	87.1	77.0	86.5	97.3	82.1
Greece	10.2	9.7	10.0	7.7	7.9	3.2
Hong Kong	5.0	6.2	4.6	7.6	23.7	21.1
India (a)	13.1	22.5	34.0	26.0	40.2	46.0
Iran (a)	10.5	6.9	4.0	4.1	6.9	5.8
Italy	117.7	109.0	118.8	137.5	144.5	121.6
Japan	175.6	173.0	142.7	152.9	145.7	109.1
Korea, South (c)	22.8	34.5	34.3	36.6	38.4	35.1
Malaysia	5.4	11.0	12.5	12.9	11.4	16.5
Nepal (c)	0.2	3.4	7.5	10.5	20.6	19.4
Netherlands	7.5	5.2	4.8	5.5	2.8	2.6
Pakistan (a)	3.2	8.1	8.0	8.3	9.3	2.8
Former USSR (c)	124.2	128.4	52.4	53.5	5.6	5.0
Spain	15.6	15.7	12.6	20.9	20.9	14.1
Taiwan	27.8	45.0	31.2	61.2	53.4	55.2
Turkey	5.7	19.9	31.4	31.0	32.3	42.2
United Kingdom	95.5	109.7	87.8	92.6	102.2	95.6
United States (c)	33.0	48.5	32.5	39.2	40.5	45.5
Former Yugoslavia	23.4	12.1	9.4	7.8	10.0	1.1
Others	83.0	59.3	46.4	54.7	55.5	48.5
Total	1 120	1 266	990	1 179	1 236	1 120

Share held by main importing countries %						
China	3	8	3	9	12	17
Japan	16	14	14	13	12	10
Italy	11	9	12	12	12	11
France	10	10	10	11	10	8
United Kingdom	9	9	9	8	8	9
Germany	8	7	8	7	8	7
Former USSR	11	10	5	5	0	0
All other	33	34	38	36	38	38
Total	100	100	100	100	100	100

(a) Fiscal year ending in year shown
(b) Combined Germany
(c) Clean content

Source: Foreign Trade Statistics

Asia

Japan

Japan has been the world's largest wool importer for decades, importing 19% of the world's wool in 1978 - 201 906 tonnes - and still 13% in 1988 (174 789 tonnes). But in the 1980s and more particularly the 1990s, Japan's wool industry has declined because of the cost of producing wool textiles, reinforced by the effects of the recession in Japan, and wool imports declined dramatically in 1992. Between July and October 1991, for example, Japan imported 482 000 bales, but only 316 000 bales in the same period a year later. Japan's wool imports have been as shown in Table 6.23.

Since the 1970s Japan has been reducing its greasy wool imports in favour of semi-processed wool in response to the increase in labour costs.

Table 6.23 Japanese imports (gross of raw wool, excluding wool on the skin, tonnes clean

1988	127 390
1989	129 279
1990	108 345
1991	115 325
1992	112 670
1993	86 964

Source: IWTO

China

In 1980, China imported only 29 110 tonnes of raw wool but by 1988 this reached 179 790 tonnes. In the 1980s, China increased its imports of most raw textiles. Raw wool was imported and increasingly wool garments were exported as the country took advantage of its low production costs, i.e. low wage levels. China was also seeking to provide textiles for its own still growing population: increased expectations about living standards coupled with higher incomes led to greater demand for woollen products. Spinning mills were turned over to raw wool imports. Between 1984 and 1988, imports provided some 60–64% of China's total raw wool consumption.

China became the dominant trading market in 1987, importing more than any individual EC country, receiving 181 290 t - 13.4% of the world total. This compares with only 11 600 tonnes in 1978. The same pattern was repeated in 1988 but following the Tienanmen Square uprising and new foreign exchange shortages, purchases almost ceased. The total was cut to only 33 303 tonnes in 1990, just 3.4% of the world total. This began to revive in the following year when China relaxed its self-imposed wool import quota from 45 000 tonnes to 150 000 tonnes because of better conditions in the Chinese textile industry, more textile exports and increased domestic demand. In 1992, imports continued and this was an eventual cause of the global wool price recovery in 1993/4. Table 6.24 shows Chinese raw wool imports.

In the 1980s, China bought less expensive coarse wool, mainly from New Zealand, to get the most wool for its money, although the wool was of significantly lower quality and relatively unsuitable for the garment industry. Imports from New Zealand were greater than from Australia by 1988. In 1978 imports from Australia and New Zealand together amounted to 99% of the total, but this fell to

Table 6.24 Chinese imports (gross) of raw wool, excluding wool on the skin, tonnes clean

1988	179 790
1989	101 369
1990	31 910
1991	103 757
1992	153 988
1993	173 523

Note: Revised official data previously assumed to be actual weight now stated to be greasy and scoured wool expressed in clean terms.

Source: IWTO

84% in 1988 as the Chinese attempted to diversify their sources of wool: imports are now coming from the UK, Argentina, Uruguay and Ireland and other origins may well be added. In the 1990s, quality demand has increased: in 1992/93 the Chinese took 24% of the Australian clip to meet the demand of their growing textile industry. The majority of their purchases are now medium micron wool for knitwear. The next strongest is for medium quality worsted yarn of 23/24 micron, and the least strong is the woollen market itself which is still weak because of over-expansion. The import structure is certainly changing, although largely in response to the devaluation of the yuan and occasional relaxations of tariffs, such as that in December 1993 cutting the tariff on imported wool tops from 20% to 15%. Between 1989 and 1994 wool yarns and scoured wool were the principal constituents of imports, but now it is expected that raw wool will account for over 60%.

Currently, imports account for about two-thirds of Chinese wool consumption, and it is generally believed that should China withdraw again from the market, especially suddenly, there would be what the BWMB call a 'dramatic' effect on the market. This explains the continuing research and forecasting attention on the Chinese market being placed by, for example, the BWMB. But as the Managing Director of G H Michell (Aus) Pty Ltd, John Michell, said in 1992, 'There is no getting around the bureaucracy. Dealing with it requires infinite patience and exporters must be prepared to wait for their returns.' Liberalisation is slow; Startoy (the wool-buying arm of the Chinese textile industry) continues to be responsible for wool buying.

South Korea

Imports of wool to this increasingly important Tiger economy have been increasing, at least until the recession began in earnest in 1993. In 1978, they were 86 020 tonnes and, in 1988, 296 119 tonnes. Despite this phenomenal rate of increase, as yet South Korea only takes imports at the level of Belgium and therefore is not a major international player in the wool market, being only the seventh largest export destination for Australian wool. Experts expect on the basis of the level of textile machinery imports in the 1990s alone that this will change. More semi-processed wool rather than greasy is being imported – in 1992/93 only 38% of Australia's wool exports to South Korea were in greasy form, compared with 64% in the early 1980s. The country is the fifth largest importer of wool tops. Table 6.25 shows raw wool imports to South Korea.

Table 6.25 South Korean imports (gross) of raw wool, excluding wool on the skin, tonnes clean

1988	36 917
1989	33 407
1990	33 374
1991	35 481
1992	37 252
1993	34 304

Source: IWTO

Malaysia

Malaysia is another steadily growing market which, although taking only a small percentage of wool imports at present, has a tremendous potential to expand in an area in which it is already strong. Table 6.26 shows raw wool imports to Malaysia.

Table 6.26 Malaysian imports (gross) of raw wool, excluding wool on the skin, tonnes clean

1988	5 166
1989	7 069
1990	8 097
1991	8 279
1992	7 320
1993	9 885*

* Based on 9 months

Source: IWTO

Taiwan

Taiwan is yet another expanding market which has doubled in size since the mid-1980s and must have the potential to grow much further. In 1978, Taiwan imported 21 279 tonnes and in 1988 35 340 tonnes. It is now a bigger import market than South Korea and even the United States in some quarters, importing three times as much as in the 1970s and being the fourth largest importer of Australian wool. Taiwanese imports are shown in Table 6.27.

Table 6.27 Taiwanese imports, m lb greasy

1989/90	1990/91	1991/92	1992/93
69	135	118	122

Source: IWTO in succession to the Commonwealth Secretariat

Hong Kong

Hong Kong imported 14 450 tonnes in 1978 and 48 913 tonnes a decade later. The country remains an important wool importer.

Europe

Western Europe

In 1978, the EC took $1473m of wool imports, compared to $2593m in 1988. In 1980, the EC as a whole was the largest import market for raw wool, taking 44.8% of the global total, 502 164 tonnes. These imports peaked in 1987 and fell thereafter as the recession took its toll on the European textile industry, declining to 450 413 tonnes in 1990. The EU (as the EC is known now), remains, however, the world's largest importer. Reflecting EU preference for fine wool types as imports, most EU imports continue to be from Australia, increasing from 30% in value terms in 1978 to 56% in 1988 and continuing to rise. Imports from New Zealand, however, mostly coarse wool, declined from 26.5% in 1978 to 12.6% by 1988. In sum, therefore, the EU as a whole - reflecting decisions ultimately by retailers and consumers in EU markets - has become more discriminating and specialist in its wool imports and the trend is continuing. Within the EU, Belgium, Denmark, Ireland and the smaller states generally are little altered in their import levels, but the reflection of production specialisation within the EU has been that Italian imports have risen significantly whilst those to Germany and the UK have declined. In 1988, Italy took just over half as much wool again as Germany - in 1992 it was almost twice as much, although it remains to be seen whether this trend continues. Imports to selected European countries are shown in Table 6.28.

Table 6.28 European imports of raw wool, excluding wool on the skin, tonnes clean

	1988	1989	1990	1991	1992	1993
Austria i	2 410	1 777	1 480	1 847	1 546	1 987
Belgium a	33 691	36 204	30 629	29 388	29 959	20 124 e
Denmark b	3 464	3 896	2 768	3 007	2 928	1 188
France c	75 467	82 272	64 943	77 820	57 536	44 529
Germany a	54 034	55 300	46 923	47 001	47 188	43 532 f
Irish Republic b	4 829	5 129	4 211	4 203	3 686	1 522 d
Italy a	73 784	71 272	80 103	92 199	90 672	83 455 g
Netherlands b	5 457	4 595	3 781	3 695	2 487	1 996 h
Poland i	14 177	10 855	2 417	2 165	2 061	–
Switzerland ai	1 530	1 605	2 248	1 853	1 102	1 84
United Kingdom c	79 130	68 460	55 000	58 900	65 120	70 099bg
Yugoslavia i	7 797	7 749	6 094	6 045	6 874	45 5

a Net imports
b Gross imports
c Retained imports
d Extra-Community trade only
e Based on six months
f Based on eight months
g Based on eleven months
h Based on ten months
i Not EC members

Source: IWTO

The CIS states and Eastern Europe

This is a dramatic story, still being written, one which has had a major negative effect on wool prices and the extent of wool trade, and one that must be seen in a historical context. The former Soviet Union's import share reached 13.7% in 1983, and fell to 6% in 1990. At their highest value, in 1988, they were worth $823.292m: a trade worth almost a billion dollars has simply disappeared from the world. Australia was the main supplier, with 49% of Soviet imports in 1978 and 55% in 1988. Imports from New Zealand rose from 16% to 21% over the same period; from Argentina they fell from 16.8% to 6.9%, and from Uruguay they rose from 4.3% to 7.7% (source: Foreign Trade of the USSR, 1978 and 1988). Table 6.29 shows Soviet wool imports. Other sources for Soviet wool were Mongolia, Afghanistan and Syria.

Eastern Europe had a 6.8% world market share in 1980, importing 87 896 tonnes of wool. Czechoslovakia, Poland and Yugoslavia accounted together for three-quarters of the total. Australia, again, was the major exporter, its share rising from 62% to 67% over the

Table 6.29 Soviet wool imports, m lb

1977/78	280 (approx)
1989/90	115
1990/91	118
1991/92	122

Source: USDA

same period, whilst imports from New Zealand fell from 24% to 15% over the same period and from Uruguay they fell slightly from 7.5% to 7.1%. By 1988 Eastern Europe's share of world imports was down to 4.4%, and less than 4% in 1992 and the years following. Czechoslovakia and Yugoslavia no longer even existed as nations. Foreign exchange shortages and the collapse of the Russian and Eastern European textile industries are responsible for this 30% plus decline in imports of wool to the region. In 1990 the Soviet Union had a $250m credit arrangement with Australia to buy approximately 15% of its production, but wool imports have fallen off dramatically now and payment terms have been difficult to agree. The New Zealand Board excitedly reported a joint venture with Russia in 1993 whereby 600 tonnes of scoured wool was shipped to be made into garments, ownership of which was to be retained by the Board until sale, but after the wool had been shipped, the Russian authorities announced new and higher duties and taxes. The wool was returned to New Zealand. Some companies such as Intex and Dowo in the Czech Republic and Kolinkho and Luibertsky in the CIS states are continuing to show an interest in large scale wool importing.

The pent-up demand in both Russia, the Ukraine and other CIS states and Eastern Europe for quality wool products is large but in the absence of sustainable credit arrangements is unlikely to lead to large trade volumes. Wools of New Zealand rightly say that for CIS countries sourcing their preferred raw materials remains a difficulty due to lack of foreign exchange.

America

The United States

The US share of the world wool market has ranged from 2.9% in 1980 to 3.8% in 1989, but has shown a gradual tendency to increase since then, see Table 6.30. In terms of origins, imports have increasingly

Table 6.30 US wool imports, m lb

1988	96.7
1989	106.9
1990	71.7
1991	86.5
1992	89.3
1993	100.3
1994	100.0

Source: USDA

come from Australia: 52.4% in 1978 compared with 28.7% from New Zealand but 65.5% and 21.8% respectively in 1988, a recognition of the US consumer preference for high quality clothing wool and a decline in the use of wool for furnishings. Imports from the EU have also shown a steady rise and since the lifting of sanctions from South Africa there has also been a revival of imports from there.

There is a consistency and stability in US wool imports. In the second quarter of 1994 they were 28m lb (12.7m kg), clean, 11% above the first quarter but 8% below 1993. Imports of 48s and finer were 21.5m lb (9.75m kg), 23% above the first quarter, but 3% below 1993. More than 90% came from two countries: Australia, 83% and Uruguay, 8%. Imports of unimproved and other grades not finer than 46s totalled 5.6m lb (2.5m kg), 16% below the first quarter and 20% below the year before. Two countries supplied 95%: New Zealand 76%, and the UK, 19%. Miscellaneous graded imports amounted to 0.62m lb (0.28m kg), with almost all coming from New Zealand. The share of raw wool imports not-finer-than 46s coming through the New England and Middle Atlantic customs districts in the second quarter exceeded the share of the finer-than-48s. In the second quarter, about 66% of the grades not finer than 46s entered through the New England and Middle Atlantic customs districts, compared with 15% of the 48s and finer. By contrast, the South Atlantic and other customs districts received 85% of the 48s-and-finer, compared with 34% of not-finer-than 46s.

The overall long-term trend in US wool imports is somewhat difficult to detect, since annual oscillations vary, but it appears to be on a slightly upward trend, especially for dutiable 25 micron wool and finer. The Chairman of the Japan Wool Spinners Association, Yukio Kurihara, observed that before wool could really increase its share of the US market, the US Government would have to axe the 40% wool tariff, which will go as part of the WTO structure, or the major protected US wool processors would have to have their protection removed. Tables 6.31 and 6.32 show imports of raw wool for

Table 6.31 US imports of raw wool for consumption, clean content, '000 lb

Year	48s and finer 1/	Not finer than 46s 2/	Misc. 3/	Total
Jan–Dec				
1988	72 323	24 418	NA	96 741
1989	77 003	29 889	48	106 940
1990	50 328	21 355	33	71 716
1991	68 242	18 166	47	86 455
1992	65 457	23 802	26	89 285
1993	76 001	21 876	2 434	100 311
Jan–Mar				
1988	26 763	6 753	NA	33 516
1989	20 166	8 815	1	28 982
1990	14 466	6 697	33	21 196
1991	18 375	4 605	5	22 985
1992	19 565	6 060	0	25 625
1993	20 206	5 244	1 006	26 456
1994	17 505	6 996	633	25 134
Apr–Jun				
1988	19 150	5 965	NA	25 115
1989	22 507	9 265	17	31 789
1990	10 962	7 070	0	18 032
1991	16 422	4 545	0	20 967
1992	18 733	6 854	0	25 587
1993	22 198	7 377	743	30 318
1994	21 462	5 875	623	27 960
Jul–Sep				
1988	9 940	6 141	NA	16 081
1989	15 328	5 500	30	20 858
1990	9 607	4 275	0	13 882
1991	16 426	4 148	42	20 616
1992	10 298	5 461	19	15 778
1993	14 675	5 287	277	20 239
Oct–Dec				
1988	16 470	5 558	NA	22 028
1989	19 002	6 309	0	25 311
1990	15 293	3 314	0	18 607
1991	17 018	4 868	0	21 886
1992	16 861	5 426	7	22 294
1993	18 923	3 968	410	23 301

NA – Not available. Numbers may not add due to rounding.

1/ Formerly 'dutiable' 2/ Formerly 'Duty-Free' 3/ Raw wool, not carded or combed, but processed beyond the degreased condition, e.g. dyed. The grade is not identified, harmonized TSUSA 5102.21.6000, 510.29.6000, and 5101.30.6000.

Source: US Bureau of the Census

Table 6.32 US imports of raw wool for consumption, clean content, '000 lb

	Unimproved and other grades not finer than 46s					48s and finer				
Country	**1990**	**1991**	**1992**	**1993**	**Jan–Jun 1994**	**1990**	**1991**	**1992**	**1993**	**Jan–Jun 1994**
Argentina	820.0	749.1	687.9	556.4	282.7	37.3	574.7	55.6	50.1	49.0
Austria	–	–	–	–	–	112.6	–	–	–	–
Australia	337.7	392.4	276.2	285.3	6.4	42 989.2	59 461.5	55 007.6	64 767.6	32 388.7
Belgium	–	34.4	19.6	–	–	184.6	43.2	–	20.3	–
Brazil	–	–	66.5	–	–	–	–	149.9	81.1	–
Canada	102.5	163.9	307.0	114.3	37.4	182.5	379.4	1 053.0	1 197.1	291.5
Chile	–	–	–	–	–	406.6	395.3	379.7	270.8	593.4
Falkland Islands	26.6		–	–	–	921.6	412.0	–	–	202.9
France	–	–	–	10.1	16.4	–	–	11.8	–	–
Ireland	115.8	–	–	264.5	–	–	–	13.5	–	–
Italy	36.7	–	–	6.2	–	–	–	–	3.5	21.6
Lesotho	–	–	–	–	–	15.2	–	–	–	–
Mexico	–	–	–	–	–	694.9	705.7	770.3	554.1	127.1
New Zealand	16 726.1	14 205.9	17 866.6	15 596.5	9 562.0	2 699.9	3 511.2	3 188.0	1 682.6	898.8
Pakistan	–	–	–	–	–	–	–	–	–	–
Saudi Arabia	–	–	–	–	–	–	–	–	56.6	–
South Africa	–	43.4	45.2	143.8	95.2	–	271.8	952.8	1 149.2	406.9
Spain	–	2,396.5	–	–	–	17.4	2.4	–	–	–
Switzerland	–	–	119.6	110.6	59.9	–	–	–	–	–
United Kingdom	3 121.4	133.7	4 196.9	4 676.3	2 364.5	318.0	217.2	331.0	264.3	630.5
Uruguay	68.4	–	75.4	70.1	325.6	1 703.6	1 705.2	3 157.7	5 853.1	3 155.4
Former USSR	–	–	–	41.5	75.9	–	296.2	2.4	4.7	119.0
West Germany	–	15.2	140.7	–	21.0	27.5	27.6	383.8	42.8	–
Other	0.00	31.9	0.1	0.0	23.8	0.0	238.7	0.1	2.7	82.6
Total	21 355.2	18 166.4	23 801.7	21 875.6	12 870.8	50 310.9	68 242.1	65 457.2	76 000.7	38 967.4

– – Not available.

Source: Bureau of the Census

consumption, and imports by country of origin. Top imports in the second quarter of 1994 were 1m lb (0.45m kg), 5% above the first quarter and 55% above 1993. Three countries were the origin of 96% – Australia 44%, Mexico 30% and Germany 22%, see Table 6.33.

Table 6.33 US imports of wool tops, '000 lb

Country	1990	1991	1992	1993	Jan–Jun 1994
Argentina	–	–	10.5	–	–
Australia	54.0	752.4	1 443.1	2 005.0	1 065.1
Belgium	–	–	71.1	–	–
Brazil	–	–	–	–	–
Canada	–	–	0.3	–	–
Chile	100.2	66.9	22.3	66.6	–
Colombia	–	–	–	–	–
Ecuador	–	–	–	–	–
France	10.9	0.3	107.4	42.6	43.2
Hong Kong	–	–	–	–	–
India	–	–	51.9	202.6	–
Ireland	–	–	–	–	–
Israel	27.5	–	58.1	377.4	–
Italy	0.2	0.7	0.5	–	–
Japan	–	–	–	–	–
Mexico	–	–	65.7	181.1	387.4
Netherlands	–	–	–	–	–
New Zealand	1.0	0.8	0.5	0.1	6.2
Peru	22.9	0.7	1.0	0.2	–
Singapore	–	–	–	–	–
South Africa	–	–	187.6	65.9	36.2
South Korea	–	–	–	–	–
Taiwan	–	–	–	–	–
Turkey	–	–	–	–	–
United Kingdom	82.9	40.0	77.3	67.4	12.0
Uruguay	58.9	–	–	38.6	30.0
Venezuela	–	–	–	–	–
West Germany	–	90.1	29.9	907.8	413.3
Other	0.0	0.2	0.0	0.0	3.2
Total	358.3	952.1	2 127.2	3 956.2	1 996.6

– – No imports or exports.

Source: US Bureau of the Census

Canada

Canadian wool imports are very slight and rapidly declining due to domestic production for domestic needs and an increasing use of

Table 6.34 Canadian imports (gross) of raw wool, excluding wool on the skin, tonnes clean

1988	1818
1989	1453
1990	1264
1991	933
1992	925
1993	1062

Source: IWTO

synthetics. Wool top imports are important. Raw wool imports are shown in Table 6.34.

Australia

Australian wool imports are small but consistent: 11m kg (24m lb) clean in 1992 compared with 10m kg (22m lb) clean in 1982. More interesting than the overall amounts are how these imports divide up, as a well-charted example of the proportions of wool imports in different categories. In 1992, 0.308m kg (0.68m lb) was imported in greasy form, whilst 10.767m kg (23.74m lb) was scoured. Some 1.24m kg (2.73m lb) was carbonised and 0.265m kg (0.58m lb) tops. Waste was 0.113m kg (0.25m lb) and woollen yarn 1.707m kg (3.76m lb). Worsted yarn accounted for another 2.674m kg (5.9m lb) and H K yarn 0.307m kg (0.677m lb). Blankets took 0.021m kg (0.046m lb) and tufted carpets 0.997m kg (2.20m lb), woven carpets 1.305m kg (2.88m lb) and knitwear 3.613m kg (7.97m lb).

CHAPTER

7

The workings of the wool trade

Auctions

Australian and New Zealand wool growers have four main options for selling their wool:

- at a public auction (through a woolbroker);
- to a private merchant;
- to an abattoir (for sale as slipe or sheepskins);
- as specialist lines (e.g. New Zealand Drysdale).

The Australian wool market is under the control of the Australian Wool Exchange. All participants involved in the transfer of ownership of wool must be a member of the exchange to do so. The functions of the Wool Exchange include the responsibility to control the auction selling rosters, for the wool selling regulations, for product quality assurance, for market reporting, and electronic data transfer. All sectors of the industry are represented on the board of the exchange - exporters, brokers, wool growers, private treaty merchants and local processors. The Garnaut report suggests that the Australian Wool Exchange should be in the private sector and, as an independent company, it is.

Auction offerings were 417 508 lots in the season to August 1993 and 368 072 in the year to August 1994, when conditions were already improving. Clearance to the trade was 85.5% in the season to August 1993 and 94.1% to August 1994 with Japanese and Western Europe buyers predominating, supported by China.

In the 1990s on average 60–70% of the New Zealand clip has been sold by auction, while sales to private merchants have accounted for 20–25%, and around 10–15% was sold as slipe or sheepskins. Three hundred lots of wool are sold every hour at the auctions through an open cry system with an average lot size of 12 bales. Wool is purchased at auction by buyers acting for wool exporting countries, local and overseas processors, and merchant scourers. While anyone can buy and sell wool at auction, to export it a company must be licensed with the New Zealand Wool Board.

Although most shearing occurs in the spring, wool is sold throughout the year, with the auction season running from 1 July to 30 June. Sales are rostered frequently throughout the season for each selling centre although they tend to peak between December and February. From the beginning of the 1988/89 season, there were only three selling centres, with all North Island wool being sold at Napier, while the majority of South Island wool is auctioned at Christchurch, sales in Dunedin being restricted to the August–November period when the bulk of fine wools are offered. From the 1992/93 season onwards national wool auctions with wool from both islands on offer were held at Napier and Christchurch and these have become part of the New Zealand auction structure. To facilitate handling and restrain transportation costs, wool is still sent to one of eight aggregation centres for pre-sale preparation. Woolbrokers also offer collection and storage facilities in additional centres, close to the production areas. It was sale by sample that made possible the centralisation of selling centres; all wool sold at auction in Australia and New Zealand is by sample, with pre-sale test certificates attached to the display box; baled wool can be stored in an aggregation centre while the auction is held in another centre – often called sale by separation.

At the beginning of each New Zealand selling season, the quantity of wool to be offered at each sale is determined by the Wool Auction Sales Committee. The maximum quantities of wool offered and other conditions of sale are contained in regulations published by the New Zealand Woolbrokers' Association. To ensure equity, wool brokers prepare wool for each sale in the order they receive it from the wool growers. On receipt of the grower's wool at the wool broker's store, it is prepared for sale either as a main lot, by grouping or interlotting, or binning. A main lot is an even line of wool which has been prepared on one farm and which is sold under the grower's brand. Although there is no set minimum number of bales to form a main lot, in order to maximise lot sizes and so reduce storage, testing and shipping charges, wool brokers aim to achieve an average of at least ten bales per lot for each sale. So when an individual grower submits only a small number of bales for sale, they may be amalgamated with similar bales from other growers (grouping or interlotting) and the lots sold under a common brand, each grower being paid by greasy weight percentage.

Similarly when a bale of grower's wool contains more than one type, or a small quantity only of a single type, all the wool is removed and each fleece individually assessed. They are then binned with other fleeces of similar characteristics until there is sufficient weight to form a full bale suitable for sale (minimum weight 120 kg - 265 lb). The weight of each sale lot should average 2000–2500 kg (4410–5510 lb) greasy. In the 1991/92 season, 98 471 tonnes (69.1%) of sale lots were main lot, 18 905 (13.2%) were interlotted, and the remaining 17.7% (25 192 tonnes) were binned.

Once the sale lots have been assembled, the wool broker arranges for them to be sampled and tested. The grab samples are displayed at the auction centres, together with the test certificates which provide evidence of the lot identification and the test results. For three days (two if the sale is less than 1600 lots) New Zealand wool buyers have the opportunity to assess the grab samples visually. This supplements the information given on the test certificate and the auction catalogue prepared by the wool broker. In New Zealand even the catalogue must give information in a form laid down by the New Zealand Wool Board: growers' brand, net weight, sale lot number, measurement data of clean wool yield, diameter, Schlumberger dry combing yield, and vegetable matter content. The reason for this precision, the Board argues, is that given the high rate of sales that occur, the buyers must have all the information they need to bid on immediate display. The catalogue leaves a column for them to record their own valuation information and their limit price, see Fig. 7.1.

On sale day, each wool broking firm in turn conducts the auction of their clients' wool. The wool broker/auctioneer identifies the lot by number and calls for bids, which cannot be advanced by less than one cent/kg (greasy). The lot is sold to the highest bidder, the buyer and price being announced by the auctioneer on the fall of the hammer. If a lot fails to reach the wool grower's reserve price, it is passed in and may be purchased by the highest bidder by negotiation after the auction, or reoffered for sale at a later auction. Payment is required within fourteen days (prompt day), at which time the wool becomes the responsibility of the buyer. Proceeds of the sale are paid to the grower up to 14 days after sale, less deductions for brokers' charges and various levies.

After the auction the broker receives instructions from the

ChCh Sale 19 Season 1991 92 Date 7 November 1991 Page 33										
Brand	Net Weight	Lot	YLD S.D.	MIC V.M.	Description	Bales	Valuation	Price	Buyer
ASCHWORTH KIWI D1179	617	CH TS 2662	74.0 71.1	18.9 0.9	X65.4 Y67.2 Z68.2 EX F MER AA	4			
	375	CH TS 2662	76.4 72.6	19.2 1.5	X66.4 Y68.6 Z69.5 MER 2TH	2			
	590	CH TS 2663	75.5 72.6	19.6 1.0	X67.2 Y69.3 Z70.1 EX F MER W AA	4			
INNISKILLEN 10 OMI GLENDALE 7	3112	CH TA 2664	75.2 73.7	33.1 0.1	X61.3 Y62.9 Z60.5 ROM H AA	17			
SEAVIEW KIWI B496	1249	CH TA 2665	79.9 78.6	35.9 0.1	X64.2 Y65.9 Z65.3 M COR H AA	9			
CAIRNHILL	1063	CH TA 2666	79.9 78.6	35.9 0.1	X60.7 Y62.4 P/S Z59.6 ROM E	7			
520 G2 MJP67	958	CH TA 2667	71.0 69.1	32.1 0.3	X55.9 Y57.4 Z50.4 X 1ST PCS	6			
543 IXU35	930	CH TA 2668	70.4 64.2	29.2 2.9	X56.6 Y58.3 Z51.6 1/2 D/F	7			
555 G5 VOC75	1704	CH TA 2668	68.8 67.1	35.2 0.2	X58.6 Y60.1 Z56.5 X CRT	10			

7.1 Example of a page from a sale catalogue (source: Wools of New Zealand).

exporter as to what is to be done with the wool. If it is to be exported greasy, the buyer's instructions will contain details of the shipping brand to be applied to each brand, the name of the ship and the sailing date. The broker in New Zealand is then responsible for delivering the consignment to one of the eight central wool facilities for preparation for shipping. If the wool is to be scoured before export, the exporter's instructions will contain details of all lots included in each delivery and which scour is to process the wool. The scour will package the scoured wool by compressing it into dense bales ready for shipment. In all cases, certificates will be required (see Chapter 2).

During the world recession, question marks were raised over the auction system and the percentage of wool sold at auction began to

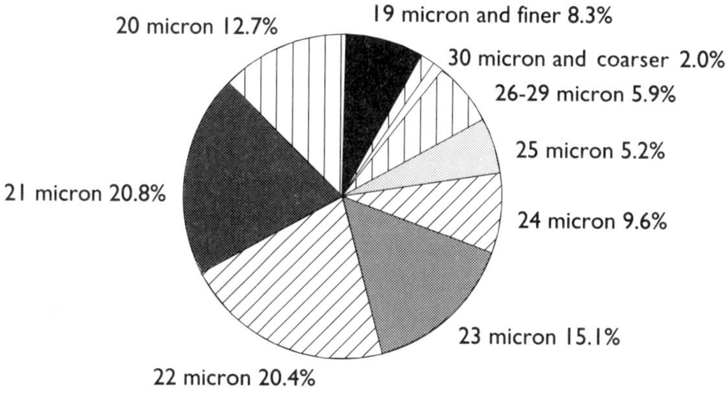

7.2 Composition of wool sold in Australia at auction, 1992/93 (source: National Council of Wool Selling Brokers of Australia).

slide slightly, but once prices started to rise again in 1994 these criticisms evaporated and the auction system remains the most important for the sale of Australian and New Zealand wool. The composition of wool sold at auction in Australia is shown in Fig. 7.2.

The rise in prices and continued scepticism over objective measurements have meant that sale by description remains a long-term goal rather than an immediately feasible achievement. Nevertheless the auction system, for wool and tea (which sell by auction) in comparison with cotton and coffee (which sell by futures and spot – an enlightening comparison) entails heavy costs. Growers have tremendous insecurity of income and the reserve price idea encourages the artificial notion of a 'fair' price for wool, making the system less responsive to demand changes. The administration is detailed and expensive, and above all the system, by comparison to a futures and spot market based system, does not encourage additional liquidity into the market and therefore make possible the laying off of risk. As Raymond Michell, chairman of the largest Australian wool company, observed: 'The dominance of the auction system means that for most growers it is simply a matter of putting the wool up when it was available, waiting for it to come up at auction and taking whatever price happened to apply on the day' (*Wool Record*, 1994).

Slipe wool

Wool from lambs and sheep sold for slaughter is the property of the abattoir, which pays the grower for the skin according to a standard schedule. The abattoir, in turn, sells it as slipe wool directly to an exporter, scourer or mill. Mazamet wools are similar to slipes but the separation process is biological instead of chemical. Most Australian and New Zealand exporters deal in slipe wool, but there are also smaller firms which specialise in all facets of slipe wool production and processing. Slipe can be purchased *tel quel* (i.e. greasy) but about 70% of production is scoured together with other wools (or slipes) to produce blends to suit the processing and product requirements of manufacturers.

Private sales

There are approximately 140 registered private wool buyers in New Zealand, many of whom are represented nationally in New Zealand by the Federation of New Zealand Wool Merchants. In Australia there are approximately 200 private treaty merchants. Private buying companies usually buy only a very small percentage (under 10%) of their own wool either from other merchants or from auctions - the rest they source direct from farmers, usually selling on to a wool exporter or directly to domestic mills. Sometimes it is reoffered in the auction system.

Sales by individual private wool buyers range from 100 to 30 000 bales a year. The percentage of New Zealand wool sold to private buyers has varied from 18–26% since the 1980s. The prices paid by private buyers are generally closely related to auction prices. While the grower may receive a slightly lower price than the wool would fetch at auction, there will be some savings on transportation costs and brokerage fees, as well as the immediate payment benefit to cash flow, rather than waiting fourteen days. The low sheep numbers and depressed prices of the 1991–94 period were undoubtedly an incentive to the private buying system. Farmers were looking for a quick return and exporters supported private buyers because they can supply wool quickly, without having to wait until the next auction and without the same exposure to market fluctuations and currency problems.

Forward trading

Forward buying and selling of wool works in the same way as for any other commodity. The purpose is to ease planning by agreeing a price in advance of the time of trade, a price which reflects mutual bargaining power as well as expectations of the future spot (present) value of the commodity. So, for example, a grower may sell his wool for delivery in three months' time at a price of A$5 per kg. A deposit may or may not be payable, which effectively slightly alters the forward price, mainly again depending on relative bargaining power – defaults in the wool trade are much rarer than in many other commodity trades, so this is not an important factor. In three months' time, the wool is supplied and all the A$5, or the balance, is payable to the grower. In the meantime, the sure knowledge of the arrival of the A$5 per kg has improved the grower's position with his bank at a time of year when there may be an overdraft; and the merchant has in turn been able to search for retail clients for the wool in the sure knowledge of when and how much wool, and at what price, he has contracted to buy.

The New Zealand Wool Board states that 'Most trades [for the export of wool] are done on a forward basis' (*Annual Report*, 1993). Even some small private wool buyers, such as Le Marquand Wools in New Zealand, buy wool forward from farmers as recommended by the Arthur D Little report. The report stated: 'Forward buying of greasy wool will be encouraged, thus allowing growers to lock in prices' (p 30) and some forward selling of wool up to three months in advance is used – in the case of Le Marquand, 20% of their clients sold wool to them on a forward basis in 1992, after having started the option in 1986, and they expected the percentage to continue to rise.

Wool futures markets

In theory, wool futures create forward pricing opportunities for wool producers, merchants, mills and commodity speculators. By using futures in conjunction with the auction system and direct marketing, wool futures advocates contend, producers and processors alike can secure the income they will receive from the physical wool. Hedging with wool futures enables growers to protect sales and stocks by locking in on the downside and merchants and manufacturers on the upside. Wool futures contracts now tend to be settled in cash so both hedgers and speculators can hold contracts until maturity without the problems associated with physical delivery. The wool can still be sold through the auction system or by private treaty.

The principle underlying the futures market is, in fact, straightforward: sell futures – at whatever price the market thinks the spot price will be at that date, a price which will converge on the spot price as the expiry date of the contract approaches – and if the price of wool falls, one benefits by the amount of the fall; buy futures, and if the price of wool rises, one benefits by the amount of the gain. Conversely, sell futures and if the price rises, one loses by the amount of the gain; buy futures, and if the price falls, one loses by the amount of the fall. The contracts are not directly between buyer and seller; there is an intermediary, the Clearing House (the Sydney Futures Exchange (SFE) has had its own since 1990), which guarantees every contract and avoids counterparty risk; all futures markets are heavily regulated. There are no disadvantages, though: changes in price are paid and required every day (so the Clearing House minimises its risk) and an initial interest-bearing deposit of about 10% is required.

The SFE published an interesting comparison – from their perspective – of the difference between forward trading and futures contracts, see Table 7.1.

So why does the international wool trade not enthusiastically adopt futures trading? At one time, it did. The SFE was established in 1960 as the Sydney Greasy Wool Futures Exchange to provide risk transfer and price discovery for the wool industry. Although not the first wool futures market, Sydney had by 1964 become the largest wool futures market in the world, overtaking the other markets in Belgium, New York, France and the UK. The success of the market was attributable to the fact that the futures market provided a regulated means of price discovery for greasy wool, an associated merchanting mechanism through physical delivery and an effective risk management system. Sources of business, of which approximately two-thirds came from outside Australia, and principally from Japan, the UK, Europe, South Africa and New Zealand, included merchants, traders, wool buying houses and mills hedging stocks or forward sales, professional commodity traders and growers. The latter accounted for only 5% of the open interest at best.

Active participation by growers was not encouraged by the banks or the majority of wool selling brokers which resulted in the majority of the growers concluding that the futures market was basically all about speculation and not hedging. Matters rolled along like this for about two decades. However, the establishment of the statutory price support mechanism of the Reserve Price Scheme and subsequent

Table 7.1 Comparing futures and forward contracts

	Futures	**Forwards**
Purpose:	Transfer of price risk to another party through forward pricing.	Transfer of price risk to another party through forward pricing.
Contract specifications:	Standardised (quantity grade, expiry). Basis adjustment for other grades.	Tailored to requirements of buying and selling parties.
Negotiation:	By competitive open outcry (price only).	By private treaty (all terms and conditions).
Price:	Reflects storage costs and seasonality of production.	Reflects storage costs and seasonality and may reflect perceived credit risk.
Market information:	On-line (immediately) and continuously available.	Not necessarily public.
Counterparty credit risk:	Minimised through Clearing House guarantee and reflected in smaller buy/sell spreads.	As assessed by the buying and selling parties and accounted for in offered prices.
Customer protection:	Corporations Law (ASC). SFE regulations. SFE Fidelity Fund.	Non-regulated market.
Market integrity:	Provided through Clearing House guarantee ($A100 million), SFE trading regulations and net tangible assets of Fxchange Members.	Determined by counterparty credit risk.
Trading flexibility	Movement in and out of market facilitated through: –role of Clearing House. –standardised contracts. –market liquidity.	Premature cancellation may incur financial compensation. Must trade with original counterparty.
Financial obligation:	Initial and variation margins (initial margin is refunded at close-out).	Usually full amount on delivery.
Cash flow:	Initial and variation margins to maintain market value.	No cash flow before maturity.
Delivery:	Seldom occurs.	Always occurs.
Marketing result:	Net price from separate futures and physical transactions.	Fixed price for deferred delivery under one contract.

Source: SFE

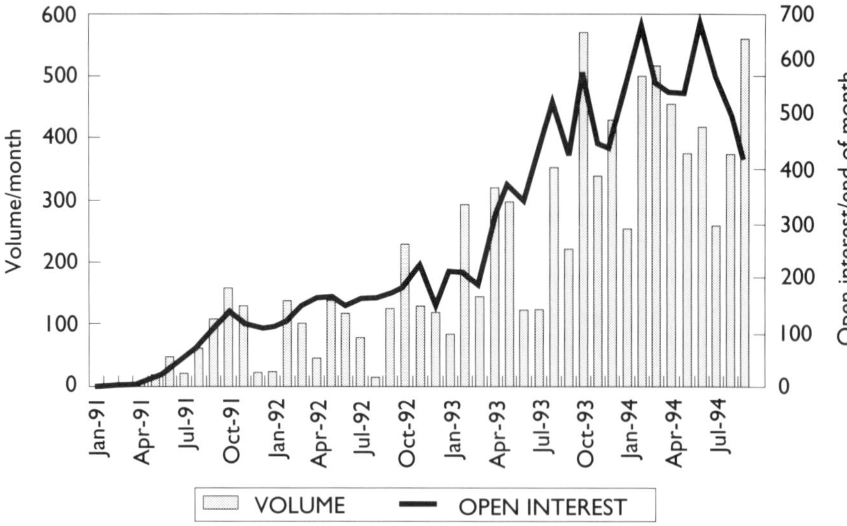

7.3 The Sydney Wool Futures Contract, 1991–94 (source: Sydney Futures Exchange).

price stability led to a steady decline in trading volumes. Having seen a record 186 000 contracts in 1973, equivalent to approximately 3m farmbales, turnover declined rapidly with only one year, 1980, appearing to turn the tide. By the mid-1980s, volume had declined to less than 7000 contracts - approximately equivalent to one week's turnover in the current auction system. In 1986, the SFE made the strategic decision to change the contract from physical delivery to cash settlement based on the Australian Wool Corporation's 22 micron indicator for the last day of trading, calculated to the nearest whole cent per kg, but by 1990 volume had shrunk to virtually nothing. Volumes for recent months have perked up variably to hover around the 400–600 mark per month, implying a daily volume of between 20 and 30. Open interest has increased too, see Fig.7.3.

There is some evidence that the volume of trade is related to uncertainty as to future prices, which is encouraging, there has been a brief inverted market (nearby trading at a premium to distant) and volumes do show a slight upward trend, but these volumes are still extremely small by comparison to the physical volume of wool produced in Australia. The SFE announced in mid-1994 that the contract would indeed return to physical delivery, based on a 21-micron fleece wool with a deliverable tolerance of wools between 20–22 microns (see specifications in Table 7.2 below). In terms of marketing, the SFE began to stress in 1994 that futures were a risk management tool for merchants and price taking financial institutions, whilst options and commodity swaps were more suitable for end-

Table 7.2 Wool futures contract specifications

Futures	Size, kg	Tick size	Months	Hours	Delivery
TCE	500	¥500	Six months	09.20, 11.20, 14.20, 15.20	Physical
OTE	500	¥500	Six months	09.20, 11.20, 14.20, 15.20	Physical
NTE	500	¥500	Six months	09.40, 10.50, 13.30, 14.40	Physical
SFE (new)	2500 of Merino combing fleece (*)	TBA	Feb, Apr, Jun, Aug, Oct and Dec up to 18 months ahead	TBA	Physical
SFE (old)	2500	A$10	Feb, Apr, Jun, Aug, Oct and Dec up to 18 months ahead	10.30 – 12.30 14.00 – 16.00 *	Cash
NZFOE	2500¢/kg indicator	NZ$25	Bi-monthly	10.00 – 12.00 13.05 – 15.00	Cash

NB: There are currently no wool options contracts traded on any exchange worldwide.
* The contract has, since 1989, been able to be traded on the electronic trading system of the SFE, SYCOM, from 4.40pm to 4.00am.

users and producers whose risk position changes only perhaps annually. But there is no option contract; however much analysts suggest that the wool industry could benefit from them, SFE has no intention of introducing them before the new wool futures contract is working properly, because futures prices determine options prices.

It is worth noting that in the meantime the SFE has diversified into financial futures markets. These have soared ahead, the exchange now having members from all the international finance houses as well as Australian companies and being one of the top ten financial futures exchanges in the world. This mirrors the worldwide advance of financial, in comparison to commodities, futures contracts. Officially the SFE remains confident, and has no intention of de-listing the contract, looking enviously at New York's cotton futures contract as an example of what could, perhaps, one day be done for wool in Australia. It was probably unrealistic of the Garnaut Committee to imagine that Wool International would manage or franchise a wool contract to Sydney or New York, however, or as the Wool Council of Australia suggested, 'play a crucial role in developing risk management such as futures, options and bonds'; that is not how it works in the futures industry: *the exchanges are the only guaranteed winners every time*. Perhaps the SFE also believes that a futures exchange in Sydney really has to have a wool contract as a symbol of the historical antecedents of futures markets.

Meanwhile in May 1991, the New Zealand Futures and Options Exchange (NZFOE) introduced New Zealand Wool Futures Contracts (WFC) but the same fate awaited it. Trading in WFC has been sporadic and only low volumes occur. The NZFOE has been owned by the Sydney Futures Exchange since 1992 and the fate of the two contracts can be considered together.

The view of the NZWB is that 'Futures trading in NZ has not been successful. This is because of grower resistance or lack of acceptance, the lack of speculators, and possibly ignorance of the benefits to be gained in risk management' (NZWB communication to the author, 19/11/93). By contrast the NZFOE, where the contract is still listed – although the options were suspended in June 1992, having only traded in May 1991 – believes that one important reason that the contract does not fly is that the NZWB was able to trade the contracts, to the suspicion of other players. Fear of the NZWB having inside information, particularly of stockpile sales, has in the past dampened most wool exporters' enthusiasm for the contract. The exchange also suggests uncharitably that exporters are also reluctant to trade the contract as the possibilities of manipulation and profit are considerably less than in the previous contract.

In South Africa, where there was a single-channel marketing system for 21 years until its abolition in June 1993, there has never been a history of wool futures.

This contrasts with the situation in Japan, the country with the only actively traded wool futures markets. The Tokyo Commodity Exchange (TCE), founded in 1958, the Nagoya Textile Exchange (NTE) founded in 1951 and the Osaka Textile Exchange (OTE) founded in 1953 all trade a wool contract. Worsted yarn is traded on these exchanges with two sessions each in the morning and afternoon daily. The Japanese Wool Importers' Association, describes these contracts as 'murky' and certainly a great deal of uncertainty hangs over them. Largely, this is the result of their history. About 40–50 years ago, wool futures trading was buoyant, accentuated by the recovery in the Japanese economy immediately after World War II. Textiles was a growth sector. During its heyday the futures exchange was used by spinners for hedging of sales and by weavers for purchase of yarn, but there was a growing perception that speculation was rampant. As a result, spinners, traders and weavers were forced to close, made bankrupt and disappeared from the market place. The futures market was biting the hand that fed it, and pressure rose for futures trading to be stopped as it was detrimental to bona fide sellers and buyers in forming sensible prices between them. There was a great deal of pressure on spinners' offer prices calculated from actual production costs from futures prices manipulated by the speculators, making planning difficult; these markets are frequently held to have been instrumental in the subsequent damage to the Japanese textile industry that followed the boom period - although rising relative costs to other Asian producers look a more plausible culprit.

Ambitious spinners in the 1970s determined that they would sell yarn on a fixed basis to protect their interests, thereby avoiding the volatile prices that the speculators were causing. Other spinners followed, and the futures markets, by contrast, lost ground as the speculators had to play one another. At the time of writing, all spinners negotiate their prices with customers on either spot or a long-term forward basis; vertical integration within the industry has progressed and yarn trading has tended to reduce as a result, focusing increasingly on speciality yarns. The wool futures markets of Japan have therefore reduced commensurately in importance, and although they still exist, T Ueno of the Japan Wool Importers Association states that their function is minimal in forming reasonable prices.

Currently, volumes on all three exchanges vary tremendously, but usually two contracts at least trade over 100 000 lots annually. The TCE state that these markets, which are in woollen yarn, are consistently 'in fact quite dull' amounting to only 1% of all commodities futures traded in 1992. Noting however that these markets have performed better than those in Auckland or Sydney, Shigeo Tanuma of the TCE suggested 'the reason might be that there is a larger amount of funds for speculation in Japan' (letter to the author, 20/1/93) and some of it inevitably finds its way into the wool futures markets. Tanuma noted that the Tokyo market tended to be consumer-oriented and that the main market users were speculators. The TCE, it is worth noting, has almost 200 member firms. In Osaka, cradleland of the spinning and yarn retailing industry of Japan, the market is produce-oriented and the users are predominantly spinners, yarn retailers and speculators. The same situation and users prevails for the Nagoya market. None of these markets is properly understood by Western traders and it is not thought likely that a very significant proportion of the trades in these markets come from Western traders. Moreover, as the markets are actually in woollen yarn rather than greasy wool, substantial gaps can open where potential hedgers could be caught both ways.

Table 7.2 shows wool futures contract specifications for the Tokyo Commodity Exchange, the Osaka Textile Exchange, the Nagoya Textile Exchange, the Sydney Futures Exchange and the New Zealand Futures and Options Exchange. Table 7.3 shows the par delivery specifications and the deliverable tolerances for the Sydney wool futures contract.

Table 7.3 Par delivery specifications and deliverable tolerances for the Sydney wool futures contract

Par delivery specifications	
Weight	2500 clean weight kilograms of Merino combing fleece
Fibre diameter	21.0 microns
Vegetable matter	1.0%
Staple length	90 mm
Staple strength	35 n/ktx
Colour	Good
T/M style	Good
Contract months	Bi-monthly structure similar to the current contract i.e. Feb, Apr, Jun, Aug, Oct, Dec out eighteen months.
Deliverable tolerances	
Weight	2400 to 2600 clean weight kilograms calculated using Schlumberger Dry T&N yield. All lots in the deliverable parcel must have yield greater than 62%.
Fibre diameter	19.6 to 22.5 microns (i.e. 1.0 microns either side of the 21 micron category). The deliverable parcel must contain wools within 1.0 micron tranches i.e. wool making up the parcel can be between 19.6m and 20.5m or between 20.6m and 21.5m or between 21.6 and 22.5m and not a combination of wools derived from different micron tranches.
Vegetable matter	Less than 2.0%.

Staple length	Greater than 80 mm and less than 100 mm.
Staple strength	Greater than 30 n/ktx (discount for wools below 35 n/ktx and no premium over 35 n/ktx). Wool of less than 35 n/ktx shall be required to have greater than 65% of position of break at the tip of base.
Colour	Good.
T/M style	Spinners, best and good (no premium for wool of spinners or best or best top making style).

Wool freight

The isolation of the major wool producing countries, in particular Australia and New Zealand, from the major consuming nations has in the past made shipping a very important part of the marketing chain; it remains so even though closer Asian destinations are taking ever larger proportions of Australian and New Zealand wool. The cost of shipping New Zealand wool alone to the market place in 1990/91 was $66m, which included dumping, and container packing, delivery to load port, ocean freight and final delivery. In 1992/93 the AWC estimated freight costs for wool at $25.74 including brokers' profits, with $9.88 additional for dumper and exporter, out of a final cost of $690 at mill. In the 1992/93 season the average cost for shipping a bale of wool – based on a container holding 120 bales of scoured wool weighing 145 kg (320 lb) each was:

- NZ$24.6 to Japan;
- NZ$29 to Europe;
- NZ$29.5 to China;
- NZ$34 to Nepal;
- NZ$35.5 to Eastern seaboard USA.

In the past, the Boards negotiated freight rates and conditions on most shipping routes on behalf of the exporters, who advised the Boards of their requirements through organisations such as the New Zealand Freight Council. In 1991 in New Zealand two replacement organisations, the Wool Industry Freight Policy Group and the Wool Industry Freight Council, were established, to provide wool industry groups with opportunities for direct involvement in the development of freight policies and shipping arrangements.

In New Zealand, to facilitate the internal handling and transportation of wool for export, wool is sent to eight central wool facilities, located in the main wool aggregation centres of Auckland, Napier, Wanganui, Wellington, Christchuch, Timaru, Dunedin and Invercargill. In Australia, similarly, there are facilities in Sydney, Melbourne, Brisbane, Adelaide, Fremantle and Launceston, and in South Africa at Cape Town, Port Elizabeth, Durban and East London; all South African wool shipments are containerised. Each of these facilities is operated by an individual company or a consortium of companies involved in the wool industry (wool brokers, scourers, shipping companies, etc). Some 50% of Australian exports are dumped by companies with a shareholding of primarily woolbrokers and minority involvement by transport companies, and a further 10% by companies based in Melbourne or Sydney with a shareholding of wool exporting or trading companies. Their primary functions are to co-ordinate the local wool flow for export and to carry out dumping and container packing. Dumping involves compressing up to three farm bales of wool (approximately 160 kg (353 lb) each) and banding them together with metal straps to form a package which takes up the space normally occupied by one standard bale. This process can be applied to both greasy and scoured wool. Depending on the size of the dump press, up to 18 tonnes (90–120 bales) can be packed into a 6m container. Single bales can also be compressed to a third of their original size, having the additional advantage that they can still be handled manually, unlike double and triple dumped bales which require mechanical handling.

The central wool facility will call for the wool from the various suppliers (wool brokers, scourers, wool stores, etc) allowing sufficient time for dumping, container packing and delivery to the container port prior to the arrival of the ship. In New Zealand there are only four fully equipped container ports – Auckland, Wellington, Lyttleton (Christchurch) and Port Chalmers (Dunedin). There is a certain amount of internal transport of wool in containers. In the past, the cost of this aggregation was usually included in the ocean freight rate charged by the shipping companies. This is no longer the case, with internal distribution costs now being charged as a separate item of freight. Costs have been cut and at least one dumping facility shut in 1993.

The Wool Commodity Group comprises representatives of the Australian Council of Wool Exporters, the Wool Council of Australia and the Australian Wool Processors' Council, together with members of the Interlaine Freight Committee, who represent European importers and manufacturers. Areas covered by these contracts are the Mediterranean, North West Continent and the UK, together with parts of Eastern Europe, amounting to about 40% of Australia's wool exports. Most Australian wool exporters seem reasonably happy with current freight rates, although there remains a belief that the overall costs could still be reduced. Currently the New Zealand Wool Board's partnership with the wool industry in respect of freighting is carried out through the Freight Policy Group and this continues to function effectively as a shipping conference although the NZWB believes that exporters should take on this responsibility entirely amongst themselves and that the Board should relinquish its long-standing rights to negotiate exclusive shipping arrangements and it is in the process of organising this.

Wool packing

After sorting wool is pressed into bales, which in New Zealand must weigh between 100–200 kg (av 160 kg - 353 lb). In the past, New Zealand wool bales had separate caps but from 1992/93 onwards these were replaced completely by capless packs. Bales are generally made of woven polyethylene fabric, and there are quality specifications laid down by the Wool Boards in each country. Bales are also almost always marked with number, farm identification and some description of the wool. Dense baling is used to compress scoured wool into a package weighing 350–500 kg (772–1100 lb) so as to maximise the quantity able to fit into a standard shipping container. The new generation high dense baling machines facilitate the packing of 17–18 tonnes of scoured wool in one 6m (20′) container. AusTop compresses tops into the same sized container and gets about 18 tonnes. The freight cost reductions of dense baling can be obtained even by those scours which do not have dense baling machines (most now do) by tripacking - using high pressure dump presses at the central wool facilities to compress up to three bales into one compact package. High density scoured wool is kept compressed by steel bands rather than the wrap itself.

Control of contamination is vital. A typical large Italian mill such as Reda can spend over $3m annually removing contaminates just from the polypropylene or hessian packaging in which wool is presented. Manufacturers, such as Rexlane Spa, are concerned at this level of expenditure. Already in Germany and shortly in other EU countries goods will not be allowed to be imported except in reusable or recyclable material. Information on what kinds of contaminants are most frequently found was collated by CSIRO from carbonised wool from two Australian mills. Plastics were a major offender accounting for a third of all contaminants. Feathers, though not man-made, also accounted for a third. Baling twine is another culprit. A study by CSIRO-Michell found contaminants in one-sixth of 132 000 bales processed during the survey period. The AWTA is screening all yield and vegetable matter tested lots for in-bale contamination free of charge during 1993–95. Plastic bags are also difficult to recycle, and this is of increasing importance, especially given the EU objective of ensuring that by as early as 1996 a minimum of 50% of all packaging waste in Europe will need to be recovered and at least 15% recycled.

All this initially led to the idea of using nylon packs, where contamination would not cause serious problems even if it occurred. But the severe cost differential – $30 per pack compared to $8–10 for a high density polyethylene pack – was always bound to limit the scope of this endeavour, and the Australian Council of Wool Exporters has rejected the proposal of a A$10 packaging fee to be paid by processors to wool growers. Some 25 000 plus bales will, however, be packed in nylon in 1994/95. In addition most scoured wool, at least from New Zealand, is to be exported to Europe by the year 2000 in woollen wraps developed by WRONZ in conjunction with Quirke Export Ltd of Christchurch, New Zealand, which are expected to be priced between nylon and synthetic bags. Exporters are keen to try to move away from the polyolefin synthetic packs which are currently used for both scoured and greasy wools. This change has been paralleled by a move towards paper bale dividers and outsorts bags, developed by AWRAP, in the mid-1990s. The problem is being taken increasingly seriously; the American Sheep Industry Association held a conference specifically on the subject in May 1993 and there is constant attention to the problem in Australia and New Zealand. The New Zealand Wool Board has continued to devolve some of its statutory powers to the wider industry, now continuing to publish industry-agreed standards but no longer checking or approving individual wool pack exports.

The industry says that all bales are inspected to ensure that their packaging meets industry standards – bales which do not are to be returned for repair or repacking. Damaged bales which give inadequate protection to their contents, or which are illegibly branded, can be refused at any point from the farm gate to the ship, the cost being borne by the last handler. The final point of inspection is usually the central wool facilities (in New Zealand) or source packers. But in Europe there remains the feeling, expressed by Luca Giovannelli of Rexlane Spa in 1993, that 'the problem has not been satisfactorily resolved and a great deal still needs to be done.' (*Wool Record*, 1993).

CHAPTER

8

The players in the international wool trade

Wool companies

Probably one of the most elusive aspects of international trade in any commodity is determining the policies, achievements and market share of the top companies involved in it. This necessarily involves matching readily available and detailed international statistics with much more skeleton company information in often different categories. International trade in wool is no exception.

In Australia, for example, the industry starts with the farmer, or wool grower, who shears and consigns his wool to a wool selling broker. Wool brokers arrange the pre-sale handling and post-sale dispatching of the wool, and conduct the auction on behalf of their farmer clients. In Australia there are some 55 wool selling brokers of which the largest are Elders Ltd and Dalgety Australia Ltd. Most brokers selling through the auction system are represented through the National Council of Wool Selling Brokers of Australia. Wool brokers do not own the wool, they only act as selling agents, charging brokerage fees which cover receiving, weighing and sampling, costs, storage, cataloguing, insurance, sale costs, delivery, etc. But they do perform a series of services: they receive wool from the grower, perform grab sampling, weighing and core sampling (under supervision of a registered test house officer), warehouse the bales, lot the wool for auction, prepare the sale catalogue, display samples, appraise the wool, deliver wool to the dump, and optionally carry out bulk classing, re-classing, interlotting, sampling of wool not sold under sale by sample and dumping prior to shipment.

There were, in 1994, ten registered firms of wool brokers in New Zealand, the two largest having branches in the main aggregation centres. Amongst these New Zealand brokers, two of the most important are Wrightsons Dunedin and Reid Farmers. The former handles 150 000 bales of wool annually - up to 2500 bales daily at the peak of the season. Wool is sorted by the company into lines, catalogued and tested. Reid Farmers is slightly smaller, handling between 85-100 000 bales annually, one-third of which is sold through the Dunedin selling centre. As brokers, both Wrightsons and Reid Farmers also offer farmers advice on clip preparations, breeding and sheep selection. They also have binning systems where wool can be sorted into particular types or by micron.

There are farmed co-operatives in New Zealand, such as the Drysdale Carpet Wool Co-operative Ltd, which sells most Drysdale wool, either directly to New Zealand or to overseas mills or their agents, administering a system of wool handling, sales and payment for some 450 growers, or the East Coast Co-Op based in Dannevirke, which has worked as a co-operative for twenty years. There are over 400 farmer shareholders, a scour, brokering service, exporting company and transport arm. The co-operative, as well as selling at auction/private sale also contracts directly with the New Zealand Wool Spinner's carpet yarn plant in Dannevirke. Growth has been steady at about 10% per annum since 1985.

In New Zealand, as in Australia, there are wool-scouring companies - some 18 in New Zealand, of which about half are commission scouts and the other half merchants themselves owned by the exporters. Commission wool scourers scour wool on behalf of local and locally based overseas wool exporters. So the wool broker generally prepares the wool for auction, although the valuation of the wool at auction is carried out by wool exporters - either merchants in their own right or brokers acting for others. There were, in 1994, 22 scouring plants in New Zealand scouring 70% of New Zealand wool and with the capacity to scour the whole clip. In Australia, there were 29 local processors. More wool is now being scoured domestically before export although over-capacity has been a problem. The IWS and domestic boards press for more wool to be exported in a scoured form as it adds value to the product and provides much needed work for the domestic scouring industry. The NZWB estimates that freight costs can be cut by 25% through scouring.

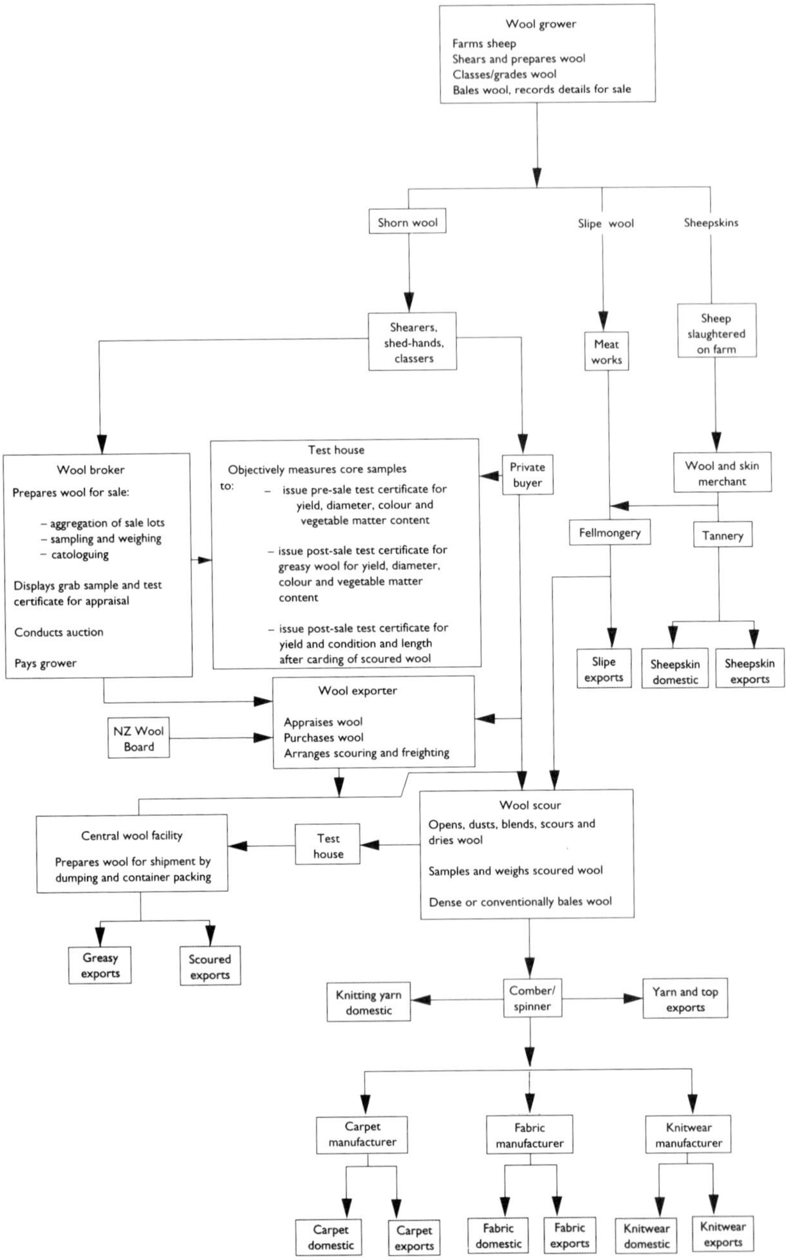

8.1 Relative positions of trading firms involved in the wool industry (source: New Zealand Wool Board).

The essential participating companies in the international trade, however, are the wool merchant companies themselves. These companies are traders who, through their representatives in different countries, trade wool in different forms (see Fig. 8.1 for the position of the trading firms in the wool industry). They live or die by the wool trade: they can neither shift into sheepmeat, or another crop altogether nor can they source an alternative fibre. The NZWB states: 'The wool exporter buys wool at auction or directly from the farmer or another buyer, and sells to the overseas end user, directly or through a network of local agents' (*Annual Report*, 1993). The wool traded can be greasy, scoured, wool tops or carbonised wool. Through close work with the mills, a series of types and samples are established, which are used as a basis for sales and purchases to that particular client. Each delivery is expected to conform to the specifications as set out in the type sample. Negotiations are carried out either over the phone, by fax or by telex.

When the market is open the major companies quote prices for their clients' preferred wool types continuously. The offer prices are made after a close study of various factors which include market rates, the availability of the type being offered (including in the stockpile), the company's own long position (stock in hand) and international currency exchange rates. Once the price has been set by the company's traders, this is then passed on to clients who may be interested in the particular type of wool. The client returns views regarding the asking price, and the business, if secured, is finalised and a contract sent by courier. A shipment date and/or a date of arrival at mill is included in the contract. Wool suitable for this order must then be allocated either from stock, auction purchases or private purchases. Whereas in the past the typical wool exporter was once a representative or agent for an overseas mill or merchant, by the 1990s, 80% of the clip in Australia was being sold on a firm basis by exporters acting as principal. The exporter typically finances the transaction up to, and often well beyond, the time of arrival of the wool at destination, sometimes for more than a year, and after the contract is signed, any fluctuations in the market, shipping delays, currency fluctuations and buyer default must be borne by the wool exporting company, which is the trading bridge between producers and users.

Computer systems are assisting the larger wool companies in their selectivity and accuracy of response to the wool auctions. These systems work by picking up the wool catalogue of each selling broker on computer link. A series of price limits are then entered by the traders in the system with parameters regarding the specifications of the different orders. Averaging is common in any parcel as almost all wool has some different qualities. The averaging must be of micron, vegetable matter, top length, yield, additional measurements and price. The final average must correspond with the client's required type. With the auction selling approximately 250–300 lots per hour, all sale room bidders must be well trained and could be operating on up to 50 orders in one day. Any purchases that the company has made are then singled out on the computer and transmitted via modem to head office; these wools can be immediately paid for and ordered out for shipping. One of the difficulties in writing about international trade in any commodity, but especially for wool where the participants are quite open about the fact, is that the quality evaluation and trading technology is both improving and becoming more intrusive in the life of a typical commodity trader.

Wool merchants themselves suggest that wool companies are no different from any commodity trading company, identifying if there was any particular special feature a tendency towards a hands-on approach, by having a long-short position controlled by direct buying at wool auctions. This applies as much to an Australian wool company, such as Namkwong Trading (Australia) Pty Ltd as to UK companies based in the Bradford area (where UK wool companies are centered) bidding at the Bradford auctions held by the BWMB. Wool companies purchase wool for a number of reasons: firstly, for forward sale contracts, secondly, for indent purchases, which involve buying wool for a client on a commission basis. This helps the buyer and the processor to determine what is needed to make the most appropriate product. This is of major importance when Australian companies deal with fine wool spinners in Europe, with whom wool trading companies in Australia have worked for decades to produce a superior fabric. Negotiations for an indent purchase are usually carried out by phone, fax or telex as with usual business. Availability of the type which the client would like to buy is advised with an estimated cost per kilo. The customer may then place an order with the wool company to buy a certain quantity or range of quantities within a certain price range – which may be very narrow, with the result that no wool is obtained. Payments are usually made with an 'irrevocable letter of credit' but other methods are used, such as cash against documents, sight air draft, sight sea draft or term draft (30, 60 or 90 days) after sight of arrival. A third reason is buying for a stock position – this is most important for any trading operation anxious to increase their trading power. It allows the company to trade under 'prompt shipment' terms and is also useful as a hedge against rises in wool prices. Fourthly, large and some small processors will buy wool to feed their machinery running at full capacity – these include BWK

Germany and the Chargeurs group. The exporter offers wool for sale, specifying the price, type and delivery date, holding the offer for 24 hours or so to allow negotiations.

In all transactions, trading conditions must be clearly stated. Generally, the IWTO *General Agreement for Transactions in Scoured Wool, Tops and Carded Sliver* forms the basis for contracts. Normally a standard clause providing for arbitration in accordance with the IWTO Arbitration Agreement is included. In New Zealand there is a *Code of Practice for Objective Measurement and Raw Wool Marketing in New Zealand* which covers all aspects of sale by sample. Trading of wool internationally is usually in US dollars, but sterling and other major currencies are often used, and are subject to agreement between the exporter and the purchaser. Credit terms, financing, currency cover and payment methods are not standardised and are matters for mutual agreement between the buyer and exporter. Wool is usually sold on a CIF (cost, insurance, freight) basis, which effectively means that for the agreed price, it is the exporter's responsibility to cover the cost of preparation, packaging, transport to load port, insurance and shipping of the wool to the port nearest to, or nominated by, the purchaser.

There are other options: delivered to mill, where the exporter's responsibilities are the same as for CIF sales with the additional responsibility of transport costs from destination port to mill, C&F, where the exporter is responsible for all charges as for CIF, excluding insurance, and FOB (free on board) where the exporter is responsible for the cost of preparation, packaging and transport to load port only; costs for shipping and insurance are the responsibility of the purchaser. Wool exporters provide advice on the most suitable types of wool to buy, on shipping and on all the commercial aspects of their business. New clients usually agree on a sample provided by the exporter; once types suitable for the product range have been established, agreed reference samples are provided, against which deliveries can be matched. It is noticeable that at this stage the trade is much closer to sale by description than it is domestically at auctions.

Not all wool companies are alike, and the capacity to trade wool is influenced by the companies' size and structure. For example, during the 1992/93 season, Itochu Australia purchased over 400 000 bales of wool through the auction system Australia-wide. Some of the smaller companies bought as little as 50 bales. The bigger companies have several divisions: administration, trading, buying, shipping, documentation and finance. Small wool companies, by comparison, operate on smaller budgets and their employees are of necessity jacks-of-all-trades – yet are still wool specialists and have useful broad knowledge across the trade. Wool companies stress that their client base is gained and maintained with 'personal service and competitiveness', which means keen prices combined with personal contacts. In that the wool business is like any other international commodity trade.

Some Australian companies specialise in exporting to either China, Japan or Europe for example (G H Michell was the first wool exporter from Australia or New Zealand to open an office in Beijing, in 1989, and has followed with offices in Shanghai and Russia) where some have a broader range of clients and specialist language skills.

Overall the success of wool companies is largely determined by the level of service that they provide, since all can access much the same wool and all are effectively in competition with one another to some degree, both in the auction and worldwide with companies competing for market share. As to ownership, wool companies operating in Australia are owned by many different national and international companies. Although several are actually Australian (Ian Laycock Pty Ltd for example advertise that the Laycock family is in its 7th generation in the business), others have head offices in Japan, Korea, China, Denmark, France, Germany, Italy, the UK, the USA and Taiwan. All the companies of any size operating in the Australian wool market are members of the Australian Council of Wool Exporters. The figures in Table 8.1 show auction purchases for the 1993/94 season and therefore represent a reasonably recent indication of the relative size of the companies involved. Some of these companies are Japanese: the Japan Wool Industry Conference states that all the big Japanese trading firms are active in this field of business, noting especially Itochu, Marubeni, Kanematsu which has a continuing large presence at Australian auctions (the first Japanese company to be established in Australia) and Nissho-Iwai.

The largest wool trading company and the biggest international manufacturer of wool tops, with the biggest and growing market share, trading and processing wool in more than 20 countries and most importantly some price setting function for raw wool and finished textiles, and hence the processing margin, is Chargeurs Textiles, which as market leader can serve as an example of a wool trading operation. Total textile revenue has fallen in recent years, from a peak of FF10.7bn in 1988 to FF6.2bn in 1993, with ample restructuring featuring in this reduction. The wool trading and processing division has similarly performed as shown in Table 8.2.

There are three 'brand names' within the company: Hart, Otegui and Prouvost. Chargeurs Textiles is in turn part of the Chargeurs Group, a publicly owned French company which has a high shareholding in other areas, BSkyB for example, although still three-

Table 8.1 Auction purchases for Australia, 1993/94 season

Buyer	Total bales	Buyer	Total bales
1 Itochu Australia Ltd	353 337	48 Scanion Wool	5 329
2 Prouvost-Hart (Aust) P/L	277 819	49 de Tuety Harold P/L	3 757
3 Kanematsu Australia Ltd	256 904	50 Dynon Wools Aust P/L	3 714
4 Standard Wool (Aust) P/L	194 521	51 Excell Wool Traders	3 582
5 Booth Hill & New P/L	187 071	52 Chadron P/L	3 462
6 Marubeni Australia Ltd	164 182	53 Dewez JR & Co P/L	3 046
7 Compagnie d'Importation de Laine	161 470	54 Amity Wool	3 019
8 Nissho Iwai Australia Ltd	161 046	55 Quay Wool Service	2 713
9 Conagra Wool P/L	154 727	56 Riverton	2 444
10 Michell GH & Sons (Aust) P/L	152 039	57 Zubo Wool	1 903
11 Bloch & Behrens P/L	147 957	58 Whitbread & Co	1 866
12 Pindar Wool P/L	144 425	59 Global	1 782
13 Dewavrin Segared A P/L	136 978	60 Peters Wool Trading P/L	1 734
14 Gedge AS (Aust) P/L	130 968	61 Georgeson & Co	1 666
15 Modiano (Aust) P/L	125 679	62 Meredith Wool Co P/L	1 488
16 Lempriere (Aust) P/L	99 987	63 Unilan (Aust) P/L	1 271
17 Laycock Ian P/L	79 292	64 Jenkin Services	1 244
18 Associated Wool Exporters P/L	61 745	65 Australian Wool Processors	993
19 Dalgety International Trading	57 702	66 Montgomery Wools	917
20 Startoy P/L	51 478	67 Desplechin P/L	668
21 Kreglinger (Aust) P/L	50 428	68 Fibres (Aust) P/L	583
22 Redstone AW & Co	50 353	69 Betta Wools	548
23 Austrawool Exports P/L	45 628	70 Patchett A & E Wool P/L	520
24 Eckels WM P/L	39 820	71 Australian Fine Wool	402
25 Hughes FW P/L	36 394	72 Devereux JB & Co	381
26 Fox & Lollie (Aust) P/L	31 110	73 Scott Wool	264
27 Daell Textile Industrial Co Ltd	30 617	74 Fujikeori	237
28 Grist (Wool)	30 610	75 Chevlot	194
29 Wright Bruce (QLD) P/L	25 269	76 City Wool Centre	194
30 O'Brien FJ Wool P/L	23 471	77 James Stedman (Wool) P/L	112
31 Belgre D P/L	22 582	78 Sydney Technical College	96
32 Dawson Sons & Co P/L	22 364	79 Rolfe Wool Services	93
33 Stirling Sorting	22 064	80 JKC Wool Buing Services	88
34 Norfolk Wool	21 449	81 Camden Wool	80
35 Allen SH & Sons P/L	21 148	82 Onkaparinga Woollen Co Ltd	78
36 Morris PJ	19 952	83 Mariston College	62
37 New England Wool P/L	12 702	84 ACF WoolTraders	53
38 Newling Phillip P/L	12 008	85 Southern Wool Traders	28
39 Techwool Trading P/L	10 779	86 Toyamenka (Aust) P/L	25
40 Vicwool	10 767	87 Canobolas Topmaking Co Pty	18
41 Wool Brokering Services	10 075	88 Smythe V & H	12
42 Schneider G & Co	9 798	89 Penwool	10
43 Quality Wool Exports P/L	8 628	90 Becu Wool Trading	9
44 Vanlaine P/L	8 610	91 Toulemonde	5
45 Cable Robert G P/L	7 330	92 Morepen	3
46 Smith Henry B P/L	7 081	93 Loropiano	1
47 Garadon P/L	6 528	94 Titanus	1
Total			3 747 587

Source: IWS

Table 8.2 Wool trading and processing division, Chargeurs Textiles, FF million

	1988	1989	1990	1991	1992	1993
Sales	2828	5958	4622	4130	4119	3316
Operating income	212	216	73	290	270	84
Capital expenditure	147	90	138	82	142	200
Employees	2189	2923	3220	2814	2766	2696

Source: Chargeurs Textiles

quarters of the Group's operations are in textiles and wool trading and processing. The company describes itself as 'the world leader in wool trading and processing ... the world's largest wool trading and processing company, accounting for 20% of international exports .... The quality of our wool combing is key to the quality of finished products at the downstream stage of the textile industrial process' (company brochure). Experts suggest that this market share may be an underestimate, but not a very significant one - perhaps of some 5%. Its market share, though, is steadily increasing, making it the most important wool company to watch in the wool trade and indicating change in the structure of the international wool trade. But although the wool of sixty million sheep goes through the company's factories every year, this compares with overall statistics of something around 1bn sheep in the world altogether which suggests strongly the truth of the well-known generalisation that the international cotton trade is commercially some ten or more times more concentrated than the wool trade. This conceals and is explained by a Gini coefficient which can measure the distribution of numbers against size and therefore express a concentration ratio which is actually much steeper for wool: there is a lack of *medium-sized* wool trading companies (see Fig. 8.2) especially when one considers that the price setting function operates in some exponential function - at least a square - of the actual volume traded.

Chargeurs Textiles, like a few international cotton firms, is a truly global one, with an increasing emphasis on Asian operations stressed by the company as the European market contracted in 1992–93. Its degree of vertical integration is what most impresses - from top manufacture to woollen garment sales - distinguishing it not only from almost all comparable cotton and other commodity trading firms but also from its own competitors. The domination of the industry, as monopoly theory suggests, is acquired not just through an absolute

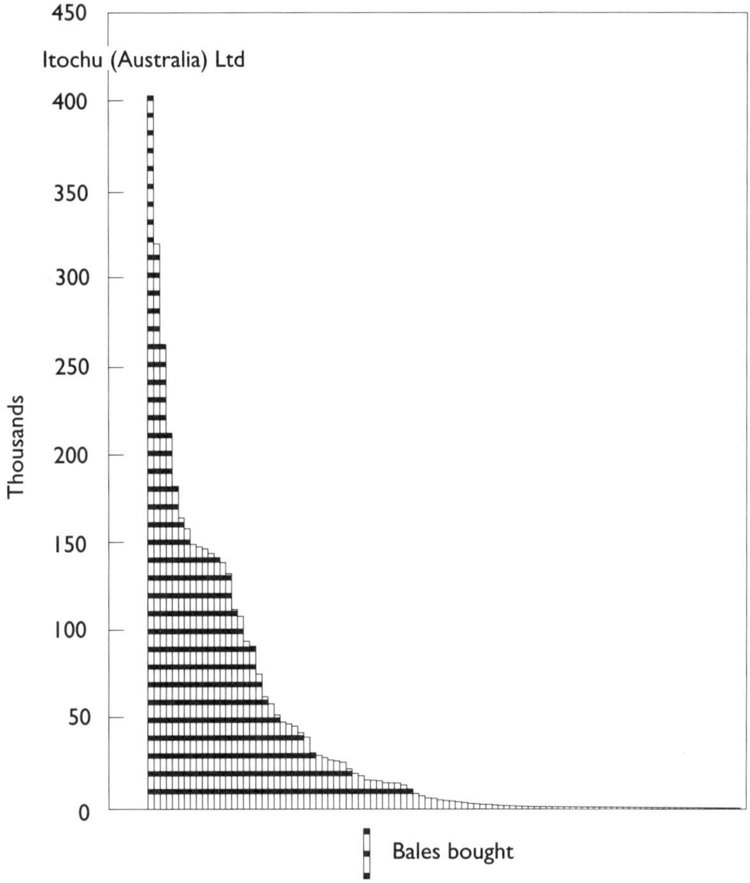

8.2 Companies at Australian wool auctions, 1/7/92–30/6/93.

monopoly (over 50%) at any one level, but through significant (over 25%) presence at a number of different levels.

In Argentina, for instance, there is Hart Wool Tops which processes some 5500 tonnes of wool tops annually, selling mainly in Asia and South America and concentrating on Patagonian wools. The Prouvost company has a production site at Jamestown in the USA, at which cut tops and shrinkproofing are two important technologies under development. Cape Tops, the commercial company of the group in South Africa, is mainly a services organisation to the South African wool industry itself, but there is also an export of greasy wool and wool tops made at the Cape of Good Hope Woolcombers plant situated near Port Elizabeth, which produces some 9000 tonnes of tops every year.

The really substantial subsidiaries, however, are still in Australasia and Europe. Prouvost Australia, the company's subsidiary, has been trading since 1920. Since 1981 the company has also been topmaking. The Riverina combing mill at Wagga Wagga has had its capacity doubled, now reaching 20 000 tonnes of combed wool and in 1994/95 a superfine combing plant is being introduced making the installation the largest topmaking plant in the entire Asia Pacific region; negotiations with BWK were taking place over this mill in 1994/95. The company is also active in scoured wool trading as well as in both standard and specialty tops such as Superwash and Soft Handle. In New Zealand Prouvost-Hart (NZ) is the country's largest exporter of greasy, scoured and slipe wools. The company wholly owns Fairlie Woolscour Ltd in Timaru, and has a substantial share in three other wool scouring companies. Auction purchases average 16 000 clean tonnes every year and further, private, purchases are made from growers in two of New Zealand's major production areas, Southland and Wairarapa. Prouvost-Hart is the company's buying and shipping subsidiary in Australia, whilst in New Zealand the company wholly owns one private buying operation and has half ownership of another, giving it a substantial presence in the market and the ability to adjust prices – bearing in mind that New Zealand is a price taker on wool (from Australia). The company themselves concede that 'As a market leader Prouvost Hart (NZ) Ltd accounts for 10% of New Zealand's total wool export sales, and ships to more than forty countries.' Industry experts have strongly suggested that 20% would be a more accurate figure, and this is an annual average. Some individual sales may be dominated by the company. The company also has a Hong Kong office which is the headquarters of the sales operation into Hong Kong itself, Taiwan, Indonesia, Korea, Japan and increasingly also Vietnam.

In Europe, Italy is still the largest importer of wool tops, accounting for almost 50% of Europe's wool consumption. The Italian subsidiary, Nuovalane, is joint owner with an Italian company of a mill near Biella, which produces 7500 tonnes of tops annually. In addition the company organises imports of worldwide tops, although the amount deliberately sourced from France against cost pressures is not disclosed by the company. The parent company is French, and France is still a leading wool processing country, producing some 80 000 tonnes of tops every year. Prouvost & Lefebvre, the French subsidiary, imports tops for French spinners from Australia, South America and South Africa, but typically for a French wool company the majority of its tops come from Peignage Amedee and Peignage de Mazamet Ausillon. The former, based in Roubaix since its formation in 1851, is the largest combing plant in the world with a capacity of more than 30 000 tonnes every year. The latter, formed in the 1970s, is based in the Mazamet area and specialises in this type of wool. Together just these two plants produce some 45% of French wool tops and have maintained their position despite the recession which has seriously affected French spinners.

In Germany the company has leapfrogged investment in the former West Germany, preferring to make major investments in the Leipziger Woll Kammerei, Germany's second largest wool processing plant, which has been re-equipped since acquisition in 1992 with plant equivalent to that in Chargeur's other French plants. There is also a specialist sales team in Leipzig, called Muffler, which is building a reputation for local spinners. There can be little doubt that the Leipzig organisation will return profits for the investment within a few years, at least by the end of the decade, and that the Leipzig operations will contribute a progressively larger element of Chargeur's European business in years to come. In Spain and also in Portugal, Prouvost Lefebvre and Peinje de Rio Llobregat have been working together to sell Chargeur wool since 1963; there is a mill near Sabadell, close to the southern French border. Prouvost Lefebvre acts as a specialist sales office for a limited range of high quality Merino tops especially suited for a weaving industry.

The UK remains the largest producer of wool in western Europe. Over 70m kg (154m lb) are produced annually. Prouvost has been established in Bradford since 1949, and a member of the Chargeur Group since 1988. Prouvost Bradford is a major producer of scoured British wool and tops, exporting annually at least 50% of its production. Hart Wool is also represented in Bradford and there is one other subsidiary company, G R Herron, which supplies wool tops to UK and overseas spinners.

The company says it aims to keep as many of its employees long-term as possible, and the published evidence of its personnel numbers suggests a core employee total of some 2000 in wool trading and processing who do indeed stay for five years or more. Numbers in the textile industry, however, predictably, are falling quite steadily. Nevertheless, some 3% of its personnel expenses annually is spent on training worldwide, whilst as with many larger trading companies – again a parallel with Dunavant is easily drawn – research and development, and above all production investment, have always been more important to market leader companies such as Chargeurs than to pure trading companies or wool producer companies. For example at present the improvement of waste disposal techniques is high on the R&D agenda and wool top plants are being expanded and improved. Substantial cash reserves held over from the 1988 period have served the company well during the decline in wool prices and the recession in the European spinning industry in 1990–92, which caused for example a 1.82% fall in the current value of sales in 1992 compared to 1991, and have placed the company extremely well to exploit the better than expected recovery in wool prices and demand seen in 1994.

In Australia the largest processor and exporter of Australian wool, including tops, carbonised wool, hides and skins, is G H Michell (Australia) Pty Ltd, which buys about 10% of the entire Australian clip annually. About half of its purchases are made privately, and the other half through the auction system. Interestingly, that percentage is approximately the same as that eventually purchased by BWK. Another large company is Lempriere (Australia) Pty Ltd, which has its head office in Melbourne, Australia's major shipping port, and other offices in Sydney, Fremantle, New Zealand, Shanghai and Prague. The company is represented in approximately 30 other countries worldwide and trades wool through both its own and representative offices. The company has been trading wool for over 140 years and remains one of the most significant in the Australian wool trade. For example the group purchased over 200 000 bales ex-auction Australia-wide during the 1992/93 season, in addition to private wool buying straight from the wool growers' shed. The company's major business is in the form of greasy wool contracts and also dealing in tops, scoureds and carbonised products.

In Australia there are 80 wool exporters in all, and there are approximately 130 licensed wool exporters in New Zealand, according to the list of those registered with the New Zealand Wool Board – Bloch and Behrens comment that 'the New Zealand wool trade is not dominated by any particular large players but is very fragmented with many small scale operators, who all do their own thing' (H Andersen, letter to the author, 1/2/94) but the Board itself states that there are about 20 key traders in New Zealand who do most of the buying and the situation is similar, if not rather more concentrated, in Australia. Before the 1950s, nearly all the major wool buying firms in Australia and New Zealand were overseas-owned. Wool buyers operated on commission, buying to order on behalf of their overseas principals, mainly large merchanting houses, processors or manufacturers in the UK, Europe or USA. Over the years the overseas based buyers have gradually been replaced by domestic exporters, although many companies still have extensive international shareholding. There are a further 30 wool exchange brokers in New Zealand. (Some of the registration for private wool buyers, wool exporters and wool exchange brokers are different registrations for the same concern.) Data for the new Australian Wool Exchange is still being assembled.

The Federacao Brasileira de Lana states that there are few

Brazilian companies involved in the international wool trade: there are 11 member companies of the Federation.

South African companies observe that as South Africa has only recently been accepted as an international trading partner, their vision of foreign trade is still narrow and they do not trade as yet a substantial proportion of the world trade in wool. In addition, many of the companies active there are subsidiaries of Australian or Japanese companies. Of the South African companies involved in the international wool trade, the South African Wool Board states that 'Stucken, OTH Beier, Cape Tops, United Wool and Modiano are the most important ones' (Ona Viljoen, SAWB, letter to the author, 29/11/93).

US wool clips tend to be small, especially in the eastern two-thirds of the USA so the farmers sell to the 40 or so warehouses - almost 100% in Texas and New Mexico - or elsewhere in the USA to wool pools. There are, according to the American Wool Council, more than 30 broker/dealers who buy wool. Some travel from ranch to ranch to buy, while others deal directly with warehouses. The US wool textile companies are predominantly importers. The top companies are Burlington, ConAgra, Fieldcrest, Forstman, Shaw Industries, Standard Commercial and Wellman. Their position is protected by tariffs, although as these steadily reduce they can be expected to emerge more as international players.

The institutions involved

Any discussion of wool marketing and the international wool trade must perforce concentrate to a large extent on the institutional framework in which wool is marketed and traded - the boards and their policies.

Australian Wool Corporation

Economists had always warned that the buffer stock scheme was doomed. They argued that for a buffer stock scheme to work, the buy-in price must be set so that demand and supply are matched in the long term. So accurate forecasting - which even ABARE cannot always manage, especially when there is substantial oscillation in price - is required. Economic events render such forecasting impossible, and there are political, interventionist rationales, generated by growers, that result in the buy-in price being set unrealistically. The schemes fail, collapsing under their own weight in the end (see Chapters 1 and 4). That is exactly what happened in Australia, and so on 1 July 1991, following the Vines Report, the Australian Wool Corporation (AWC) that was established in 1973 was replaced by three separate bodies: the Australian Wool Realisation Commission (AWRC), charged with disposing of the stockpile, the Wool Research and Development Corporation (WRDC), and the Australian Wool Corporation chaired by Mac Drysdale. Three bodies were funded by the wool tax and approved borrowings. For 1991/92 the tax was 12% and was apportioned 0.5% to the WRDC, 2.5% to the AWC for international promotion, marketing and quality assurance, and 9% to the AWRC for debt management and asset disposal. For 1992/93 the tax was 8.5% and was apportioned 0.5% to the WRDC, 3.5% to the AWC and 4.5% to the AWRC, all for the same purposes as before. In exchange for this bureaucratic reorganisation, which was described at the time by Jim Maple-Brown, Chairman of the controversial *Wool into the 21st Century* committee, as 'about as bad as it could be' and which proved shortlived, the Australian government agreed to guarantee the borrowings of A$2.7bn, leaving the producers to pay interest and storage costs. In 1991 outgoing AWC Managing Director Jim Young put on record his belief that the AWC had achieved important other successes, overlooked by the collapse of the Reserve Price Scheme, such as improvements in shed hand training, classing standards, contamination control, the market indicator, successful freight negotiations, and specifications for wool packs.

The Australian Wool Corporation had never been above criticism from within the Australian wool industry. Some argued that in the period to 1992, for example, the AWC and the IWS together cost the industry $2bn in promotion and all the industry received in return was the worst crisis for a generation. As a result of the Garnaut Report, the Australian Wool Research and Promotion Organisation (AWRAP) began operating on 1 December 1993, formed from merging the AWC and the WRDC, with Mac Drysdale again in charge. The plan at that stage was for AWRAP to handle R&D, quality assurance, international market development and international promotion, with former AWC functions (see below). The final step in this series of changes was the announcement in mid-1994 of an institutional, but not a legal, merger between the IWS and AWRAP, with again Mac Drysdale in charge, following a review of the two operations' activities by the Boston Consulting Group. The idea is for consumers to deal with one integrated organisation by the end of 1995.

Wool International

The AWRC has now been in turn replaced with Wool International as a result of the Australian Wool Research and Promotion Act and the Wool International Act. The aim is for Wool International to be privatised itself in 1997 if there are positive net assets and for shares in Wool International to accumulate in proportion to the wool tax paid between 1 July 1993 and 1 July 1997. The Garnaut Report has led to a fixed selling schedule being imposed on the stockpile, in a solution very similar, though less rapid, to that proposed by Jim Maple-Brown in 1991 (see Chapter 4).

Australian Wool Exchange

The changes have also in turn led to the Australian Wool Exchange (AWEX), of which the mission is to 'enhance the global demand for Australian wool for the benefit of buyers and sellers by providing and facilitating fair, efficient, innovative and informed trading systems in an environment which fosters competition and self-regulation' (*Initial Report*, 1994). AWEX from 1 February 1994 in principle took over the functions of the pre-1993 AWC and subordinate committees such as the Wool Industry Advisory Committee so far as marketing, quality, auction programmes and wool sales are concerned. The industry is finally moving towards self-regulation. AWEX is to control auction facilities, sales rosters, the development of electronic trading, rules for private treaty sales and its wool exchange rules. Since 1 July 1994 AWEX has overseen clip preparations and showfloor inspection, show floors and sampling site registration and contamination screening. Arbitration, communications, clearing, quality assurance, inspection and the quality mark for wool are all part of the package, to follow in due course. 'The difference is that there will be no government involvement in AWEX activities. Instead of these activities being funded directly by Wool Tax levies via AWC budget allocations, they will now be funded by AWEX membership joining fees (set at A$4000 for 1994/95), annual membership fees (A$500 for 1994/95), trading fees applied on a per kilogram basis (0.2 ¢/kg for 1994/95), plus fees levied on a user-pays basis for services provided' (Wool Exchange Brochure, Chairman's Introductory letter). The new Chairman argued that the removal of government control also brought commercial accountability, hence the need for such a formal structure. Exporters, processors, brokers or merchants who want to sell wool at the Exchange's auctions must now be members and 95% are; growers are now also members. In 1994 there were suggestions that the new Exchange would centralise all sales, possibly as early as 1995/96, would reduce competition at auction and introduce sale by description or electronic trading. According to the 1994 *Annual Report*, 'The Wool Exchange has developed plans for the introduction of industry description and improved market reporting'.

Cotton seems to have managed perfectly well in the United States without a physical cotton exchange to which all cotton traders are supposed to belong. Freeriding must also be a problem here: membership is not compulsory, and although today's wool traders will certainly join (95% already have: as of the 1994 *Annual Report* there were 113 Foundation and 15 Ordinary Members), there seems no pressing reason why everyone should, especially if auctions can be circumvented or an Exchange member used as a proxy buyer. Already the smaller wool brokers have been pressing for a membership fee based on traded volumes. Also AWEX seems to concentrate on selling: will the IWS take on responsibilities for the types of achievement that Jim Young looked to in 1991? What also is to become of the functions of the multiplicity of other organisations in Australian wool, all dominated by specific personalities, such as the Australian Wool Industry Council, yet another body formed after the 1991 reorganisation, or the Wool Council of Australia, which is the wool group of the National Farmers Federation formed in 1979 from two other organisations with a prime objective 'to maximise returns to woolgrowers by developing policies which will ultimately achieve this goal and to represent woolgrowers in dealings with industry bodies and the Government?' Sir William Gunn, doyen of the Australian wool industry, observed in May 1991 that: 'A disjointed wool industry management structure didn't work back in the late 1950s and it won't work in the 1990s' (*Wool of Australia*, 1991).

Table 8.3 shows wool sales and government-owned stocks.

International Wool Secretariat

The International Wool Secretariat is the wool growers' worldwide promotional body. It acts as the overseas extension of the Australian Wool Corporation, and has now been merged with it. It was established in 1937 with the aim of optimising the long-term returns to wool growers in its member countries by increasing worldwide demand for wool. The founder members were Australia, New Zealand and South Africa, Uruguay joining in 1970. These countries continue

Table 8.3 Wool sales and government-owned stocks, major exporters

	Australia			Wool International	New Zealand			South Africa		
Year	Auction offerings, thousand bales	Sold to trade, %	AWC purchases, thousand bales	Ending stocks, thousand bales	Auction offerings, thousand bales	Sold to trade, %	NZWB ending stocks, thousand bales	Auction offerings, thousand bales	Sold to trade, %	SAWB ending stocks, thousand bales
1987/88	4288	96.1	34	8	1560	85.0	94	592	99	17
1988/89	4609	88.9	240	189	1406	85.1	100	618	94	60
1989/90	5771	47.3	2949	3065	1307	56.6	490	661	70	242
1990/91	5471	61.9	1926	4624	1293	80.3	558	690	54	164
1991/92	4512	89.8	1584	4070	1263	92.2	401	534	84	46
1992/93	4298	88.1	–	3950	1164	82.7	343	463	81	45
1993/94	4154	90.2	–	3667	1201	85.3	173	425	98	1

Source: International Wool Textile Organization in Succession to the Commonwealth Secretariat.

to account for some 80% of internationally traded wool. The National Wool Boards of Australia, South Africa and New Zealand retain control over the marketing of wool domestically, although in the Australian case this distinction is now otiose with the merger. They launch periodic wool awareness campaigns domestically. The UK is the largest wool exporter outside the IWS system.

The IWS budget is contributed mainly by the wool growers of each country, from levies on their wool sales, with additional funding by the Australian government. The IWS aims to build wool demand for members' wools in all major manufacturing and consumer markets. Its official aim is to promote wool and wool products directly to consumers and to work with selected manufacturers and retailers, aiming to develop innovative wool products and to improve the efficiency of wool processing. It is worth noting that just one synthetic fibre manufacturer, Dupont, spends four times as much on R&D as does the whole international wool industry. The IWS international branch network covers 29 countries, and is supported by marketing and services groups operating from the IWS headquarters at Ilkley.

The IWS is responsible for promoting the Contractwool programme in Western Europe. Manufacturers sign a partnership agreement to develop new Woolmark and Woolblendmark - the trademarks promoted by the IWS for garments made from pure new wool and a recognised blend respectively - carpets containing wool at least 60% from IWS partner countries. This effectively used to mean New Zealand, as other IWS countries produce very little carpet wool. IWS does not have the ability to reach retailers and users, they believe, hence the importance of direct relationships with manufacturers and the promotion of the Woolmark since its inception in 1964 and the Woolblendmark, of which there are now more than 1800 users worldwide just for interior textile alone. The IWS claims 90% consumer recognition worldwide for the Woolmark.

The IWS's role encompasses technical back-up and the transfer of technology developments from the wool industry to manufacturers, process and product development, design and styling, market information, quality control, product marketing, advertising and promotion, and administration of the labels given to wool products. The IWS also co-ordinates a global strategic plan for wool research and development, which sets priorities and ensures co-operation of activities between IWS and grower country research establishments.

Since the late 1980s the IWS has moved to chase the high-volume markets dominated by cotton and synthetics; but at the same time as early as 1990 it was realised that cotton and synthetics were in turn 'moving to grab wool's share of the lucrative luxury end of the clothing trade' (Vernon Graham, in *Wool Australia*, op cit, p 18) and controversy continues to rage over whether the IWS should stay with traditional support for formal apparel wear.

Considerable dispute exists over the performance and indeed the role of the IWS, for example where some of the IWS is sited (in England), over past so-called 'generic' promotion of wool itself rather than garments or uses, on whether too much research funding has gone into production research and too little into process and product research, and over the proportion of its funds that are spent on marketing in Europe and the USA compared with Asia. In 1991/92, Australia contributed 78%, New Zealand 13%, South Africa 8% and Uruguay 1%. The *Wool into the 21st Century* report said that the IWS had a power base for promoting wool with which virtually no other group with an interest in wool can compete. The continued decline of wool's share amongst fibres and the collapse in wool prices and of the reserve price schemes in Australia and New Zealand has led this promotion to be constantly under scrutiny and indeed the promotional budget was cut more than 60% between 1990/91 and 1993/94. The Australian contribution fell from $A155m in 1991/92 to A79m (proj) in 1994/95. Costs have accordingly been trimmed and staff numbers have been cut by more than half.

In 1993 the Wool Council of Australia recognised 'the critical funding shortage facing the IWS ... IWS global promotion effort is under threat' (*Annual Report*, 1993). One of the more successful of recent promotions was the 'Cool Wool' idea of the early 1990s (see Fig. 8.3), by 1994 having been extended by companies such as Forstmann to the USA, followed by 'Soft Wool' representing another technical improvement, but all these trademarks have their critics as well as their supporters, notably in Japan, who query their effectiveness and opposed the idea of paying to use them. But as from mid-1994, in response to the funding crisis, manufacturers are being asked to pay a flat fee of $7000 to use the Woolmark and Woolblendmark from 1 May 1995. The IWS has also appointed advertising agency Abbott Mead Vickers BDDO in succession to Merkley Newman Harty to administer the actually very small amount of $45m that is to be spent on marketing in 1994/95 subject to the success of charging for licences. It will be very interesting to see whether there are any improvements as a result of these changes.

8.3 Cool Wool promotion in Germany (source: International Wool Secretariat).

New Zealand Wool Board

The New Zealand Wool Board was established in 1944 under the Wool Industry Act, and reconstituted under the Wool Industry Act 1977, amalgamating with the New Zealand Wool Marketing Corporation (successor to the New Zealand Wool Commission) in 1978. Its key objective, defined in the Act of 1977, is 'to obtain, in the interests of growers, the best possible returns for New Zealand wool'. It is 80%-funded through a levy on wool growers on the proceeds of their wool sales, amounting to 6% in 1992/93, together with income from investments and other income and has approximately 70 staff, with directors appointed by the industry as well as by the government, spending NZ$75.2m in 1992/93, of which NZ$11m (on the OECD definition) went to research (WRONZ).

The Arthur Little report argued that it was excessive price instability which was creating market resistance and grower uncertainty in New Zealand. The report argued that it was the raw wool marketing system itself that was causing the problem, and not the NZWB. Hence, it was argued, the removal of the Board's Support and Minimum Price schemes (which were aimed at smoothing out fluctuations in auction prices and at guaranteeing a minimum price for wool growers respectively) in February 1991 would not solve the industry's problems.

The New Zealand Wool Board, in common with other such organisations worldwide, continues to argue strongly for the role of such organisations in setting quality control regulations – not believing that the market can do this job effectively unaided – and allowing its marketing funds to be channelled through the International Wool Secretariat. The Board continues to have a number of joint ventures and wholly owned subsidiaries, such as New Zealand Wool Services International established in 1992.

The NZWB believes that it also performs important work in helping farmers become more competitive, in negotiating shipping rates, in regulating the sale, sampling and export of wool, in registering exporters (the term licence is misleading as it is automatically granted), in training woolhandlers, in developing new export markets (since 1993 the Board has had an office in Beijing, for example, and its technical staff work with manufacturers in such countries as India, Nepal, China and in the Middle East) and in initiatives which have improved the packaging and distribution of wool. This has not stopped criticism (e.g. the Hussey Report in 1992) of the role of the Board and claims that its activities should be limited to R&D and promotion.

Competition between the different wool marketing organisations is continuous, if not intense. In 1992, 59% of the IWS interior textiles budget - 90% funded by New Zealand - was spent in Europe and 18% in Asia. Despite the fact that China and East Asia only attracted 3.6% of the IWS apparel budget, they took almost 30% of New Zealand's apparel wool usage. These factors must have contributed to the New Zealand decision to establish their own marketing organisation: in mid-1994 as part of the international institutional reorganisation a new organisation, Wools of New Zealand (WNZ), took over the marketing of non-apparel New Zealand wool, with offices in Atlanta, Tokyo, Beijing, Brussels, Dusseldorf and Ilkley as well as Wellington and Christchurch.

The NZWB budget for 1994/95 was NZ$54.3m, of which NZ$4.5m was for research. There is also a new trademark, Wools of New Zealand, which does not have a licence fee attached and it is planned that up to 250–300 companies will be become licencees in the next few years; WNZ also owns the Decorwool (which encompassed 260 carpet ranges in 1994 and 3000 retailers in Western Europe), Decorwool Prestige and Contractwool trademarks. New campaigns, including 'woolcentres' in stores for the use of New Zealand wool in carpets have been launched in the UK, Germany, the Netherlands, Belgium and France. Domestically in New Zealand the slogan was 'Let's get real'. In the USA 'Partners in Profit' was launched and now encompasses over 300 retailers; in Japan the Home Wool Carpet programme was launched. All this is partly aimed to ensure greater transparency in the use of wool growers' funds. But all former IWS Interior Textiles staff now work for WNZ in the same locations. New Zealand apparel wools remain under the IWS and its trademarks.

This is further evidence of the ending of the phase of 'generic marketing' of wool.

British Wool Marketing Board

The British Wool Marketing Board is a farmers' organisation working on behalf of 90 686 registered wool producers in 1993 - a 2.7% fall from the previous year. It was established in 1950 to market all fleece wool produced by sheep farmers in the UK. Since the 1950s it has also run a training scheme, a ram fleece assessment service and arranges grading training courses. The real essence of the Board's existence however is the marketing system. All registered producers - anyone with four or more adult sheep must register with the Board - may sell their wool to the Board. The clip is allocated to a merchant in the area, and the merchants provide containers ('sheets') for shorn wool. The merchants then make their own arrangements to transport the wool to auction via warehouses where the wool is sorted and graded. Details are sent to be registered on the BWMB's computer system.

In practice, sales still occur through the fortnightly Board sales, which since 1992 no longer take place in Edinburgh but only in Oak Mills, Bradford twice monthly. These are conducted on behalf of the Board by the Committee of London Wool Brokers (CLWB). Depending on the sale, about thirty purchasers can be expected and about 1.6m kg (3.5m lb) of wool in 5000 kg (11 000 lb) lots bid in pence per kilo in a similar way to the Australian and New Zealand auctions with reserve prices, 28 days billing and payment by the CLWB to the Board of the total sale price. The majority of participants are professional wool buyers from the Halifax and Bradford areas who in turn sell on to the carpet industry and other producers, although some producers send representatives themselves. The Board supplies and charges the merchants for the containers and carries out technical inspection of the wool.

The withdrawal of the Wool Guarantee was not a surprise to the Board as the Government stated its intention to do so in 1988. However, it did come initially at a bad time for UK wool producers as it meant a large reduction in wool-derived income as the market price was less than the Guarantee, which was already operating on a delayed payment system for four years beforehand. The Board and the Farmers' Unions tried to persuade the Government to postpone withdrawal of the Guarantee or to phase it out, but the Government went ahead. The current system is that the Board collects the wool from the farms in its eleven UK regions, grades it for quality at nineteen handling depots throughout the UK and prepares it for sale by auction.

There are storage charges levied of 1 p/kg for wool delivered up to four days after 31 August, ranging to 4 p/kg for wool delivered in late December. The advance payment is made with the balance from the previous season, now based on market value. Although the advance (the wool cheque, set at a 'realistic' level, based on the average price achieved last season) no longer pays for shearing, there has been no immediate collapse in the number of farmers, as some were already predicting that the price supports would be removed. The BWMB retains, at least for the time being, its statutory powers of purchase. To some extent the BWMB must walk a tightrope: aggressive marketing of British wool is continual but the Board must bear in mind that if the British wool price differential widens too far, a renewed import of lower quality wools from Pakistan, India and China can be expected. Relative prices have to be restrained therefore, at the same time as securing satisfactory returns for UK farmers. In May 1994 the structure of payments was as shown in Table 8.4.

Table 8.4 The structure of BWMB payments in May 1994, p/kg

Grade	Balance '93	Advance '94	Total payment
430 Cross E & W	42.0	49	91.0
434 Cross E & W Cast	38.9	44	82.9
707 Swaledale & D'bred	41.7	38	79.7
709 Swaledale & D'bred Grey	36.0	33	69.0
718 Light Herdwick	37.9	24	61.9

Source: BWMB

The BWMB announced in Spring 1994 that handling charges had again fallen, and had been set at a maximum of 18 p/kg, of which 15p was the cost of grading paid to the merchants, and 3p covered the cost of promotion, finance and administration. The Chairman, Alun Evans, said that he believed the BWMB was 'the most efficient and cost effective wool handling operation in Europe' (promotional literature, 1994). Partly this was because transport (in the previous season 4.5 p/kg) had been made optional.

Amongst the associated organisations of the Board are the Joint Advisory Committee from the industry, the Agents' Negotiating Committee, the Users' Committee, the British Wool Promotion Committee, the Valuation Appeal Tribunal and a government-appointed Consumers' Committee. There is also the Confederation of British Wool Textiles Ltd, the Wool Federation of Scotland, the

Country Wool Merchants' Association, and the UK Wool Growers' Federation. There must be some suspicion that the work of these Committees overlaps, and that the structure of the Board does to some extent reflect the previous price support regime.

The BWMB argues that support for its Marketing Scheme is almost unanimous, and that buyers and users of British wool, the Farmers' Unions, the major political parties, wool handling agents and the great majority of producers (this last the most doubtful of the assertions) want the system to continue as they consider it to be the most efficient way to collect, market and distribute British produced wool. Given that the average farm production is only 450 kg and that Britain produces more different types of wool than any other country – 200 grades are quoted by the BWMB Annual Schedule published in April – the Board does have a strong case for centralising the marketing and selling function in order to provide medium and high volume manufacturers with the qualities they want in the quantities they need. There are also ample opportunities for wool quality in the UK to be improved, for example in respect of artificially stained, bloom-dipped or paint-marked fleeces.

The BWMB, by contrast to the IWS, targets manufacturers as well as retailers in the limited UK carpet market in which it operates. The 1993/94 BWMB promotion, for instance, involved over 1650 retailers in distributing literature to potential customers. The sustained marketing campaign costs about 1 p/kg of wool and the BWMB believes that it is necessary in order to raise the profile of wool. The Shepherd's Crook symbol is being increasingly used by the UK carpet industry for carpets with at least 50% British wool. The BWMB has a wide remit to encourage manufacturers to use wool, show consumers the wide range of available wool products, provide educational material and show British wool producers what is being done on their behalf at fashion and trade shows and exhibitions and through catalogues and other promotional material.

South African Wool Board

The South African wool scene changed dramatically on 1 July 1993 when the single-channel pool marketing scheme operated by the South African Wool Board since 1972 under the Agricultural Marketing Act was abrogated and wool marketing was made subject to the free market. The South African Wool Board no longer has the function of raw wool marketing and farmers are free to sell their wool to anyone they choose whether by auction, private treaty or otherwise, for local processing or export. A pooling system was introduced by Cape Mohair and Wool (CMW) in 1994, to operate on an advance/supplementary payments system. Now the SAWB must dispose of the remaining small South African stockpile and reduce the accumulated debt under the previous system of R166m, 70% government-guaranteed and the rest to be funded through the liquidation of assets. The SAWB remains armed with a remit to encourage wool production and industry development, support R&D, provide market information, market wool in South Africa and liaise with the IWS. The levy has accordingly been reduced by 33%, from 7.5% to 5% on gross proceeds, with the Board also having other income, for example from property. There are over a dozen listed members of the South African Wool and Mohair Buyers' Association (SAWAMBA) and they are all computer linked to the SAWB.

United States Department of Agriculture

The USDA operate in effect much the same system until the provisions of PL 103-130 come into force; they provide for a phase out of the wool and mohair programmes over the 1994 and 1995 marketing years and repeal the 1954 National Wool Act as amended by the Food, Agriculture, Conservation and Trade Act of 1990. Support prices in the 1994 marketing year announced by the Commodity Credit Corporation of the USDA were $2.09/lb for shorn wool, producers receiving only 75% of their calculated payments. Wool on unshorn lambs was supported in the 1994 season, as in the past, at a level based on the hundredweight of live, unshorn lambs marketed. In 1995 they will receive only 50%.

Even in the USA there is a move towards a free market in wool. The American Sheep Industry Association has a wool division, the American Wool Council, which represents the (over 100 000) sheep producers in the USA since 1955. Its headquarters are in Denver, Colorado and it also has an office in New York. The AWC has proposed ambitiously to inflict a 2 ¢/lb tax on clean wool used by processors and on the wool used in all imported wool products, but in 1994/95 the US mills believed that the plan would be a 'very tough sell' to the US industry. Overseas marketing funds available from the USDA FAS in 1994/95 are minuscule by comparison with cotton, a mere $210 000.

Critics have suggested for many years, but especially since the role of the government boards has been cut, that the marketing problems of wool are deep set and not amenable to marketing remedies, and perhaps this thinking permeates the USDA where outsiders certainly do get the impression that cotton is much more central to their thinking than wool ever could be - purely in financial terms this is quite understandable. The 1992 Arthur Little report on the New Zealand industry suggested that the marketing pipeline was too long and that there was too much of a focus on greasy rather than clean wool prices at auctions and private sales. *Wool into the 21st Century* argued that wool marketing costs were excessive, and drew some telling comparisons with cotton in respect of the number of layers of middlemen, the level of political interference, and the psychology of those involved in the trade to demonstrate the point. Change is underway in these areas: the real question is whether wool can catch up, or whether there are yet more improvements that cotton can make to continue to lead wool in these important areas. Just about all the wool promoters and marketing operations have a long way to go, however, before they reach the professionalism and the commitment of resources demonstrated by the National Cotton Council of America, which wool industry sources in the USA freely admit is partially responsible for the difficulties that wool has in making headway in the USA.

It is, however, very difficult to see how the situation where growers are price takers at the end of a long chain can ever be avoided, and in the absence of effective government support schemes, forward contracting and perhaps eventually proper futures markets would seem the only alternative.

CHAPTER

9

The international woollen industry

Wool weaving and manufacture

Woollen manufacturing processes are similar for Merino, cross-bred and other apparel wools, but depend on whether they are to be used for felt, woollen or worsted yarn. In all cases, there is a trade-off between lower cost yarn and the risks of so doing, which include weak yarn, unevenness, knots and poor colour, which can outweigh the savings.

Carbonising

Scouring does not always eliminate vegetable matter such as burrs and seeds, and so heavily contaminated wool is treated with a mild sulphuric acid solution first, to break down the burrs and then heat to convert the disintegrated material into carbon. The burrs are finally removed, first by crushing and then shaken out of the wool by a machine rotating at high speed. Any remaining impurities are therefore blown out of the fibre.

Blending

Blending provides flexibility, allowing substitution of one wool type for another, or even a change in the ratio of each type in the blend, all without materially affecting the desired yarn characteristics. Blending enables the processor to improve the performance of the raw material, ensure a continuous supply despite seasonal variabilities in price and availability, improve product performance and appearance, and generally get better value for money from the wool - although these savings need to be balanced against the cost of the processing itself. Careful selection and blending of wools compatible with the processing system to be used will ensure the best processing performance. Uniformity of yarn quality depends to a great extent on the thorough mixing of the wool components before, after and during scouring to ensure an even distribution of fibre characteristics throughout the blend. Manipulation of different wool types within blends allows for special effects, such as using lustrous wools or improving resilience in carpet yarns by introducing medullated fibres into the blend. 'The move towards higher output machinery, semi-automated and linked processes are making the selection and blending of raw materials more important than before and the final cost of material in the finished product *the* consideration.' (Bruce Rainsford, letter to the author, 28.11.94).

Worsted system

The worsted system produces a smooth, lean, compact yarn constructed from parallel fibres of reasonably uniform length and fineness. It uses fine long stapled wools with low levels of vegetable matter contamination (burrs and seeds) to produce fine smooth finished products such as suitings and fashion fabrics. Worsted yarns are used to produce clearly defined light and medium weight woven and knitted fabrics. The key stages in the worsted process are carding, gilling, combing and spinning, see Fig. 9.1. The process provides several opportunities for blending in between carding and spinning, and as the blend comprises wools which are quite similar in character, the initial opening and blending stage is less critical than for woollens. Worsted fabrics are made from the more lustrous wool qualities and short fibres, known as noils, are combed out. The fibres are combed to bring them, as far as possible, into being parallel: worsted yarns have a characteristic, even appearance. The ropes of parallel fibres are called 'tops', which are then drawn out into progressively finer threads in the spinning process. Quality use does overlap. There is now also a 'semi-worsted' system in which there is no combing, demanding a minimum of short fibres and a minimum of vegetable contamination. Clearly manufacturers would like to cut out steps in production.

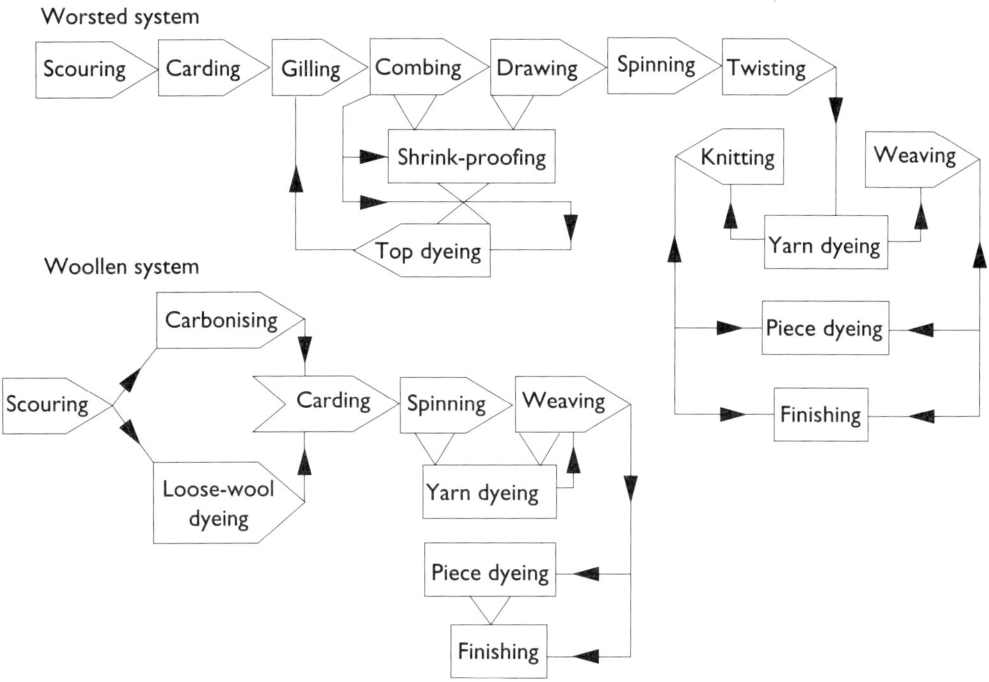

9.1 Stages in the manufacture of wool textiles (source: Dept of Primary Industries and Energy and Wool into the 21st Century).

Carding

The wool then goes into a carding machine which opens the entangled scoured wool, as gently as possible, and removes the burrs and seeds, leaving the wool as a continuous thread, known as a sliver.

Carding was originally done by hand – like so many aspects of the woollen and worsted industry it has become capital rather than labour intensive. Two flat cards with convenient handles, covered with teeth or card clothing, served as the means of teasing out the wool lock by lock, fibre by fibre, reversing root to tip and tip to root, so that the fibres were properly mixed. Carding then became more mechanical, using rollers instead of flats. Carding issues include the size of the rollers, their speed and inclination and the shape of the teeth and the density of the card clothing. Carding is a highly technical operation not well understood outside the industry and even within it; for example carding for long wool does not have teeth that run into one another, whereas short mungo carding does.

Worsted carding straightens, makes parallel, cleans and blends the fibres, to make a sliver of uniform quality, thickness and weight. This uniformity is required for a strong, fine worsted yarn: it is a matter of great care in production. Long fibres need to be whole and short fibres must not curl up despite later combing. All extraneous substances must be taken out so that they cannot prevent effective worsting. Worsted carding, unlike woollen, is performed on one long card. The carding machine is divided into three: feeding, carding and delivery, and they consist mainly of sets of rollers moving at different speeds and in different directions. The vegetable matter/burrs in the wool can be removed in various ways, either by crushing, chemically or with revolving burr knives but usually with burr beaters and Morel rollers turning at about 2000 rpm (mid-1990s). Carding is completed with the fibres being formed into a heavy sliver or rope for further processing. Impurities not removed by scouring, and those added in preparation, are removed through backwashing, which is done before combing. Many balls or cans of card slivers are fed into the backwashing machine simultaneously; the machines wash and then dry the slivers. The bowls contain olive or olein soap full of suds, at least one bowl contains warm rinsing water to which ammonia or blueing is sometimes added. The slivers are squeezed and dried, usually with hot air. Oil is added to prevent the fibres from becoming too brittle.

Gilling

The gilling and combing steps which follow in the worsted system, as well as contributing to the further blending of the fibres, are designed to ensure that the fibres are increasingly aligned parallel to each other. Gilling involves passing several slivers through a series of coarse pinned combs (fallers) to produce a single aligned sliver of similar weight to each of the input slivers, thereby combining the different qualities of card sliver together. The sliver is then combed by rows of pins mounted on revolving cylinders, which start off coarse and get progressively finer. During this combing process, short or broken fibres and most of the vegetable matter remaining after the carding process are removed. The slivers leave the gill boxes faster than it enters – the draft rate measures the ratio. Measuring devices keep the sliver length uniform. Successive gilling makes the fibre thicker and more uniform in weight and stock.

Combing

The wool is then combed, in order to eliminate short fibres of a given length and also further to straighten the fibres and cut out impurities. This is the key operation in the production of worsted yarn. Combing continues the gilling process, using a fine toothed roller comb to remove the remaining vegetable matter and the fibres broken down during carding. There were four comb types: Noble, Lister, Holden (square motion) and French (rectilinear). The first two were used in the English combing system and the latter two in the French system. Each of the comb types has different advantages, and is suitable for different lengths of wool. The Noble circular comb was the most widely used, but it required considerable moisture in the wool and the Heilman straight comb is cheaper to use, although not suitable for medium staple wool. Current machines such as the Schlumberger PB31 produces 30 kg (66 lb) of wool per hour and requires one person for every ten combs. It has 750 moving parts and can comb each individual fibre in a sliver of wool with an accuracy of 30 microns at a rate of 210 beats per minute. Other manufacturers include Sant'Andrea of Italy and Leisnig of Germany. Recombing is rarely performed and then only because dyeing can cause fibres to curl. Often it is done when different coloured slivers are required, although this is usually done in the gill boxes. The combed fibres are again drawn out and reformed into a sliver of level and uniform thickness for another gilling stage. This completes the worsted process, forming a parallel sliver, which is wound into a large ball, called a top.

The rejected short fibres, known as noils, are collected and can be used in woollen blends, felts, etc; they are worth only some 40% of the value of the top. Mill Romaine results are calculated as the weight of the noil × 100/weight of top + noil.

Tops are the intermediate product of the worsted system, and much wool as noted above is traded internationally in this form. An increasing amount of processing of wool to this stage is being carried out in Australia.

Drawing

The wool coming from the combing or carding machine is gathered into loose ropes called slivers and then washed. Drawing the fibre, which comes next in the textile production process, produces the fine roving that can be spun into an even yarn. It thins out the sliver to make it uniform, the problem being to keep the fibres straight and parallel. All systems use drafting rollers and a winding up of the original sliver. There are English, French and cone systems in use, the English for long coarse lustre and cross-bred wools, the French for unoiled tops of short fine wools and the cone system for oiled tops. The process is repeated several times, reducing the diameter of the top at each stage. At the last drawing process (roving or finishing) a small amount of twist is added to increase strength as the sliver is diminished in thickness. In its reduced form the sliver is called a roving.

Woollen system

This uses coarser, shorter stapled wools with higher levels of vegetable matter contamination, to produce heavier, hairier products, such as upholstery, bulky knitwear, blankets, flannels and tweeds.

Woollen carding involves passing the wool over revolving cylinders where it is disentangled and mixed together until an even veil or web of wool fibres is produced. Unlike the worsted system the fibres are not laid evenly. The final section of a woollen carding machine is the condenser which divides the veil of wool into strips and rubs them together to form a slubbing. The slubbings are then wound on to condenser bobbins ready for spinning.

Spinning

Once the roving has been obtained it must be spun into yarn. The basic principles of spinning and weaving machinery are the same as centuries ago. The medieval loom remained in use until after 1733 when John Kay invented the flying shuttle, which was driven mechanically across the warp, without having to be thrown by the weaver. Automatic spinning followed. There are four methods of spinning – flyer, cap ring and mule. Flyer spinning, invented by Sir Richard Arkwright in 1769, driven by horses at first and then by water – the water-frame – produced smooth, lustrous fibre. The speed of the flyer is slow and the method is not used any more.

James Hargreaves in 1767 invented the spinning jenny, with multiple spindles positioned alongside one another. With this development one spinner was able to operate up to 120 spindles concurrently. Crompton's spinning mule combined the principles of the water-frame and the jenny. The spindles were not stationary; they were mounted on a movable carriage which travelled away from the rollers, drawing out the wool threads which were concurrently twisted by the spindles for strength.

Other machines were invented to prepare the wool for weaving, for example the combing machine, used in the worsted industry for combing the long fibres parallel and removing the short fibres, and the carding machine for opening out, blending and straightening the wool fibres after cleaning. All these operations became mechanised. At the beginning of the 19th century woollen cloths were made of high quality and the steam engine had begun to be introduced to Yorkshire mills. The cap spinning method, invented by Charles Danforth in 1828, was used for English system worsteds. The speed of the machine is high but quality remained a problem. Mule spinning produced exceptionally fine, soft yarn with short wools.

By the end of the century hand weaving had all but disappeared. The use of ring spinning, formerly used for cotton, is now used for almost all worsteds. Quality yarns are produced at low cost. Very few knots are found in the yarn, which is superior to cap spun yarn. The yarn is fed through an eye, and on to a traveller which is dragged around a ring, oiled to reduce friction, and then fastened to a static ring rail. The yarn goes at right angles from the traveller to the bobbin; the bobbin motion inserts the twist and the traveller runs slower than the bobbin to ensure tension. The speed of the spindles is decreased to compensate for the loss of tension due to the bobbins filling up.

The English system used ring, cap and flyer spinning, although now according to the Confederation of British Wool Textiles there is very little cap and flyer spinning left in the UK; US mills use ring spinning. Flyer spinning is used for carpet wools. In all systems there are three steps to spinning: final drafting, twisting the roving and packaging – these are continuous operations except for worsted mule spinning. The yarn as delivered by the mule is single and will serve as a warp or weft for most woollen cloths, warp usually twisted harder than weft. Sometimes for fibre strength or colour the yarn must be doubled or further thickened, which is done through attachments on ring frames. There is always a wide variety available. In the woollen system, the yarn is spun directly from the slubbing made during carding. The slubbings are drawn out to the thickness of yarn required while rotating spindles add a designated amount of twist as the yarn is spun, although woollen yarns are not twisted as tightly as worsted yarns.

Recent improvements in spinning processes have seen, for example, the Plyfil process – the adaption of techniques previously used only for synthetics and blends at speeds of up to 300 m/min for blends and 250 m/min for pure wool. This is about fifteen times faster than those normally attained in classic wool spinning. Another good example is the Repco spinning system, which is in use in a number of mills. Another slightly less recent example was SIROSPUN, a technology developed by CSIRO which reduced the cost of spinning fine wool by 56% by eliminating one step in the spinning process. It has produced yarn with unusual properties and has allowed the development of the very successful 'Cool Wool' fabrics. A final example of such new developments is the wrap frame (hollow spinning) process produced for example by Gemmill & Dunsmore which also makes twisting frames. Ring-frame spinning machines in the mid-1990s reach speeds of 16 000 rpm for spinning worsted fabrics, with up to 640 spindles (double-sided). What worsted spinners, and weavers and knitters are looking for, however, remains little changed: a clean spinnable sliver of wool top, of which the micron is the most important characteristic. The weight or thickness of the final cloth depends on the fineness or thickness of the yarn that goes in to it.

Warping

Large spools of yarn are wound into a beam which is used for weaving, a process known as warping. Spun yarns may be used as a single yarn or twisted together with others (folded) depending on their end use, for example to supply a hosiery knitting machine, to provide both warp and weft for weaving on a loom, or for handknitting.

Weaving

This is the oldest way to produce fabric from yarn. The basic principle of interlacing yarns to produce fabric has not changed for centuries. Weaving interlaces yarns at right angles to one another forming the fabric. On the loom, lengthwise yarns are called the warp. These normally demand a higher degree of twist than the filling yarns, which are interlaced horizontally with them. Historically, cloth has been woven by a wooden shuttle moving horizontally back and forth across the loom, interlacing the filling yarn with a vertical warp yarn. Most mills now use high speed shuttleless looms operating at up 1200 picks/minute and produce a wide variety of fabrics but for wool these speeds are excessive and not suitable for wool fabrics.

There are several types of looms. Some have metal arms which pick up the falling thread, carrying it halfway across the loom to where another metal arm picks it up and carries it the rest of the way; other types use small projectiles picking up the yarn from large cones and then shooting it across the warp and back from the other side by means of compressed air. The trend is also towards quieter as well as faster looms. The latest Sulzer machines, for example, support six weft colours and are capable of weaving cloths made from low tenacity yarns at speeds of up to 470 picks per minute.

There are three basic types of weave, although there are many variations. Wool can be used in all three: (i) the plain weave where the filling is alternately passed over one warp yarn and under the next; (ii) the twill weave where the yarns are interlaced to form a diagonal ridge series across the fabric and (iii) the satin weave - this is the least common, made with fewer yarn interlacings and with either the warp or the weft yarns dominating the cloth face. In addition there are composite weaves such as the leno or terry.

In most advanced mills, optical scanners monitor the production process continuously, searching for flaws in the cloth emerging from the loom. Computers identify the source and it is automatically removed before posting the order. Diagnostic systems then operate to rectify the fault.

Knitting

This is a way of constructing fabrics by using a series of needles to interlock loops of yarn; machine knitting production is often more flexible and faster than woven production. Lengthwise rows of these loops, comparable to the warp yarn in woven goods - are called wales - and crosswise rows comparable to wefts are called courses. Weft knit and warp knit fabrics are different and require specialist machinery. Warp knitting gives stable knitted structures, for example for curtains. There are three weft stitches, plain, purl and rib, plain usually for jumpers, hosiery and underwear fabrics, rib for socks and underwear as well as the wrist and neck bands for jumpers and purl - which is a combination - often for childrens' wear.

There are many similarities between knitting done by hand and machine knitting, but there are also key differences. A typical hand knitter using two needles and forming one stitch at a time may produce 60 stitches a minute, but a modern knitting machine may use up to 1600 needles and produce over 3m stitches a minute. In place of a single yarn cone, a knitting machine may have 8–148 cones, each feeding more than 700 feet (213m) of yarn/minute into the fabric. Most wool is knitted on circular machines which have needles fixed to the rim of a rotating cylinder. As the cylinder turns, so the needles work their way from stitch to stitch, producing a tubular fabric. The width is regulated by the size of the cylinder, which is usually 1–2 inches (25–50mm) in diameter.

Another basic type is the flat knitting machine. This is designed with a flat bed, and has dozens of needles arranged in a straight line and producing a knit fabric that is flat like woven goods. Such machines produce over 1m stitches/minute, can be set to drop or add stitches automatically, and can narrow or widen the fabric at certain points in order to make particular shapes. As with weaving machines, knitting machines can be programmed to make a wide variety of fabrics and shapes.

Dyeing

Most wool goes through a further series of chemical treatments and finishing processes to meet specific end-use requirements. Wool dyes well: the scales on the wool's surface tend to diffuse light giving less reflection and a softer colour. Because the protein core of the wool is strongly reactive, it soaks up and combines with a wide variety of dyes. Some mills undertake the job of dyeing and printing the fabric in addition to spinning and weaving. Some mills sell undyed wool to converters, who finish the cloth in separate plants. Finishing includes cleaning and preparing the cloth, dyeing it, and then treating it with chemicals, or mechanically, to get the necessary texture and performance characteristics: there are numerous finishing processes reflecting the vast range of colours, textiles and qualities demanded by the competitive Western retail market.

Dyeing colours the wool and can be carried out on scoured wool, top, yarn, fabric or garment. It normally involves batch treatments in boiling dye liquors for longer than an hour. Most dyeing of wool occurs at the yarn stage. To colour wool it is either yarn dyed or piece dyed, and increasingly computers are being used to make and match colours more quickly and accurately. Yarn dyeing is done before the cloth is woven or knitted and is used to produce gingham checks, plaids, woven stripes, and other special effects. In 'package-dyeing', which is one of the most frequently used methods of yarn dyeing, the yarn is wound around perforated cylinders or packages, and placed on vertical spindles in a round dyeing machine. Dye solution is forced alternatively from the outside of the packages and vice versa; the dye reaches the core of the fibre and is less liable to run than piece dyeing. This final method is conversely used for fabrics that are to be all one colour. A continuous length of cloth is passed through a trough of hot dye solution. The cloth is then squeezed through rollers, spreading the colour evenly across the cloth and removing the excess liquid. In a variant of this method, the fabric is made into a rope-like coil which is processed on a reel passing through the dye beck or vat.

The printing of colour designs on to woollen cloth is a similar technique to printing on paper. Long runs of the same fabric design are usually made on a roller print machine, making 1–200 m/min, printing up to 16 different colours together. Such a machine has a large padded drum or cylinder, surrounded by a series of copper rollers, each with its own source of dye and a 'doctor' blade to remove excess dye. The number of rollers depends on the fabric design: each colour in the fabric is applied by a separate roller. The cloth moves between the rotating drum and the rollers under great pressure. It acquires colour from the engraved areas of each roller sequentially. The printed cloth is immediately dried and moved to an oven where the dye sets.

The other main way of putting colour designs on to cotton is automatic screen printing but this is not successful on the thicker wool fibres.

Finishing

This describes a number of processes designed to impart the necessary drape, handle and aesthetic properties to a wool fabric. There are hundreds of different mechanical and chemical finishes that can be applied to wool, and many are simultaneously applied to the same fabric. Wet finishing involves liquors and chemicals being applied to the fabric, while dry finishing involves mechanical treatments. The aim throughout is to improve the appearance of the fabric and also to improve such characteristics as durability, water or fire resistance, control of shrinkage, or colour-fastness. Woollen cloth must be shrunk and felted by being passed through rollers and soap solutions. The nap (surface) is raised by passing the cloth through drums set with the heads of teasels and then cropped by a kind of mowing machine. Raising and cropping are not needed for worsted because the aim there is to display rather than conceal the weave pattern.

In the 20th century, woollen cloths have come to be made from every type of material: noils (Australian, cross-bred, English, alpaca and mohair), mungo, shoddy, extracts, flocks, fud (short mill waste), cotton sweeping, silk waste, etc. However not all woollen cloth is of inferior quality: in England the West Country still produces impressive woollen fabrics, and Batley, Dewsbury, etc, produce woollen fabrics which are inexpensive but not obviously so.

The industry is subject to rapid technical development. New carpet technologies include yarn bonding, which improves tuft definition and yarn bulk and reduces fibre shedding, and new dyeing technology, which reduces the amount of setting resulting from dyeing and improves process performance and yarn properties. Upholstery techniques have been improving in respect of fire resistance and treatments which allow the use of coarser wools in finer yarns as well as pollution-free insect resistance for carpet yarns - the minibowl process - which cuts effluent volume and reduces the release of insect resistant agents to the environment.

The scope of the industry worldwide

Wool fibre is sold internationally with comparatively few restrictions. However as it progresses through the various forms of processing and refinement from scouring, through sliver or top, to yarn, to product it meets progressively more restrictive practices. Table 9.1 gives exports and imports of worsted and woollen yarns.

The IWTO provides a wealth of statistical detail on the import and export of wool yarn, and woollen *fabrics,* which are outside the scope of this book but which represent a balance and a reciprocal to international raw wool exports (whether greasy or scoured). The 'great debate' over the likely future significance of raw commodity exports applies as much to wool as to cotton. The statistics show that New Zealand, for example, exported (according to the then provisional statistics of the New Zealand Government) $NZ900.3m of raw fibre in 1993, of which the great majority was scoured wool export revenue. Sheepskins accounted for a further NZ$66.8m, and wool waste a mere NZ$1.7m. Intermediate products (including yarns, tops and slivers) made up NZ$85m, and final products NZ$90.9m. New Zealand already exports a quarter of its carpet production annually and most of its rugs, for example, with a value of $64.7m, 90% to Australia - more than the value of yarn exports, and this figure rose again in 1994. In the early 1990s, for New Zealand, raw wool exports remain approximately 83–79% of the total wool sector's exports.

Table 9.1 Exports and imports of worsted and woollen yarns, tonnes

					Jan–Sept		Jan–Dec	
	1988	**1989**	**1990**	**1991**	**1992**	**1993**	**1992**	**1993**
Exports								
Worsted yarns								
Austria	1 309	1 214	1 221	1 848	1 244	1 124	1 601	1 611
Belgium	4 693	4 391	4 304	4 071	3 005	2 601b	3 895	3 431b
France	7 759	6 860	5 347	6 100	4 863	4 615	6 097	5 971
Germany (West)	16 684	17 492	16 059	18 767	16 436	13 164c	20 693	17 527c
Italy	10 593	9 778	10 916	13 869	11 804	13 156	14 557	16 906d
Japan	1 420	1 668	2 078	1 889	1 105	1 228	1 275	1 422
South Korea	7 089	4 547	3 202	5 808	4 074	1 293	4 579	1 761
Malaysia	79	371	2 076	2 602	1 958	2 704	3 045	3 605a
Switzerland	6 693	7 337	7 425	8 297	6 308	5 435	8 254	7 316
United Kingdom	4 646	4 621	4 519	4 950	4 008	4 922	5 391	6 672d
Netherlands	841	877	481	484	289	329	387	454
Woollen yarns								
Belgium	5 896	5 648	5 455	5 045	3 172	2 945b	4 157	3 963b
France	1 936	1 900	1 520	1 584	1 630	1 371	2 175	1 753
Germany (West)	2 682	2 805	2 523	2 449	1 676	1 426c	2 445	1 913c
Irish Republic	4 317	3 713	3 348	3 557	2 593	–	3 742	–
Italy	4 867	4 207	4 307	5 717	5 117	7 250	6 855	9 060
Japan	8 204	6 906	6 861	7 661	5 232	3 328	6 211	3 703
South Korea	48 383	10 225	7 285	8 440	6 495	4 766	7 770	5 498
Netherlands	1 736	1 592	1 316	1 322	814	353	977	455e
United Kingdom	9 187	9 146	9 386	8 892	7 927	7 894	10 721	10 194d
Malaysia	26	3	10	1	41	13	44	18
Switzerland	152	211	59	365	200	142	310	165
Worsted and woollen yarns								
Hong Kong	25 159	26 813	22 262	29 839	30 559	27 232	36 529	34 092
Irish Republic	5 311	4 370	3 923	3 829	3 671	–	5 021	–
Taiwan	6 145	4 551	5 927	8 912	6 485	6 658	7 837	8 045
Imports								
Austria	2 596	2 431	2 618	2 790	2 077	1 926	2 702	2 585
Belgium	6 973	6 850	6 674	6 325	4 357	3 627b	5 627	4 869b
China	–	5 180	7 973	10 850	43 257	37 893	51 244	45 783
Denmark	4 022	3 235	2 966	3 260	2 532	–	3 322	–
France	5 524	6 086	7 342	7 133	6 737	5 646	8 667	7 010
Germany (West)	14 202	14 451	13 639	16 719	13 186	11 003c	17 150	15 139c
Hong Kong	32 765	34 396	28 822	42 064	41 898	32 495	49 901	38 690
Irish Republic	3 845	3 154	3 596	3 360	3 825	–	6 028	–
Italy	10 606	11 409	10 596	12 498	11 677	9 209d	14 624	12 233d
Japan	9 711	6 685	6 812	12 934	8 998	4 263	10 001	5 610
Netherlands	7 430	7 819	7 146	5 810	3 918	4 517	5 145	6 245e
Switzerland	3 808	3 597	3 409	3 750	2 630	2 184	3 395	3 011
United Kingdom	15 196	14 520	12 107	13 054	11 081	10 027	14 468	13 563d
United States	5 366	4 602	4 090	3 916	2 655	3 565	3 428	4 675
Total of above	122 024	124 415	117 790	144 463	152 471g	126 355g	186 355g	159 413g

a Estimate based on data for 9 months.
b Estimate based on data for 6 months.
c Estimate based on data for 8 months.
d Estimate based on data for 11 months.
e Estimate based on data for 10 months.
f Including re-exports.
g Excluding Denmark and the Irish Republic.

The main factors supporting the raw wool trade is the lower wage costs of Asian countries and the fashion industries of Europe. By the mid-1980s, almost half of all textile fibres were being spun in developing countries compared with somewhat over a third in the mid-1970s. The East Asian countries' lower production costs, physical proximity and own expanding markets render them well suited to providing Japan with intermediate products, including high quality wool yarn produced on new machinery, and fabric. Taiwan, South Korea and Hong Kong are the leaders, reflecting their significance in world wool imports and now developing joint ventures in China, Bangladesh, India, Indonesia, Thailand and especially Vietnam. Textile products are, for example, Taiwan's second largest export; the country is now a major centre for the early stage processing of wool and has a large wool spinning sector. Textile products are South Korea's largest single export item. Moreover, the governments of developing countries normally give financial support to their textile industries as a way of obtaining foreign currency as well as imposing judicious tariffs (such as that imposed by South Korea in February 1994, raising its duty to 19% on imported fabrics) where required to protect domestic industry. As the IWS readily admits, most textile market growth, as well as production, is occurring in developing countries where the market is for cheap, basic textile materials. In addition these countries place high tariffs themselves on textile imports, in some cases such as India and Pakistan doubling the cost to the customer.

In the early 1990s all textile industries worldwide went into a severe recession. Production of textiles worldwide fell by 1.7% in 1990 and 3.8% in 1991. The collapse was especially notable, and longer term, in Russia and the other CIS countries. This decline, Comitextil noted, was only exceeded in severity by 1981, and gradual recovery had to await the end of the Gulf War, the US Presidential election and OECD economic recovery generally beginning in 1994. The recession served to deal further blows to the relative status of the European textile industry, which lost hundreds of thousands of jobs. Bernard Florin, Chairman of the Comité Central de la Laine, told the 1993 IWS wool conference that '... when I started my career in the late fifties, there were in France alone 33 combing mills producing a total of 66 000 tonnes of tops. There are now only three left producing 70 000 tonnes. There were 150 spinning plants, only 33 are left for a much lower production.'

The strongest parts of the European industry emerging in the mid-1990s were the specialist, fashion-conscious fabric areas. The EU remains an important export destination for fabric and garment exporters, however; these, especially garments, increased in value terms throughout the recession of the early 1990s at double figure rates each year. A similar story applied in Argentina, where in 1993/94 domestic consumption of wool fell by 14% due to increased imports of wool products. By contrast, Japanese textile imports fell throughout the early 1990s in response to the recession. The Japanese textile industry, however, remains of tremendous importance to the international wool trade and with the dominance of Australian wool exports by Japanese companies, which are themselves very closely tied to the textile industry, arrangements between these companies are a source of considerable concern to Australian wool producers and woolbrokers. Table 9.2 gives Japanese wool textile industry statistics.

In mid-1993 there was some evidence of a recovery in world textile production, and wool consumption increased sharply in most markets, even those such as Western Europe where overall apparel purchases actually fell. The Wool Business Conditions Survey (WBCS) published quarterly showed continued improvements in 1994 both in Europe and Japan, especially in the worsted sector. Figure 9.2 shows European worsted and woollen industry production. Top production in selected textile manufacturing countries is shown in Table 9.3. World textile shares are shown in Fig. 9.3.

It is generally agreed that, despite the siting of the IWS in Bradford and the existence of the industry-levy funded National Wool Textile Export Corporation (the UK produces less than 12 000 pieces of top quality cloth a year, a fraction of that produced in Italy) it is Italy which leads the international wool industry – despite the importance of Japan and China. The Biella area of Italy is the centre of the Italian wool industry. There is a national Italian wool promotion committee, responsible for example for the 'Cool Wool' (Lana Fredda) motif. Italy is especially noted for its promotion and use for fashion purposes of high quality wool which it has been argued has lifted the consumption and eventually also the price of wool internationally. There are 14 members of the GINTEL in France and 9 members of the Syndicat Negociants Transformateurs de Dechets (wool top makers). There are 4 members of the Federation Francaise des Peigneurs de Laines (combing mills) and 25 members of Syndifil (worsted mills). There are 8 members of the Union Nationale Française des Filateurs de Laine Cardée et Autres Fibres (woollen spinners). There are 27 members of the Federation Française du Tissage de Laine et Autres Fibres (wool weavers).

A typical US industry review of the industry featured in the USDA market news for the week of 11 August 1994: 'Worsted mills continued to operate near capacity, however, many woollen mills are on reduced work schedule or closed for vacation.' The United

Table 9.2 Japanese wool textile industry statistics (year ending 31 December except where noted)

	1970	1980	1988	1989	1990	1991	1992	1993
Raw wool imports from Australia								
m kg greasy equivalent	262	166	174	157	113	132	144	113
$A (million)	257	422	1197	1295	816	733	726	510
(year ending June 30)								
Net domestic absorption (m kg clean)	176	147	199	205	176	199	200	n/a
New domestic absorption per capita (kg)	1.7	1.3	1.3	1.4	1.4	1.6	1.6	n/a
Scoured wool production	175	90	68	62	48	49	49	n/a
Scoured wool imports	20	43	60	67	61	66	68	n/a
Scoured wool exports	0	0	0	0	0.1	0.3	0.3	n/a
Scoured wool consumption	200	113	115	109	94	97	96	n/a
(m kg clean)								
Wool top production	151	76	82	78	68	72	72	n/a
Wool top imports	2	9	28	28	24	31	34	n/a
Wool top exports	51	0	0	0	1	0	0	n/a
Wool top consumption	138	87	98	94	88	96	92	n/a
Wool top stock	12	9	12	13	11	9	11	n/a
(m kg clean)								
Worsted yarn production	132	74	84	82	77	81	80	n/a
Worsted yarn imports	1	1	9	5	6	12	9	n/a
Worsted yarn exports	14	6	4	5	6	6	7	n/a
Worsted yarn stock	22	20	20	21	20	21	27	n/a
Woollen yarn production	50	46	36	36	29	26	26	n/a
Woollen yarn imports	1	0	1	1	1	1	1	n/a
Woollen yarn exports	3	11	11	10	10	11	10	n/a
Woollen yarn stock	7	7	8	8	7	6	5	n/a
(m kg clean)								
Worsted fabric production	361	238	295	296	285	298	272	
Worsted fabric imports	0	9	19	24	20	17	16	
Worsted fabric exports	44	8	10	12	16	17	22	
Worsted fabric stock	117	101	132	137	134	139	135	
Woollen fabric production	65	75	59	55	50	47	63	
Woollen fabric imports	0	3	9	9	8	5	5	
Woollen fabric exports	2	4	5	6	6	9	9	
Woollen fabric stoc	29	35	37	36	32	28	32	
(million sq m)								

Sources: Australian Bureau of Statistics, International Wool Secretariat, Japan Wool Spinners Association

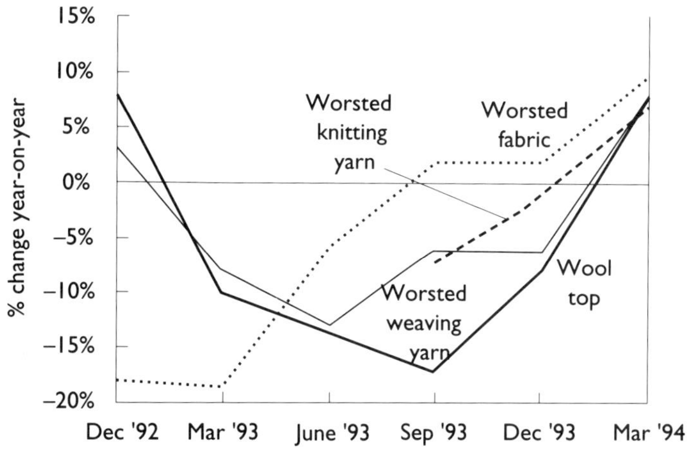

(a)

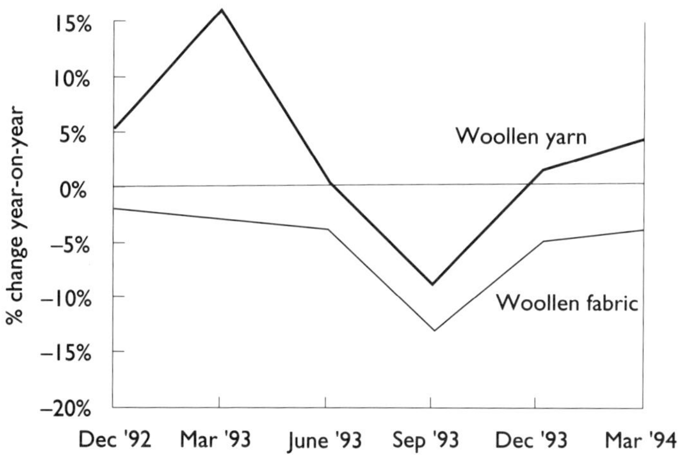

(b)

9.2a) European worsted industry production; b) European woollen industry production (source: WCBS).

Table 9.3 Production of tops of wool or fine hair (included carded sliver), tonnes

	1989	1990	1991	1992	1993
Argentina f	8 552	11 755	12 549	11 257	12 429
Australia	23 421	21 017	31 503	37 677	37 576
Austria e	–	–	–	–	–
Belgium	20 115	15 798	14 429	17 808	10 210
Brazil	9 500	8 400	8 300	8 500	7 300
of which exports	6 544	6 977	7 704	7 741	–
China	93 290	59 005	72 800	75 000	90 000
Columbia	911	–	–	–	–
Denmark	–	–	–	–	–
Egypt	2 489	2 678	2 867	2 769	–
Finland	1	1	1	1	–
France b	71 958	60 421	66 808	71 697	55 711
Germany (East)	(8 000)	(7 000) }			
Germany (West)	33 426	25 837 }	42 595	46 314	43 226
Hungary	1 565	751	458	627	–
Iceland i	44	53	–	–	–
India	13 500	12 870	13 680	16 380	19 890
Irish Republic d	–	–	–	–	–
Israel	3 300	2 500	3 100	3 000	–
Italy	59 772	52 670	57 008	61 833	53 074
Japan	77 989	67 778	72 426	72 226	54 105
Korea (South)	15 871	12 019	14 169	15 227	11 598
Netherlands	–	–	–	–	–
New Zealand c	–	–	–	–	–
Poland	9 536	3 779	1 766	–	–
Portugal	5 610	5 305	3 260	3 190	3 148
South Africa	19 234	18 496	21 994	23 553	20 725
Spain	15 300	12 500	14 000	14 000	13 016
Switzerland	900	849	802	693	472
Syria h	–	–	–	–	–
Taiwan	12 516	13 695	19 967	23 785	23 122
Turkey	23 800	25 300	22 350	23 850	22 000
United Kingdom	38 667	34 213	35 990	38 606	36 442
United States i	32 032	29 630	33 433	32 574	31 657
Uruguay	–	42 642	53 298	53 842	48 649
of which exports	26 694	42 910	48 051	47 274	43 663
Estimated total g	643 690	553 064	625 464	662 733	609 471
of which EEC (the Twelve ag)	253 348	214 244	234 590	253 948	215 327

a Excluding Greece.
b Includes production of carded sliver, in tonnes, 7 494 in 1989; 5 856 in 1990; 4 242 in 1991; 1 531 in 1992; 860 in 1993.
c 3 091 in year ending March 1973.
d 334 tonnes in 1972.
e 244 tonnes in 1975.
f Exports.
g Including estimates in cases where full returns are not available.
h 1 522 in 1979.
i Includes some mmf tops.

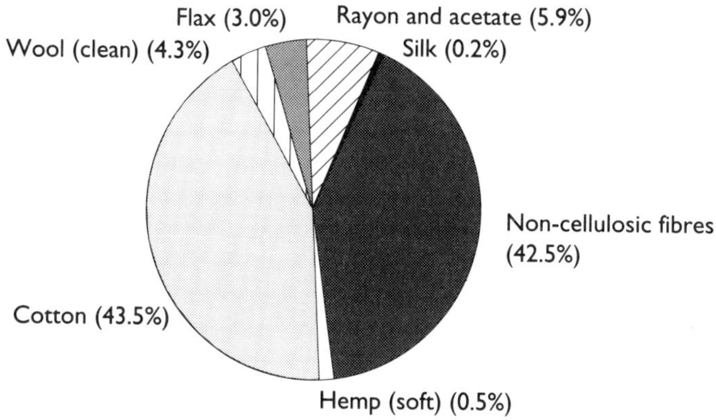

9.3 World textile shares, 1993.

States is a major importer of woollen garments, and the international wool trade is less significant for the USA than the import of finished woollen garments. Wool itself, for example, constitutes only some 1% of US mill use, only some 0.6 lb (0.27 kg) per capita consumption in the USA but woollen garments *in toto* constitute some 1.6–1.8% of total consumption. The size of this import trade, driven by the lower cost of manufacturing wool garments outside the USA and by fashion, somewhat limits the extent to which the USA is an important import market for raw wool. Another way of looking at this fact is that the USA imports approximately twice as much wool in the form of finished garments as in raw wool, and that if the USA imported no finished garments but made all its own, raw wool trade would increase by 5%. Statistics for the US textile products trade are shown in Table 9.4.

Table 9.4 US textile products trade, m lb

Wool	Exports	Imports
1990	59.6	205.8
1991	63.3	210.9
1992	72.2	237.4
1993	77.6	260.5
1994 (Jan – Jun)	44.7	125.7

Source: USDA

CHAPTER

10

The future of the international wool trade

Competition for wool

To read the advocacy of wool from successive wool marketing organisations - but perhaps most especially from the 1991-93 AWC, one would be forgiven for believing that wool was a dominant world fibre with a secure and perhaps even increasing market share. This is absolutely not the case.

Competition for wool has come, since World War II, from rayon and other man-made fabrics as well as cotton, see Table 10.1. Reliable statistics on market share are difficult to obtain (see Helen Egan: The market share of wool, AWC April 1991). Under any set of approximate definitions, however, it is clear that wool's share of world fibre production is under 10%, has been since 1959 and will remain so. In 1950 wool constituted 10.1% of wool fibre *production*; in 1960 9.5%; in 1970 7.4% ; in 1980 5.5% and in 1990 5%. As a percentage of total fibre *consumption* it has fallen similarly, from 6.9% in 1970 to 5.3% in 1980 to 4% in 1990. Increased specialisation in the use of fibres, notwithstanding efforts to promote wool as a fashion fibre - responding to the increased percentage of apparel sales being fashion-related, and not just for the purpose of keeping clean, dry and warm - especially by the Italians, and the heavy promotional expenditure of the IWS, seem certain to keep wool in very much a

Table 10.1 Wool textile production, lb

Year	Rayon and acetate	Silk	Non-cellulosic fibres	Hemp (soft)	Cotton	Wool (clean)	Flax
1980	7147	123	23095	569	31427	3675	1389
1981	7064	126	23869	492	30474	3719	1347
1982	6493	121	22368	459	31993	3656	1437
1983	6457	121	24418	406	31560	3759	1733
1984	6605	123	26023	443	42552	3831	1512
1985	6462	150	27533	481	38541	3816	1642
1986	6304	139	28499	485	33880	3924	1605
1987	6229	139	30293	474	38891	4000	2108
1988	6385	141	31784	465	40514	4134	2039
1989	6488	146	32512	397	38280	4348	1799
1990	6078	146	32877	364	41747	4273	1570
1991	5313	148	33691	439	46076	3845	1541
1992	5044	148	35192	432	39730	3724	1484
1993	4952	150	35675	425	36496	3633	2536

Source: USDA

fourth place in world fibre use. Perhaps without such expenditure, as the *Wool into the 21st Century* report suggested, wool would have disappeared altogether.

In the early 1990s it was recognised that wool was a 'mature' market, with brand, quality image and product perception all-important – but without the comfortable inelastic demand curves with respect to price that most mature products enjoy. Market changes ranging from central heating and air-conditioned buildings to the decreasing tolerance of individuals in Western countries for hand-washing woollen garments, blankets, etc – the AWC went so far as to issue a pamphlet on 'The Care of Wool' which outlines six long and tedious steps to handwashing wool: it is difficult to imagine many people actually doing this – and the creation of specialised synthetic garments for outdoor use have almost all worked against wool.

The IWS believes that the main reason for wool's declining market share has been the growth in the textile market for products for which wool is totally unsuitable, such as tyre cords, and industrial and medical textiles. Mac Drysdale says that the wool industry should therefore ignore overall textile market share statistics as 'invalid and irrelevant' and look to markets where wool is successful. But this is a circular argument. *Most people in the world now do not wear any wool at all.* A sympathetic appreciation of the relative merits of the different fibres was presented by the AWC in the 1980s, and even that pointed to the difficulties that wool faces in respect of laundry and durability by comparison to synthetics , see Table 10.2. The Superwash process developed by CSIRO, and associated standard, an assurance

Table 10.2 Fibre attribute comparisons

	Wool	Cotton	Nylon	Polyacrylic	Polyester
Appearance attributes					
Drape	1	3	3	2	3
Texture	1–2	1–2	3*	2*	3*
Colour	1–2	2	2	1	3
Crease retention	2	4	2	3	1
Wrinkle recovery	2	4*	2	3	1–2
Comfort attributes					
Moisture absorption	1	2	4	5	5
Elasticity	1–2	3–4	2	3	4
Porosity	1–2	1–2	4	4	4
Permeability	1–2	1–2	4	4	4
Performance attributes					
Water repellency	1–2	4–5	2	3	2
Abrasion resistance	2–3	2–3	1–2	2–3	1
Shrinkage resistance	4*	2	1	1	1
Laundry performance	4*	2	1	2	1
Dryclean performance	1	1	2	4	3
UV stability	1–2	2–3	3	1	1
Safety attributes					
Flame resistance	1–2	5*	3	5	3
Insulation	1	1–2	4	4	4
Acid resistance	1–2	5	4	1	1
Anti-static properties	1	2	4*	5*	5*

* Performance can be improved by applying special treatment.

Ratings: 1 = Excellent 2 = Very Good 3 = Good 4 = Moderate 5 = Poor

Source: AWC, 1988

that the garment so labelled can be washed by machine without damage, must be the start for any defence in this critical area.

But surely there must be a floor to this fall in relative share? Forecasts of almost any kind, without any technological input, would however suggest that wool is set to fall consistently below 4% of total world fibre production and consumption by the turn of the century. Price is not the driving force behind this: the Australian Price Index for wool and cotton, taking 1965/66 as 100, shows 185.9 and 267.6 respectively in 1978/79, compared with 283.9 and 271.4 in 1992/93. In the late 1980s cotton certainly became a great deal cheaper relatively than wool compared with the situation in the mid-1980s, at least until the rapid price falls of the early 1990s, partly caused by lower marketing and distribution costs, see Fig. 10.1. Certainly some marginal wool consumers will have been driven off wool, possibly

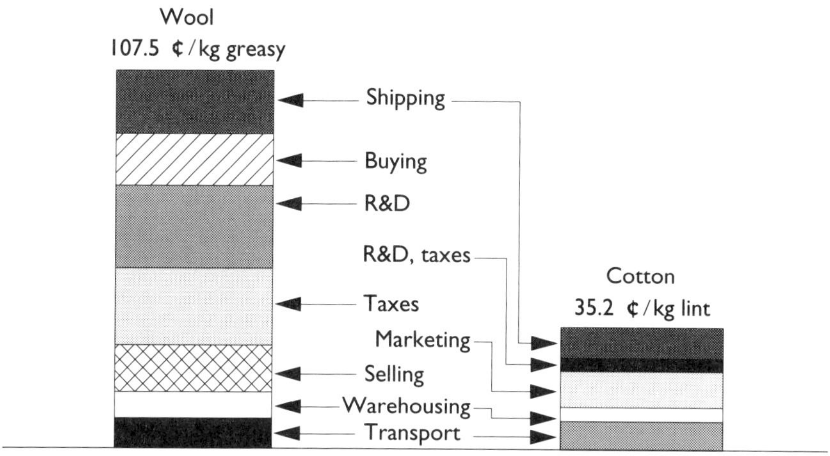

10.1 Cost of marketing cotton and wool in 1990 (source: AWC).

permanently. This, however, masks the changes that occurred in the period between the 1960s and the 1980s and does not explain the long-term trend which saw wool lose market share despite being relatively cheaper than cotton in every year since 1965/66 until 1985/86 and then again in 1990/91. The effect of this switch has been more heavily felt in non-apparel wools, which have faced stiff competition from synthetic fibres.

Wool has not done badly, increasing production by 6–8% comparing the early 1990s as a group with the early 1980s – but other textiles have done better, and so wool has lost ground. The Arthur Little report concluded in 1992: 'Wool's position in premium fibre markets remains severely threatened by synthetic fibres. Wool's share of the total textile market has declined dramatically over the past sixty years; from 20% in 1930 to around 4% today. Just under 2m tonnes of raw wool were produced in 1991, whereas international man-made fibre production reached record levels of over 19m tonnes' (p 9). Nothing has substantially improved since 1991, although there are at least signs that wool has reached the nadir of its decline and with wool prices having risen substantially in 1994/95, production levels were likely to follow them up in 1995/96.

Table 10.3 shows an indication of the balance of US mill consumption of different fibres. Cotton's dominance is clear as is the very small – but relatively consistent – percentage of total mill use obtained by wool. In US terms, wool takes very much a fourth place behind non-cellulosic synthetics, cotton and cellulosic synthetic fibres in that order. And in terms of overall per capita consumption it is very small indeed – consistently under 2% and in 1993 1.7%, compared

Table 10.3 US mill consumption of cotton wool and man-made fibres

Year		Cotton	Wool	Cellulosic	Non-cellulosic	Total man-made	Total fibres	Wool's share of total
							m lb	%
1989	1Q	949.9	37.3	165.8	2 174.2	2 340.0	3 327.2	1.1
	2Q	1 033.3	35.9	159.9	2 234.0	2 393.9	3 463.1	1.0
	3Q	1 054.1	31.7	140.9	2 134.5	2 275.4	3 361.2	0.9
	4Q	1 008.7	29.8	134.2	2 074.1	2 208.3	3 246.8	0.9
Total		4 046.0	134.7	600.8	8 616.8	9 217.6	13 398.3	1.0
1990	1Q	1 056.6	35.4	141.5	2 088.1	2 229.6	3 321.6	1.1
	2Q	1 071.1	34.7	144.7	2 163.0	2 307.7	3 413.5	1.0
	3Q	1 037.6	30.0	159.2	2 089.4	2 248.6	3 316.2	0.9
	4Q	950.0	32.6	153.5	2 107.6	2 261.1	3 243.7	1.0
Total		4 115.3	132.7	598.9	8 448.1	9 047.0	13 295.0	1.0
1991	1Q	1 032.9	34.7	128.3	1 898.1	2 026.4	3 094.0	1.1
	2Q	1 109.5	40.2	141.1	2 173.1	2 314.2	3 463.9	1.1
	3Q	1 108.3	39.1	145.8	2 244.0	2 389.8	3 537.2	1.1
	4Q	1 096.8	37.5	141.3	2 230.6	2 371.9	3 506.2	1.1
Total		4 347.5	151.5	556.5	8 545.8	9 102.3	13 601.3	1.1
1992	1Q	1 169.2	40.9	140.7	2 207.2	2 347.9	3 558.0	1.1
	2Q	1 178.7	38.7	144.4	2 320.1	2 464.5	3 681.9	1.1
	3Q	1 219.6	36.7	140.3	2 323.5	2 463.8	3 720.1	0.9
	4Q	1 194.1	34.5	132.3	2 334.2	2 466.5	3 695.1	0.9
Total		4 761.6	150.8	557.7	9 185.0	9 742.7	14 655.1	1.0
1993	1Q	1 255.1	40.1	144.7	2 313.7	2 458.4	3 753.6	1.1
	2Q	1 260.1	40.3	158.3	2 463.2	2 621.5	3 921.9	1.2
	3Q	1 249.1	38.1	152.2	2 422.6	2 574.8	3 862.0	0.9
	4Q	1 173.4	38.3	139.2	2 375.5	2 514.7	3 726.4	1.0
Total		4 937.7	156.8	594.4	9 575.0	10 169.4	15 263.9	1.0
1994	1Q	1 240.4	40.8	144.8	2 504.0	2 648.8	3 930.0	1.0
	2Q	1 331.0	39.1	134.2	2 623.1	2 757.3	4 127.4	0.9

Sources: US Bureau of the Census and Fiber Organon

with 1.6% in 1979 and 2.6% in 1986 when cotton's rapid resurgence had only just begun.

The competitive position of wool must be considered as part of the overall future position of international wool production and the international wool trade.

What does the future have in store? A report from CIRFS, the synthetic fibre trade organisation, suggested the following scenario in which in Western Europe at least wool was expected to retain market share because it was both less affected by imports from third world countries and also continued to perform relatively well in some large

Table 10.4 World fibre consumption, m tonnes

	1990	%	1995	%	2000	%
Cotton	18.70	48.8	20.75	48.7	23.40	48.2
Wool	1.95	5.1	2.04	4.8	2.18	4.5
Synthetic fibres	14.90	38.9	17.29	40.6	20.50	42.3
Polyamide filament	2.99	7.8	3.24	7.6	3.69	7.6
Polyester filament	4.13	10.8	5.15	12.1	6.45	13.3
Polyester staple	4.90	12.8	5.41	12.7	5.92	12.2
Acrylic staple	2.30	6.0	2.56	6.0	2.91	6.0
All others	0.57	1.5	0.94	2.2	1.55	3.2
Cellulosic fibres	2.75	7.2	2.53	5.9	2.43	5.0
Total consumption	38.30	100.0	42.60	100.0	48.50	100.0

Source: CIRFS

end-uses, such as carpets and knitwear, but even here European yarn production was expected to fall by 11%, Table 10.4.

The situation in the mid-1990s

The international raw wool market is awaiting the outcome of a number of different issues, all of which appear to be bullish in their orientation. Firstly there is the question of the possible revival of the Russian market. There has as yet been no word from the IWS on their expectations for this market, although RER cautiously expects that the overall take-up for woollen yarn in Russia could rise by about 10% in 1995/96. This is based on an analysis of expected economic growth and Western relationships between demand and growth, however, which may not entirely apply in the new Russian context.

The second issue is the role of China. Even more than at the start of 1994, wool analysts, just as those in the silk and cotton markets, are looking at Chinese economic growth and textile demand. Part of the problem with the current flow of information and forecasts about commodity markets is that there are two 'layers' of analyses: on-line daily information, such as that provided by Reuters and Knight-Ridder, and detailed forecasts and studies which are usually released only in written form. They are often out of date by the time they reach their audience, but they still have an effect in the market. Such may be the case with the long awaited International Wool Secretariat China 2000 report, which in predicting that China will take up some 25% of the world's available wool supply by the end of the century overlooks both the current restrictions that the Chinese are just beginning to place on their runaway economy, and also the possibility of a fully fledged recession in China, perhaps induced by Deng's death.

However, as Western economies start to pick up there is undoubtedly continued upward pressure already being felt on wool prices. Prices may have reached their ceiling but forecasts from ABARE are continually being revised on the basis of fresh supply information. The shortage of fine micron wool has been especially concerning: the Southern hemisphere weather has been relatively rainy for the past few seasons, reducing the production of fine micron wool. Improvements in the economies of developed countries mean that textile demand slides further towards wool fabrics utilising the higher quality wools, and this has what has been described as a 'tractor beam effect' on other microns: partly through a collective mentality without practical justification, but partly because those traders with forward positions that they find difficult to honour in exactly the right micron will seek to do so using the next most fine available and so on in a trickledown effect. There is now a serious danger of undersupply in the market and world production is still falling: Russia, Uruguay and Argentina are all reporting production falls which will not be compensated by slight increases in production in China.

The result is that since 1993/94 there have been huge price increases of 100% for fine wools, and further massive increases followed towards the end of 1994 or beginning of 1995. Clearly the Japanese are using the physical wool market as a commodity trading market, which they are freely allowed to do, buying up supplies and then releasing them when the price has risen. Some brokers are even going out of business due to defaults from suppliers and their inability to take covering positions against forward supply commitments, wool magazine sources reported at the time.

Major purchasers of wool and those in the retail chain actively expressed their concern to the Australians in particular - who regarded the price increases as merely returning them to profitability - that matters were in danger of getting out of hand. There is a serious danger that, faced with such dramatic increases in raw material prices without any such increase in consumer demand, let alone overall consumer income, consumers will shy away from quality wool products. Once manufacturers start to glean this impression they too will shy away from wool and a great deal of the marketing effort that, for example, the British Wool Marketing Board and others have placed in wool, will be completely wasted. Once this all happens the market can be dislocated for a number of years, as has happened before on two occasions. Some experts have expressed concern that if it happens a third time it will not be elastic on the rebound but will permanently wedge out consumers.

In an effort to avoid this, the Australians were being urged not to rush to dispose of their stockpile this season but to structure their sales so as to ensure smooth and moderate price rises. Understandably this view is not yet accepted in Australia. The difficulty of achieving this has been reinforced by the administrative changes that have been effected in Australia. The new IWS/Wool International organisation is still finding its feet, and attempting - for example - to divest itself of responsibility for research and development, training and standard setting. *Wool Monitor* (or its equivalent) is still published but the IWS appears to have stopped publication of *Wool Compendium*. It is undoubtedly an organisational state of flux. In Europe, consumers of Australian wool have been stressing that although this may be the IWS mandate, it has a more general responsibility for the reputation and quality of Australian wool and should not act hastily.

The difficulty is reinforced by the method of selling wool at auction. Without an active futures market, and with the withdrawal of the price reserve scheme, farmers are facing auctions where prices are rising and falling some 50% during the course of a single day. Their whole year's income is being decided in a matter of minutes when their clip is sold. This is encouraging profit taking and the development of auction trading strategies by farmers to bid up prices. Reserve prices and the withdrawal of wool actually during the course of a single auction is quite common, although there are rules governing how this can be done. The result is that price oscillation at auctions is increasing and the uncertainty is itself helping to drive up prices. The whole market is an excellent example of the volatility that can be induced by the absence of an effective hedging mechanism, and it seemed likely that prices would continue to rise until lack of demand chokes the rises off - perhaps much sooner than the Australians were expecting.

The future of the market

Forecasting is sometimes just extrapolation of trends. Does a forecast of the international wool trade for the next decade or more see another roller-coaster of prices accompanied by further frenetic institutional change? Perhaps the easiest forecast about a commodity trade to make, just as it is the most accessible historical data set to obtain – along with global and national yield production information, is overall trade levels.

The level of world exports was 1.796bn lb (814m kg) in 1988/89, 1.566bn lb (710m kg) the next season, 1.448 bn (657m kg) in 1990/91, 1.815bn (823m kg) in 1991/92, 1.598bn (725m kg) in 1992/93 recovering to 1.772bn lb (804m kg) in 1993/94. Experts expect this total to increase for at least a couple of seasons as the stockpiles are run down and economic activity in Europe and the Far East mounts. In the short term, Wool International was probably right in August 1994 to say that the market fundamentals were improving rapidly, with the Eastern Market indicator forecast to average around 700 ¢/kg clean in 1994/95, in a range of between 650 ¢/kg and 750 ¢/kg. Wool International went on to say that economic growth and retail demand in the six major wool consuming countries would strengthen in 1994/95; wool textile industry activity was improving, commercial stocks are returning to long term levels and confidence was rising among wool users. Wool International expected lower production and fixed WI stock sales of 96m kg in 1994/95 to tighten supplies. The scene was being set, at least according to concerned wool buyers from retailers, for another repeat of the boom and bust cycle of the late 1980s. It is much to be hoped that the international trade has learned from these mistakes and that after the 1994/95 season the total volume of trade and prices settle back a little, the extent of which being determined by whether the current worldwide economic recovery takes firm root or not. All this is likely to be accompanied by a recovery in sheep numbers and hence wool production towards the later years of the decade, although Jo Modiano foresees a drastic decline in Australian sheep numbers, down to 123m by March 1995 and a clip of 650m kg. This in turn would put tremendous pressure on supply and force up prices. Forecasting a definite boom-bust cycle is hazardous.

As to the regional distribution of trade, in the short term that again is reasonably easy to forecast: towards Asia. Whilst Japanese wool imports look set to decline or at least not rise as rapidly as in the past, and China's rise may be subject to unpredictable changes, those of other Asian economies look likely to hold their position and some hitherto small importers of raw wool may, due to their lower production costs, come to the fore in the next decade. Textile Intelligence in 1993 saw a 20% consumption rise in developing Asia, Latin America, Africa and China in the period 1992–2002. As early as March 1994 it was recognised (in *Wool News*) that 'Emerging countries, such as India, China, Turkey, Mauritius, North Africa, Egypt and Madagascar offer major opportunities for Australian wool.' The international wool trade will be in the 21st century primarily an Asian-Australasian trade, with Europe playing an unsteadily and gradually decreasing role in the physical side of the trade - CERFS 11% forecast decline in wool yarn production in the 1992–2002 period is relevant here - although giant European-owned companies such as Chargeurs will obviously still have an important role to play.

Specific forecasts of regional trade distribution are fraught with danger, but it seems perfectly possible that by the first decade of the next century, China will take as much Australian wool as Western Europe, at least in some years, whilst other Asian destinations excluding Japan will take more. New Zealand is already looking primarily to Asia, and by the first decade of the next century Europe's share of New Zealand exports could be less than 20%. The wild card is the possible economic regeneration of Russia and the other CIS states/ Eastern Europe, but forecasts of this regeneration are postponing the date every time they are issued, and a timeframe of beyond the first decade of the next century now looks realistic rather than cynical.

The Todhunter thesis is appealing, plausible and probably also likely to accelerate. The fact that retailing in general and other textile production internationally either already has or is currently following this line redoubles the likelihood. Countries all seek to refine and process their own resources as far as possible, adding value before exporting them. The lure of reduced costs and even in this case a less contaminated product is bound to appeal to overseas manufacturers, although producers must face increased risks, depending on who runs the risk of default due to strikes, storms, etc. Others suggest that manufacturers will rely on overseas sources of supply for tops only for a percentage of their needs. But as communications improve and decrease in cost, and transport costs fall as a percentage of overall cost, international shipment of wool will become quicker and more direct between country centres. Interestingly, the NZWB said in 1993 that their target by 2000 was to scour 85% of the clip domestically and add 10% net value to the clip to the value of scoured output through specialised processing, and secondly to process 10% of the clip beyond scouring to intermediate product stage and a further 10% to final product stage. WRONZ in its 1992/93 Report stated that it was 'entirely focused on a target New Zealand clean wool price of $8/kg and a growth in the on-shore added value sector to $1210m by 2007.'

Direct contact between the evolving 'country dealers' working between Australian and New Zealand farmers and northern hemisphere - or increasingly, Asian - industry is increasing gradually. Todhunter believes that the traditional large brokers' power is fast diminishing, and that there is a burgeoning development of small more cost effective wool selling brokers, but traditional brokers are remarkably resilient, especially when backed up with Japanese money, and the large wool trading companies such as Itochu and Chargeurs are surely here to stay. Indeed, certainly in regard to mills and probably also in respect of wool exporters there will be some rationalisation, as the negotiations between BWK and Chargeurs over their respective mills in Geelong (Vic) and Wagga Wagga (NSW) indicate. And the market is still a long way away even from the Arthur Little 'Fibre Firms', which encompassed pooling of wool and objective measurement. There are just too many wool firms in the 1990s chasing too little business with the result that economies of scale are difficult to achieve.

It has to be right, though, to argue that 'it is not impossible to see the development of air freight and "Just in time" deliveries to spinners which are likely to be brought about by onward processing in Australia' (*Wool Record*, March 1992) ready for computer design and controlled manufacturing which could take only weeks to appear on the shelves rather than the current estimate of Chargeurs that 'It takes approximately two years from the time the wool is shorn from the sheep till it reaches the consumer in the form of garments'. As early as the evening of 25 June 1811, after all, Sir John Throckmorton wore a coat made from a fleece that had been on the sheep's back in the morning. It may take two centuries for the practice to be widespread. In any event, changes designed to speed up and simplify the physical trading process, combined with ever more complex private sector trading documentation and contract structure, alongside a gradual decline in the status and involvement of controlling boards and agreements, appear to be the late twentieth century rule of the development of international commodity trade.

Institutionally, the NZWB for example plans no further involvement in direct wool selling once the stockpile is sold, or in freight rate setting. The Board will then concentrate on promotion, research and product and market development: exactly what the new commercialisation of the South African Wool Board is intended to do and what the IWS does. The research priorities of the Boards will include fibre quality and other programmes to distinguish their wool from its competitors, alternative production systems such as combining fine wool and meat production, and improving efficiency with genetics – for example the development of the so-called Superfibre in Australia which seeks to produce finer, more uniform fibres, softer handling and more elasticity with greater tensile strength. Another example is that in mid-1994 a French company announced an improved method of protein absorption for sheep leading to higher yields. More wool from fewer sheep is a relatively predictable development.

Equally important will be a greater attention to environmental issues, which has arrived a little tardily in the wool industry but which is bound to accelerate in importance along with animal welfare issues such as sheep transport and sheep slaughter, which the EU at least has a view on. Chargeurs noted as early as 1992 that 'environmental concerns are stepping up pressure on producers to reduce the ecological impact of wool cleaning' (publicity literature, 1992) and this can be expected to intensify. No textile has an automatic right to environmental plus points; scouring effluent is currently about 50 times stronger than domestic effluent and that cannot continue. There are many other examples from the wool industry and considerable improvements can be expected throughout in the long term and in response to legislation. The future will see still greater attention to the 'engineered' design of yarns and fabrics as well as aesthetic design, to the measurement of performance and subsequent establishment of standards during processing and in the final product; indeed, it has been observed that ' ... there is so much happening in domestic, medical, industrial and environmental textiles that it is difficult to know how to strike a balance between what is happening and what is perceived to be' (Bruce Rainsford, epis. cit).

The IWS is bound to have similar commercial priorities although Australian wool appears less threatened by competition in strength. In its 1992 Annual Report the AWC identified the 'Challenges for the Future' as increasing demand, improving efficiency within the industry, managing debt and value adding. With the third objective now probably satisfactorily achieved, the remainder of the decade and the next decade will see greater attention placed by the new IWS on the other three objectives. It seems very unlikely that the reserve price schemes will be reintroduced in Australia, New Zealand, South Africa, the USA or the UK, although further institutional change as self-regulation settles in must be ranked highly likely.

As mentioned earlier, one of the difficulties in writing about international trade in any commodity, but in fact especially for wool where the participants are quite open about the fact, is that the technology is both improving and becoming more intrusive in the life of a typical commodity trader. In accordance with this rule it can be expected that such innovations as on-farm bale pooling for export by growers, and objective sampling and testing can be expected to gain ground steadily. In December 1992 the NZWB claimed that 'Today we are close to having a set of standard tests that very effectively describe most textile processing characteristics. More development work is still needed … New tests, such as length after carding, length/strength and bulk, are being introduced or further developed' (NZWB *Wool Report*, December 1992, p 4) but the Board noted that the industry had not yet put these tests into action: notably, although growers are already required to have all wool sold at auction tested, export delivery contracts in the mid-1990s are far from uniformly incorporating these results.

Nor is there yet a standard description system for internationally traded wool. As Mac Drysdale, IWS Chairman, observed also in the Annual Report of 1992: 'Machine speeds in the textile industry have increased at a rapid rate in the past ten years. Fully automatic plants becoming common in cotton and synthetic yarn production are possible only because of the complete specifications and high-quality condition of the fibre in process. The lesson for wool is clear'. In the medium term, however, despite the encouragement of all the Wool Boards and the impeccable logic presented by the SFE, it seems unlikely that the auction system will be threatened precisely because of the continued prevalence of the sale by sample system. The international wool market is a slow-changing one – except institutionally – and sale by sample has only had twenty years in operation.

Traders, especially, realistically expect such a change to be a long while coming, as the overwhelming majority of the industry retains the need to see a sample before purchasing any wool and the wool trading companies must guarantee their delivery. Eventually the objective of the NZWB, that 'all exports of New Zealand Wool be accompanied by test certificates based on the existing set of industry-approved tests' (*op cit*, p 4), an objective shared by the IWS, is bound to come about, along with the highly desirable situation of objective measurement, universal high quality, sale by description and electronic trading. The economics of the trade in the long term, however, demand that they will eventually do so, but most expectations are that it may be quite some way into the new century before this actually happens.

It is easy for boards and other non-commercial organisations, or for that matter commissioned researchers such as Arthur D Little to recommend changes as improvements. Prescription in the wool industry should be carefully distinguished from forecasting, which it not always is in the face of determined wish-fulfilment. In fact, institutional or academic prescriptions can take decades to work through into practice. Nevertheless they are often good guides to what eventually happens. The NZWB sees electronic wool trading, for example, as 'an important future link in the marketing chain that would give more options to growers' (*op cit*, p 4). The Board claims that although electronic trading may not, of itself, lead to fundamental improvements in the wool marketing system, 'it should reduce volatility by allowing wool to be on offer for a longer period of time'. Raymond Michell argues that the Wool Exchange concept is 'an interesting development in the marketing of wool'. He saw a continuous movement to alternative selling systems. The broker was tending to become a trader, and traders were going straight back to the grower. Manufacturers such as Luca Giovanneli are sceptical of the idea, believing that it will not take the place of the current auction system. Michael Moss, President of the New Zealand Council of Wool Exporters, opined that electronic trading depended on developing an objective length after carding test for cross-bred greasy wools. And evidence from the use of electronic trading in other markets, such as commodity futures markets, suggests that for the foreseeable future, the effect of electronic trading is to reduce liquidity in markets, not to increase it. Wool on offer for a longer time is not a merit in itself: it only benefits the international trade if it is actually sold.

What about a really rejuvenated futures market in Australia and/or New Zealand to complement sale by description and electronic trading and to utilise some of the enormous potential additional liquidity that the international finance and commodities companies could bring to the international raw wool trade? There has been a slight revival in SFE wool trading and there is undoubted enthusiasm from Wool International and IWS officials. The SFE's official position is that they are very confident that the erosion of the Australian stockpile will produce a role for an active futures market and there is some evidence with the enthusiastic support of Wool International and the introduction of a physical delivery contract that this may at last occur. They state: 'This is a need which is universally recognised among wool industry participants, however it is not something that can be achieved overnight, as it represents a fundamental change to the way wool is priced and subsequently traded. SFE says it is very confident in the future of the wool contract, and is undertaking programs to re-educate the marketplace as to the role of the futures market ...' but efforts to restart commodities futures contracts, even with different contract specifications, such as for rubber, have not proved successful in the past. In general, the 1990s have not proved happy or suitable times for the launching or rejuvenation of commodities futures contracts, as the failure of the New York International Cotton Futures contract demonstrated. Liquidity is and will continue to be at a premium and suspicion of commodities futures, especially from auctioneers and their supporters, shows little sign of diminishing. Hopes from the SFE of a close relationship with the new Australian Wool Exchange may be over-optimistic; but it is certainly not unrealistic to see a steady revival of volume on the contract, especially a successful physical delivery contract.

The forecast that this book offers for the international wool trade in the short and medium term is therefore conservative. There seem no insuperable obstacles, especially now that the market is reviving, to a continuation of existing arrangements and evolution of trade volumes, national and company market share and processing. In the long term, however, everything that the international wool trade does will be subject to upheaval and rejuvenation.

Select bibliography

Because of the institutionalised nature of the international wool industry, information is plentiful and tends to come in the form of annual reports from a variety of public and private bodies. Articles in the journals published by these bodies, usually monthly (the names of which change frequently) are also useful. The International Wool Secretariat in Ilkley and Melbourne remains the single most important source of data and public analysis on the international wool trade.

Annual Reports

Australian Wool Exchange
British Wool Marketing Board
International Wool Textile Organisation
New Zealand Futures and Options Exchange
New Zealand Wool Board
South African Wool Board
Sydney Futures Exchange
Wools of New Zealand
WRONZ

Cotton and Wool Situation and Outlook Report
Cotton and Wool Update

Published quarterley and monthly respectively by the United States Department of Agriculture Economic Research Service

IWTO

Monthly journal on the international textile industry published by the International Wool Textile Organisation

New Zealand Wool Industry

Report for the New Zealand Wool Board by the Arthur D Little consultancy organisation, 1991.

Non-wool contamination in carbonised wool

Report G73, 1992, CSIRO, division of Wool Technology

Wool Australia

Published in Melbourne and available through the IWS.

Wool in the 21st Century

Radical report published by the Centre for International Economics/ Wool into the 21st Century Committee, Australia, 1991.

Wool Market News

Published weekly by the United States Department of Agriculture.

Wool record

Published monthly by World Textile Publications, 76 Kirkgate, Bradford: the best monthly summary of developments in the industry and trade.

Index